D1711623

James Macpherson

Twayne's English Authors Series

Bertram H. Davis, Editor

Florida State University

TEAS 467

JAMES MACPHERSON
Copy in the National Portrait Gallery, London after the 1772 oil painting
by Sir Joshua Reynolds.
Courtesy of the National Portrait Gallery, London.

James Macpherson

By Paul J. deGategno

North Carolina Wesleyan College

Twayne Publishers
A Division of G. K. Hall & Co. • *Boston*

James Macpherson
Paul J. deGategno

Copyright 1989 by G. K. Hall & Co.
All rights reserved.
Published by Twayne Publishers
A Division of G. K. Hall & Co.
70 Lincoln Street
Boston, Massachusetts 02111

Copyediting supervised by Barbara Sutton
Book production by Gabrielle B. McDonald
Book design by Barbara Anderson

Typeset in 11 pt. Garamond
by Compset, Inc., of Beverly, Massachusetts

Printed on permanent/durable acid-free paper
and bound in the United States of America

Library of Congress Cataloging-in-Publication Data

DeGategno, Paul J.
    James Macpherson / by Paul J. deGategno.
       p. cm.—(Twayne's English authors series ; TEAS 467)
    Bibliography: p.
    Includes index.
    ISBN 0-8057-6975-7 (alk. paper)
    1. Macpherson, James, 1736–1796—Criticism and interpretation.
2. Ossian, 3rd cent., in fiction, drama, poetry, etc.   3. Literary
forgeries and mystifications.   4. Mythology, Celtic, in literature.
5. Gaelic poetry—Adaptations.   6. Celts in literature.   I. Title.
II. Series.
PR3544.D44   1989
821'.6—dc19
                                        88-35166
                                            CIP

For Rhonda

Contents

About the Author

Paul J. deGategno, associate professor of English and chairman of the Division of Humanities at North Carolina Wesleyan College, was educated at Norwich University, the University of Rhode Island, and The Pennsylvania State University. His primary scholarly interest has been the eighteenth century, and he is the author of articles on Rochester, Defoe, Smollett, Macpherson, Radcliffe, and Scott. He has been a National Endowment for the Humanities Fellow at the University of Minnesota and a Lilly Scholar in the Humanities at Duke University.

Preface

Two centuries have passed since the publication of a group of poems that set in motion a controversy unrivaled in the rich history of English literature. James Macpherson's *The Poems of Ossian* (1760–63) caught the European mind and fed the longings of the preromantic age. The heroic code, natural and noble wild imagination, gloom, mystery, sensibility—all of these Ossianic qualities proved irresistible to an audience whose sense of primitivism and sentimentalism had been stimulated by earlier antirationalist statements. Sharp reactions echoed from Edinburgh to Moscow. Critics called the Ossian poems revolutionary, a work of genius, a literary achievement of a Homer of the North; many who refused to join the cult of Ossianism, however, argued that the poems were not only intrinsically worthless, but were, in fact, forgeries. With such a diverse reception, a bizarre controversy was launched that would extend into the next century and affect the work of the major men of letters, as well as dozens of lesser writers, for some decades.

The controversy over the poems' authenticity has long since been settled satisfactorily; however, the debate over Macpherson's achievement continues, though the temper and quality of that discussion have, of course, changed since the height of critical awareness of Ossian in the nineteenth century. The issues and facts concerning Macpherson, these poems, and, indeed, the controversy itself have become enmeshed in a rich tangle of confusion: what has not been forgotten has often been misunderstood.

Happily, contemporary as well as excellent modern editions of the poems still are extant. Available, also, is a modern reprint of the influential work of Hugh Blair, *A Dissertation on the Poems of Ossian* (1763). Primary materials such as letters, essays, reviews, and reports can be readily secured by interested readers. The appropriate time has come for a critical introduction to Macpherson's life and work. Scholars and, especially, students may read the poems with keener and more informed interest for such a study.

This critical study has three purposes: to provide as much information about James Macpherson, his poetry, and his age as the student will require for an understanding of the poems; to read the poems freshly, as literary works; and to analyze the poems' reception by Macpherson's early and late contemporaries, as it reveals certain shifts of taste in the last half of the eighteenth century. I begin with a chapter on Macpherson's theories of literary composition and analyze his early work, which culminated in 1760 with the publication of the *Fragments of Ancient Poetry*. Chapters 3 and 4 examine Macpherson's chief poems, the epics *Fingal* and *Temora*, as well as the lesser pieces. The poems are discussed in the order presented in their first editions, not in the order Macpherson contrived for the corrected edition later, when his purpose was, in part, to deter accusations of forgery. Chapter 5 describes the nature and intensity of the Ossianic controversy, and chapter 6 explores the influence the poems have had upon literature, painting, and music. Chapter 7 surveys Macpherson's work as a historian, pamphleteer, and translator.

For their kindness in allowing me to use their resources, it is a pleasure to thank the librarians of the National Library of Scotland, Edinburgh University, Duke University, the University of North Carolina at Chapel Hill, Williams College, North Carolina State University, the University of South Carolina, and North Carolina Wesleyan College. I especially wish to thank Dianne Taylor of the Wesleyan College Library for locating various materials for me.

I am happy to acknowledge the generous and patient support of the Wesleyan College Faculty Research Committee for a grant that permitted me to travel to Edinburgh and the Highlands. In Scotland, I appreciated the assistance of Andrew Macpherson, Curator of the Clan Macpherson House Museum, Newtonmore, and the hospitality of the present residents of Belleville, Colonel R. T. S. Macpherson and family. For freely offered information and advice, I am indebted to Professor Derick S. Thomson of Glasgow University. I must also thank the Clan Macpherson Association, United States Branch, for allowing me to join their spirited gathering.

Among my colleagues I want to thank Professors Leverett T. Smith and David Ketchiff for their encouragement and example. For careful criticism of the entire work I am deeply obligated to my colleague, Professor Linda Flowers and to Professor Lewis Walker of the University of North Carolina. Professor Bertram H. Davis of the Florida State University has been all that an author could desire of an editor; without his faith in my abilities this study could not have been written.

My debt to my wife may be understood by my dedication of this study to her.

Paul J. deGategno

North Carolina Wesleyan College

Chronology

1776   The widely read pamphlet *The Rights of Great Britain Asserted Against the Claims of America*.

1778   Assumes the post as deputy to and agent in London for Mohammed Ali, the Nawab of Arcot, a wealthy Indian prince.

1779   *A Short History of the Opposition During the Last Session* and *The History and Management of the East India Company*.

1780   Elected member of Parliament for Camelford, Cornwall.

1784   Purchases land for a house at Balavil, Inverness-shire, in his home district. The design for the home, which he renames Belleville, completed by Robert Adam. Reelected to the House.

1790   Reelected to the House.

1796   17 February, dies at Belleville; 15 March, buried at Westminster Abbey.

1797   The Highland Society of Scotland initiates an investigation into the authenticity of the *Poems of Ossian*.

1805   *The Report of the Committee of the Highland Society of Scotland* published; Sir Walter Scott writes an influential review; the Ossianic controversy appears settled.

Chapter One
James Macpherson

Writing in his journal for 8 February 1763, James Boswell recalled an afternoon visit to the London home of the Irish actor and elocutionist Thomas Sheridan, where the topic of discussion was the poems of Ossian. "He preferred Ossian to all the poets in the world," wrote Boswell, "and thought he excelled Homer in the Sublime and Vergil in the Pathetic"; he added that "Mrs. Sheridan and he had fixed it as the standard of feeling, made it like a thermometer by which they could judge of the warmth of everybody's heart."[1]

The object of such literary devotion was the work of James Macpherson, an obscure schoolmaster and unsuccessful poet from the Highlands of Scotland, who had burst upon London's cultural scene with purported translations of ancient Gaelic poetry. The effect on literary taste and judgment of his 1760 *Fragments of Ancient Poetry,* and of the epics *Fingal* and *Temora* that followed, is difficult to exaggerate. Well into the next century the body of poetry eventually collected as the *Poems of Ossian* fueled a controversy that, by the time it was over, had involved nearly every important writer in Europe and America.

The conflict raged over the authenticity of these works, with commentators holding widely divergent views. Samuel Johnson declared Macpherson a base forger who "found names, and stories, and phrases . . . and with them compounded his own compositions."[2] At the opposite extreme Hugh Blair assured his fellow Scotsmen and the world that the texts were translations of actual Gaelic verses. The debate has long since been definitively settled: scholars agree that Macpherson did collect a number of Gaelic Ossianic ballads, sometimes using original characters and ideas but more typically altering these, while adding modern, non-Gaelic characteristics of his own.

Despite their lack of authenticity, the fact remains that these tales of Celtic heroes and adventure met with immense and near-universal acclaim throughout Europe. The *Poems of Ossian* would influence, would indeed help shape, the romantic movement itself. Goethe, Schiller, Klopstock, and Lessing found the poems provocative and inspiring in their exotic wildness. The misty romanticism of the Celtic hero-world and the struggle of the Celts to repulse foreign invaders and retain their freedom appealed to Napoleon Bonaparte, whose copy of the *Poems* (in Italian) still exists. Among French writers, Voltaire admiringly called Ossian "the Homer of Scotland," and Chateaubriand is said to have been willing to defend the bard's life with his own.

The appeal of *Ossian* to eighteenth-century primitivism and sentimentalism proved irresistible. Although he was re-creating a dim Celtic past, Macpherson avoided uncouth language and barbaric impulse, and this delicacy contributed to the success of *Ossian*. The beauty and unexpected charm of the poems displayed the author's genuine imagination and poetic sensibility. In a curious way, he became a pioneer who offered the writers that came after him a vision of a world where feeling was elevated over thought and instinct over education.

Early Life

Macpherson was born at Ruthven, Inverness-shire, Scotland, on 27 October 1736, the only son of an indigent farmer, Andrew Macpherson, who had married Ellen Macpherson of the same Highland clan. The Macphersons lived in the Spey River valley, the traditional home of the Macpherson clan. For over seven hundred years the clan Macpherson had held preeminence over rival clans by the strength and shrewdness of its warriors.

In the sixteenth and seventeenth centuries Macphersons had supported various Catholic monarchs and fought on the royalist side in the Civil War. Though punished for its loyalty, the clan continued to prosper; it remained influential until 1746, when the Duke of Cumberland's English army, chasing the defeated Jacobites, ravaged the clan stronghold. Young James, nearly ten years old, observed with insatiable curiosity the heroic struggle of the Highlanders, assembled at Ruthven for the last time.

Macpherson's early education had begun at home with daily readings from the Bible. For the next six years he received an excellent education in the Badenoch parochial school and may have finished his secondary schooling thirty miles to the north in Inverness. Andrew Macpherson, who cherished the idea of his son becoming a gentleman, urged a career in the ministry. In the autumn of 1752 James traveled to Aberdeen, the center of civilization in northern Scotland, matriculating at King's College in February 1753. His studies were marked by periods of idleness and truculence, but "he read widely and made himself a fair classical scholar."[3] In 1755 he was forced to leave without a degree since he could not afford the increase that year in tuition. He transferred for a time to Marischal College, Aberdeen, and then to the University of Edinburgh, where he was a student in divinity. Unable to secure a degree, he returned to Ruthven in 1756 and began teaching in the charity school there.

During his college years, and particularly on returning to his village, Macpherson was writing poetry, producing nearly four thousand lines of verse. His teaching duties were not demanding, and his eagerness to escape the drudgery of familiar surroundings lent further encouragement to his ambition to succeed as an original poet. Seven poems in hackneyed neoclassical verse were published at various times in these years; none can be considered distinguished, though *The Highlander,* published in Edinburgh in 1758, does exhibit a tentative sublimity suggestive of *Fingal.*[4] He soon recognized the poem as a failure, and asked the publisher to destroy any remaining copies. It would be hard to imagine a less promising beginning in poetry. But seemingly undiscouraged, Macpherson immediately began cultivating other projects.

He had long admired the Celtic traditions of the central Highlands: the customs, poetry, and songs of the region. At first, from simple inquisitiveness, Macpherson spent hours listening to his neighbors reciting Gaelic poetry. Later he transcribed a few fragments, a task made more difficult by his knowledge of Gaelic which was "bookish rather than native." Determined in this effort and yet uncertain of the ultimate value of what was still just an amusement, he left Ruthven in the spring of 1758 for more advantageous surroundings in Edinburgh.

His return to the capital was prompted by a desire to establish himself as a writer, discarding forever his prospects for the ministry, and to widen his circle of literary friends. Macpherson began serving an apprenticeship as a man of letters by doing literary hackwork for various booksellers and copyediting for Balfour, a publishing house. His entry into Edinburgh society was inauspicious; without adequate funds, Macpherson found it necessary to seek employment as a private tutor for the children of wealthy families. His first position, as tutor to Thomas Graham, the son of the laird of Balgowan, was to prove fortunate. The boy, a willing and able student who prospered under Macpherson's instruction, insisted that his teacher accompany the family on its travels.[5]

In the early months of 1759, while traveling in Scotland with his pupil, Macpherson was introduced to Adam Ferguson, a clergyman, soldier, gentleman, and, most significantly, the favorite companion of nearly every man of letters in Edinburgh, lay and clerical. This "Man of Sense, Knowledge, Taste, Elegance, and Morals" responded with increasing interest to Macpherson's enthusiasm for Gaelic poetry. Intrigued by the fragments shown him, Ferguson offered to introduce Macpherson to his friend, the dramatist John Home, and the meeting took place the following September at Moffat, a watering place for Edinburgh society. From this beginning, Macpherson would emerge as the translator of Ossian and the catalyst for a literary movement that would involve Scotland, England, and eventually much of Europe.

Middle Years

The acquaintance between the twenty-three-year-old Macpherson and John Home quickly ripened into a close friendship since both men shared an interest in finding ancient "national works." Ten years earlier the English poet William Collins had presented to Home the manuscript of "An Ode on the Popular Superstitions of the Highlands of Scotland, Considered as the Subject of Poetry," as a mark of his appreciation for the Scot's enthusiasm for primitive poetry. More recently Home had won the respect of his literary colleagues for his play *Douglas,* which had created a sensation in Edinburgh in 1756, as well as in London the following year.[6] When Home asked Macpherson for examples of Gaelic verse, Macpherson readily supplied him with a rhapsodic monody in English entitled "The Death of Oscar." Delighted by this discovery, Home promised to show the fragment, and any others Macpherson translated, to the learned Hugh Blair, soon to be professor of rhetoric and belles-lettres at the University of Edinburgh, and one of the founding members of the Select Society, Edinburgh's foremost club for men of letters.[7]

Encouraged by Blair's response, Ferguson's, and that of the philosopher and historian David Hume, the historian William Robertson, the economist Adam Smith, and other patriotic Scots, Macpherson published anonymously in Edinburgh his fifteen *Fragments of Ancient Poetry collected in the Highlands of Scotland, and translated from the Gaelic or Erse Language* (June 1760). Not only did Blair write a prophetic introduction to this book, he directed fund-raising in town to pay Macpherson's expenses for traveling through the northwest Highlands and outlying western islands in search of more Gaelic verse. David Hume, not usually one to allow his emotions to overcome his reason, wrote in August 1760 "that we have endeavoured to put Mr. Macpherson on a way of procuring us more of these wild flowers."[8] In January 1761 the young man returned with two epics about the Celtic hero Fingal, which he said had been written in the third century by Fingal's poet son, Ossian. One such epic was issued in six books as *Fingal: an Ancient Epic Poem,* together with fifteen other poems by Ossian, in December 1761; and early in 1763 appeared the second Ossianic epic, *Temora,* in eight books along with five shorter poems. To both works, Macpherson appended essays on the methods of his research and assured his readers of the poems' importance as social history.

Fingal, published in London by Thomas Becket, was dedicated to an unnamed "certain nobleman of exalted station." Later, in the dedication to *Temora,* Macpherson named as his patron John Stuart, Earl of Bute, the Scottish Tory grandee and former tutor of George III. Bute was then prime minister of England and at the height of his power.

Throughout 1762 nearly every writer and editor in London and Edinburgh praised *Fingal* as a great success, though some were soon suspicious of a translator who would not produce the original documents. Macpherson's claim for the authenticity of the poems was buttressed by the support of Bute and other Scots, which made any discussion of Ossian's history a matter of national pride. As skepticism grew in England and Ireland, the debate was inflamed by the vehement defense of Hugh Blair, whose *Critical Dissertation on the Poems of Ossian* appeared posthaste—in 1763. Blair argued with patriotic fervor that Ossian was the Homer of the Highlands, his work the equal of the *Iliad.* The debate would grow in furor, with Hume demanding that Blair make a more thorough investigation into the various charges of forgery. But most readers were not so skeptical, and Blair's *Dissertation,* which was frequently printed with later editions of the poems, did much to shore up Macpherson's claims. His defenders "indulged the pleasing supposition that Fingal fought and Ossian sang," and spoke, admiringly of the pathos, sublimity, and delicacy of emotion revealed in the work. Disbelievers refused to grant any distinction between the historical authenticity and the literary worth of the poems. If they were not ancient, they had no value as literature. The dispute rose and fell in three stages: an early phase of disbelief lasting five years, a middle period of furious moral debate sparked by Samuel Johnson after his tour of Scotland in 1773, and a final, though for Macpherson unfortunate, disposition with the publication in 1805 of the *Report* of the Highland Society of Scotland.

Macpherson, in the meantime, became wealthy; he stood "in the eye of the great world." His popular success as a translator of two epics in two years had brought him £1,200. In addition, Bute secretly sent him £300 a year, though, as Hume's biographer comments, "that situation could not long endure, and soon Bute found a means of disposing of the truculent translator." Since anti-Scottish feeling had reached new heights in London with John Wilkes's and Charles Churchill's vigorous attack on the government in the *North Briton,* Bute used his influence to remove a major cause for English resentment of Scots. On 15 June 1764 Macpherson was sent to America as provincial secretary to George Johnstone, the new governor of West Florida, a colony recently acquired by England in the Peace of Paris marking the end of the Seven Years' War. On arriving in Pensacola, Macpherson also assumed responsibility as clerk of the Governor's Council and later justice of the peace. These colonial offices proved time-consuming and tedious; moreover, the poet missed the amusements of London. After fifteen months and involvement in numerous arguments between the civil administration and the military, Macpherson returned to England with the understanding that he would retain his £300 a year for life if he remained in the service of the government.[9]

By the beginning of July 1766 the Rockingham ministry was tottering, and George III, employing his royal prerogative, decided to send for William Pitt, now Earl of Chatham. Determined to destroy party groups, Chatham selected his own cabinet and followed his own policy but met with a number of rebuffs. In this charged atmosphere Macpherson began work as a political writer for Lord Shelburne, Chatham's secretary of state for the southern department. Shelburne had begun his political career as a supporter of Bute, gaining a reputation as an accomplished debater and one of the most enlightened statesmen of his time. Within a year Macpherson had attracted the eye of Frederick, Lord North, who had replaced the infamous Charles Townshend as chancellor of the exchequer. A shrewd and practical man of business who pursued moderate and general policies, North put Macpherson's ready wit and vitriol to work replying to the audacious *Letters of Junius* (1768–71).[10] Though the extent to which Macpherson's letters to various journals influenced popular opinion is unclear, North found the poet's efforts valuable in representing the tenuous position of the cabinet, particularly in the Wilkes affair.

Ministerial instability and royal obstinacy continually plagued the social order; the people clamored for parliamentary reform. What they got instead was Lord North as the First Lord of the Treasury and, in 1770, prime minister; thus, Tories and the "King's Friends" in Parliament provided an unshakable majority. With his new Tory minister George III was able to rule almost as he pleased for twelve years (1770–82). During these years, however, unprecedented difficulties arose as a result of the approach and onset of the American Revolution.

In June 1776 the Second Continental Congress meeting in Philadelphia moved a resolution declaring independence, and formally approved the declaration in July. Macpherson, who had been supervising ministerial newspapers, was charged by Lord North to draft an immediate reply stating the government's view on the impudence of the rebels. In three months his pamphlet, *The Rights of Great Britain asserted against the Claims of America: being an Answer to the Declaration of the General Congress,* was issued to great popular acclaim. Macpherson was again to realize fame and wealth from his writings as his government salary rose from £600 to £800 a year.

The years 1771–79 were profitable in other ways for Macpherson. Catering to popular taste, he began writing histories. The research for his first book focused on the Celtic past of England and Ireland, a logical extension of his interest in the Ossianic material. Intended for little else than glorifying Celts and demonstrating the efficacy of religious and political institutions, *An Introduction to the History of Great Britain and Ireland* (1771) received scathing reviews. Hume, calling Macpherson's "the most anti-historical Head in the Universe," decried his lack of impartiality in examining persons and events.[11] Nonetheless, the work sold so well that Macpherson's publisher requested an enlarged edition for 1772, and a third, "revised and greatly enlarged," appeared in 1773. After extensive travels to gather documents in Paris, London, and Edinburgh, Macpherson published *Original Papers, Containing the Secret History of Great Britain, from the Restoration to the Accession of the House of Hanover* and the *History of Great Britain from the Restoration to the Accession of the House of Hanover,* on 10 March 1775. As far as British history is concerned, both works make significant contributions to the body of historical knowledge of these periods. The histories do have a strong Tory bias, however, and Macpherson realized in advance that his work would draw the Whigs' wrath. To forestall criticism, he went so far as to leave the original documents on display at his publisher's. Defending himself, he claimed, in an anonymous reply to a letter that declared him a biased impostor, that ". . . his

apparent and uniform attachment to the rights of human nature . . .
have met with the unanimous approbation of the judicious and unpre-
judiced of all parties."[12] As a result of the publicity from these two
histories and a recent fourth edition of the *Poems of Ossian,* by now made
even more famous by the quarrel it had occasioned with Johnson, Mac-
pherson possessed considerable bargaining power with his publishers
for the copyright to the *History of Great Britain.* Strahan and Cadell
paid him the enormous sum of £3,000 in order to issue the second
edition only a year later.

His only real failure during this period came with a translation of
the *Iliad* (1773). Though interesting as the only extended Ossianic
prose translation that is comparable to the original, it was severely
censured for dressing Homer in tartan colors. For once critics' opinions
held sway over public taste as the work sold very little, but the poet
took no apparent notice; always ignoring his failures, he fixed his gaze
unswervingly on success.

Macpherson's prosperity and fame during the seventies culminated
with the painting of his portrait by Joshua Reynolds. The impression
created by the pose and bearing of the poet is surely one of dignity and
warmth. The sitter does not look at the spectator but appears in easy
contemplation; his expression is spirited yet touched by sentiment. His
clothes are those of a fashionable man of his day. The half-portrait
reveals neither his great height—over six feet three inches—nor his
unruly temper. What one sees is Reynolds's assured touch for combin-
ing realism with a classicist's respect for human dignity. The work
must have met with Macpherson's full approval for it gave him the
well-bred, well-born look of an eighteenth-century gentlemen.[13]

Last Years

Macpherson approached middle age having accomplished many of
the goals he had set for himself as a young man: literary fame, wealth,
and social acceptance. The only major challenge of the years ahead was
how he would consolidate (even improve) his gains.

His *Poems of Ossian,* translated into ten foreign languages, had in-
spired countless readers and been read by the famous and near-famous.
The literati of Germany, Italy, and France stood in awe of the sublimity
and the magnificence of the language. He had survived, though in
somewhat bedraggled fashion, a verbal drubbing at the hands of no
less imposing a figure than Samuel Johnson. *Ossian* managed to thrive

even under the stigma of being a forgery. Macpherson doggedly continued to maintain the authenticity of his work. Agreeing in 1789 to the Highland Society's request for publication of the Gaelic originals, Macpherson began arranging his fragments and transcripts of oral recitations, bringing what originals existed into agreement with his own version, and supplying a Gaelic text. Seemingly, he had no intention of publishing his materials, wishing only to quell any rumor of being uncooperative. At his death this work remained incomplete and unpublished. In these last years he hinted more openly about his role in the success of *Ossian,* in a somewhat pathetic attempt at further glory. Except for this bit of recklessness Macpherson would never again make revelations that might threaten his fragile hold on fame.

With remarkable tenacity he had made himself indispensable to his publisher and to his patrons in government and thereby gained a fortune. All that remained was insuring his wealth by one further investment of his talents. About 1777 his opportunity came when a cousin, John Macpherson, an agent of the East India Company at Madras, was forced to resign his post. The agent had been secretly serving as a lobbyist in England and in India for Mohammed Ali, the Nawab of Arcot, an ally of the British Crown whose financial debts to the Company were enormous. With the encouragement of his kinsman, the poet accepted a position in 1778 as the Nawab's deputy in London, defending Ali's interest in the ongoing struggle between the Company and Parliament. Meanwhile John Macpherson (who later became governor-general in India) bought a seat in the House in order to press the Nawab's claims on the legislature. James published the letters from the Nawab to the Court of Directors of the Company in hopes of urging them to cancel the large interest debts incurred by his client. In 1779 he completed *The History and Management of the East India Company,* which served no other purpose than objecting to the Company's mistreatment of the Indian prince.

Since Parliament was divided on the question of just what authority it might exert over Company affairs, the time seemed appropriate for the seating of the Nawab's agent in the House of Commons. Accordingly, in 1780 Macpherson joined his kinsman in the House as a member for Camelford, Cornwall, paying £4,000 for his seat. Because of his association with the Indian prince, he was one of six members openly suspected of conflict of interest.[14] Macpherson countered this slander on the grounds that he had been instrumental in reconciling the difference between the Court of Directors and the ministry. He held his seat for life, winning reelection in 1784 and again in 1790. Before he began his second term in Parliament he received handsome gifts from his prince, sufficient to make him by any standard an exceedingly wealthy man.

In recognition of his standing and influence, the government offered Macpherson in 1783 the lands of his clan chieftain, Ewen of Cluny, whose house had been burnt to the ground and estates forfeited after the rebellion in 1746. Unwilling to tamper with the rights of traditional clan inheritance, Macpherson refused but began the next year making plans for building a mansion on an estate in his native parish. His parliamentary duties and services for the Nawab allowed him only six months away from London, but this was sufficient time for him to fulfill his final ambition. Land was purchased on a dominant knoll above the Spey, and the leading architect of the day, Robert Adam, was asked to design a house appropriate for an enlightened Scottish laird.[15]

Macpherson named the late-Palladian villa Belleville and announced through a series of lavish parties that a new period of sophistication and amusement had begun in the valley. Reports of his wealth, generosity, and amiability became legend; his five children, though born illegitimately in London, were raised in the house and received every kindness from his clan neighbors.

Nearly sixty years old, Macpherson had spent four decades hungrily pursuing recognition and wealth. In his eagerness he had damaged his health, leaving himself unable to enjoy fully the honors he had achieved. In poor health during the summer of 1793, he instructed the executors of his will to have him buried in Westminster Abbey. Money was set aside for this purpose and for the erection of a marble monument near his birthplace. In each of these matters he was to have his wish. With careful deliberation Macpherson completed the final requirements of fame and faced death calmly, revered by many as the discoverer of ancient epics indicative of a new order in the Western world and despised by others as a forger who had perpetrated a vicious hoax. He died at Belleville on 17 February 1796, confident in his own mind of posthumous distinction as the translator of the *Poems of Ossian*.

Chapter Two
Apprentice Work and First Fame

The dominant scene of Macpherson's early life was the pathetic sight of the Highland clans straggling past his home in full retreat from Culloden. The picture of these beaten men contradicted the young boy's vision of his countrymen as heroes—men whose humanity blended with courage in all their actions. Though his sentiments were shaken by the reality of the scene, Macpherson would never abandon his belief in the valor and nobility of the Highland warrior.

It was fortunate that his passion for the ancient traditions of his race would find an outlet in his love of poetry. In the early 1750s Macpherson was developing his creative spirit and acquiring a sense of the poetic process. His verse of this period reflects, however, the difficulty the poet had in producing the regular meter, syntactic clarity, and antithesis and balance characteristic of neoclassic poetry. Unwilling to trust his poetic instincts, which favored a diffusion of sense, he instead applied himself to imitating the predominant forms of his day with their concentration of reason and judgment. Samuel Johnson, while not referring to this topic, remarked during his trip to Scotland in 1773 that the Highlanders "have inquired and considered little, and do not always feel their own ignorance."[1] This general criticism typifies the response of most subsequent readers to Macpherson's early work. But whatever misgivings may exist, in the majority of the seven poems known to be his, the poet demonstrated a genuine desire to come to terms with the mysterious resonances of his Scottish heritage.

First Experiments

Macpherson's earliest extant poems date from the period 1753–58, when he was a college student in Aberdeen and Edinburgh and later a naive schoolmaster in his native Ruthven. These poems show his fondness for heroic sentiment, nationalistic pride, tragic gloom, melancholy, generosity, and compassion.

Malcolm Laing, an early nineteenth-century editor of *Ossian,* was responsible for securing and publishing the first poems, *Death* and *The Hunter,* in 1805. Laing received the rough manuscript from a sometime acquaintance of the poet, a minister of the local parish church in Kingussie. As far as the editor was concerned, the supporting documents found in the crude notebook established the poems as the poet's earliest work. Macpherson's biographer, Bailey Saunders, is convinced the poet had no intention of publishing the poems and believes Laing's compulsion for revealing such "rude work" was to discredit further the "translator" of Ossian. It does seem that Laing's aim was to chart Macpherson's development from an inexperienced and technically incompetent adapter of neoclassic convention to a poet of consummate skill quite capable of forging the Ossianic poems.[2]

A review of *Death* suggests how inept Macpherson could be when forced to complete a poetic exercise. Consisting of 512 lines of blank verse, the poem is a tepid imitation of the mortuary reflections of the Scots clergyman Robert Blair's *The Grave* (1743) and similar to Edward Young's *Night Thoughts* (1745). These more famous works have often been associated with the poetry of melancholy graveyard brooding, but their real purpose and attitude were quite different. They preached the somber message that religion alone can reconcile us to the inevitability of death. Macpherson followed thousands of other sentimental readers in ignoring the austerity of the verses and instead misinterpreted them as a wistful appeal to sensibility.

In *Death* the poet adopts the role of a melancholy figure meditating on the macabre tragedy of life. The general theme is the inevitability of suffering and death for man in a world torn apart by war. In contrasting pictures of war and peace, the poem is divided into three sections: the dismal prospects for achieving lasting peace (ll. 1–222), the certainty of war and a depiction of battle scenes on land and sea (ll. 223–378), and the return of peace with opportunities to mourn the dead (ll. 379–512).

If the poem has redeeming qualities, they exist in the descriptions of the fighting between rival armies and the destruction of a fleet at sea in the second section. Macpherson's language and imagery, though at times pompous, give eloquent support to the view that valor, nobility of soul, and an ability to bear sorrows with courage give meaning to the unceasing warfare:

> See! bright in arms, along the iron field
> The stately young Philanthes drives the foe;
> No thirst of fame, no lion-hearted thought
> Prompts on the youth—nought but his country's love.[3]

But the rarity of such clear, straightforward poetic vision condemns the work to an interminable series of clichés, unfortunate puns, mixed metaphors, and conventional figures.

Superficial resemblances to *Ossian* may be seen in the violent death of the young hero, the poet's lament at the passing of noble comrades, and the description of the world as a dangerous place where sorrow is certain and happiness transient. What Macpherson cannot accomplish in *Death* is a believable, intensely personal relationship between the sensitive, contemplative bard and the mysterious, tragic world in which he finds himself.

The cold intensity of perception required of an artist who intends to reveal man's weakness in the face of unmanageable forces would again escape Macpherson in his second work. *The Hunter,* Laing's title for this rambling narrative, contains nearly seventeen hundred lines in heroic couplets divided evenly into ten cantos. The weaknesses of the poem are inescapable, particularly in the disorder of the narrative and the clumsy manipulation of supernatural forces in the natural world. The difficulties become more stark since the poet uses a verse form and poetic tradition reminiscent of the early Augustans but conveys his subject matter in a later style given to ornateness, hyperbole, and violent exclamation:

> A place there is, where the cerulean main
> Glides up through earth, and forms an azure plain;
> The Hunter stood astonish'd, to survey
> The roaring billows on the watry way,
> How liquid mountains dash against the shore,
> The rough rocks rumble, while the billows roar.
> He stretched his limbs along the murmuring deep,
> And the hoarse billows lull his soul to sleep.
>   (2:476–77)

Reacting to these characteristics, a modern editor, John Macqueen, believes that Macpherson's earliest poems remain examples of a first step in a remarkably consistent development. "From the beginning his concern was with natural man and the expression of natural feeling, as feeling, as the terms were understood in the middle eighteenth century."[4]

Donald, the rough-hewn hero of *The Hunter,* seems to gain his strength from the ruggedness of the natural spectacle. The setting offers blissful scenes of "rough brow'd rocks" that surround "the hut, the heathy wild, the barren fold."[5] The hunter is at first satisfied with the simple challenge of survival, but becomes disenchanted after a series of visions, brought on by a vengeful fairy princess, haunt his sleep. No longer able to respond to the beauty and simplicity of the landscape, the hunter seeks in "vile ambition" the "High-tower'd" city of Edin with its stores of riches and fame. His arrival at court is most propitious because the English have invaded and threaten destruction and "hateful slavery"; Donald, embracing the Celtic ideal of love and loyalty to king, follows a code that requires the individual to act for the common good, not for his own glory. With magnificence and "terror, commixed with soul-attractive grace," he becomes, as Carlyle was later to say of the hero, "the living light-fountain, which it is good and pleasant to be near."[6] Just as in the Old Testament battle between David and Goliath or the Homeric combat of Achilles and Hector, the Highland warrior defeats in single combat the Saxon hero, who "greatly stood . . . bear[ing] a spacious shield, / Glittering with iron terrour o'er the field" (2:483).

Macpherson was attempting, with juvenile enthusiasm, to restore the pride of the Highlanders. In reawakening the memories of liberty, the power of the clans, and the courage of the Scot, he spoke without disguise of his oppositions to English tyranny. But if a tone of revolutionary zeal exists in this and the later poems, it is only for a moment. Macpherson's intention was not to create political heroes but to present modern sentimentalists. As J. S. Smart comments, "the heroes of Macpherson . . . love 'the enchanting tale, tale of pleasing woe.' They call for the minstrel and cry, 'Send thou the night away in song; and give the joy of grief.' "[7]

The Hunter possesses a similar brand of fatalism: at the moment of greatest victory comes the moment of deepest sorrow. Donald's soul finds no pleasure in fame; because of his ignoble birth, he remains unworthy of the princess Egidia—his great passion. The narrative pauses here, while the "hill-born hero" sings "his toils, his woes," and then tumbles haphazardly from canto 6 to the end with revelations that disclose his noble ancestry, one which permits the lovers to marry with blessings from both the fathers, who are present at court. There is no doubt that Macpherson means to draw attention to the artificiality of the happy ending. Each canto balances joy with gloom and fertility with desolation; nature is beautiful and beneficient, but also cruel and destructive. Donald's final acceptance in the Edinburgh court and union with the weak Egidia suggests no reassertion of liberty but the imprisonment and corruption of the natural man. Macpherson's immaturity would not permit a more coherent and less conventional close; instead, he only suggests his true attitude:

> In vain, in vain I sooth my glowing care,
> In vain elude thy venomed pangs, Despair!
> Even now, perhaps, the seamen ply the oar,
> And waft my soul into the farther shore.
>   (2:521)

The poet had probably meant to use this effort merely as a first draft for *The Highlander*, which he published two years later; nevertheless, he created a notable character in Donald, who possesses "all the qualities that can ennoble human nature; that can either make us admire the hero, or love the man."[8] When Hugh Blair wrote these words, he was praising Fingal's moral excellence, but they apply equally to Macpherson's prototype of Fingal in this poem.

The publication of *The Highlander* in April 1758 brought no recognition to the poet. In fact, he became rather embarrassed shortly after its appearance since his publisher, Walter Ruddiman, Jr., did not see fit to review the work in either of his two journals, the *Scots Magazine* or the *Edinburgh Magazine*. Saunders believes that Macpherson made a special effort to suppress the work. Macpherson's preface to his translation of the *Iliad* suggests that he recognized even as a youth that imitation carried to excessive length curbed the imagination and dulled one's judgment.

His most severe critics, while censuring the poem, believe that it reflects "a genuine and serious desire to fashion an epic on a Scottish theme."[9] *The Highlander* is an original narrative about prehistoric Scotland, written before Macpherson had realized in *Ossian* that such fantasy might prove profitable. With his knowledge of early Scottish history derived from John Fordun, John Major, and George Buchanan, he creates a framework of six cantos where an unknown warrior, Alpin (the name of an early ninth-century Scottish king long celebrated in elegiac poetry), appears and rallies the Scots in a fierce defense of their

homeland against Danish invaders. Later, when victory is assured, the
present king, Indulph (an historical figure, who was the seventy-sev-
enth king of Scotland), singles out the hero for praise; Alpin, speaking
of his youth, reveals characteristics that Indulph recognizes as those of
the lost son of his dead brother, King Malcolm. Alpin, now called by
his true name Duffus, refuses the offer of Indulph's throne in order to
retain the status of warrior while pursuing and marrying the princess
Culena. In a rapid change of fortune, Indulph is killed by marauding
Danes; Duffus, with his new bride, becomes king.

By combining history and legend with nationalistic fervor, Mac-
pherson rediscovers the ancient traditions, thereby attaining prestige
for his people. He never plays down the importance of warfare to the
Celts; moreover, he paints an entire nation as war-mad, both high-
spirited and ready for battle. With measured phrasing, he describes the
trappings of the Celtic warrior and the elements that together symbol-
ize the full responsibilities of manhood. The poem displays quite ef-
fectively the two complementary and essential facets of Celtic
aristocratic life: fighting and feasting. The first three cantos describe
the fighting, an athletic event where the participants compete for per-
sonal prestige and social position. The final three offer an extended
feasting period when the exploits of the warriors are recounted with
proper embellishment that stresses their nobility. "The Caledonian
court is a model of openness based on benevolence, honesty, and
trust."[10] As a recorder of this generosity and heroism, the bard enum-
erates the essential moments until they become part of tradition:

> To keep in song the mem'ry of the dead!
> They handed down the ancient rounds of time,
> In oral story and recorded rhyme.
> The vocal quire in tuneful concert sings
> Exploits of heroes, and of ancient kings.
>   (2:573)

The similarities between *The Hunter* and *The Highlander* leave little
doubt that the former was an early draft of the latter: the unknown
warrior of mysterious lineage emerges through acts of valor and bravery
as champion of the Scots in a war against the invader; he conquers not
only the enemy, but the hearts of the nobles, including that of the
king's daughter, and his noble ancestry is revealed. In comparison to
The Hunter, the later poem has undeniable strengths, particularly in its

coherent narrative and use of natural settings. At the same time, it anticipates *Ossian* in its use of nature as an emotive power and in its tuneful bard as a singer of "the melody of woe"; it suffers artistically, however, from a poorly controlled clash between the poetic impulses of two different periods. Nonetheless, Macpherson's impulse in this poem, as C. S. Lewis finds, was sincere; he was "seeking in the past that great romantic poetry which really lay in the future, and from intense imagination of what it must be like if only he could find it he slipped into making it himself."[11] His desire to rescue the pride of the Scots from the gloom of Culloden brought him through the composition of these flawed epics to the extraordinary *Ossian*.

Later Experiments

By the autumn of 1758 Macpherson had been in Edinburgh at least two months after resigning his teaching position in Ruthven. The metropolis had fascinated him since his student days there, and now he became thoroughly familiar with the lower town of the Canongate and the high town or Edinburgh proper. He was drawn to it as a paradoxical place of medieval historic associations and modern cosmopolitan aspirations where his ambitions might prosper.

The contrasting urban environment and the beautiful natural surroundings of the Firth of Forth, the Lomond hills, and Arthur's Seat were a reassuring reminder of the Highlands. Macpherson might have joined Boswell in praising "that lofty romantic mountain on which I have so often strayed in my days of youth, indulged meditation and felt the raptures of a soul filled with ideas of the magnificence of God and his creation."[12] The poet, however, was not merely satisfying some agreeable whim, but exploring every opportunity for recognition as a man of letters. Through his contact with Walter Ruddiman, Macpherson began sending the printer occasional verse for publication in the *Scots Magazine,* a leading monthly in the kingdom and a literary journal of some repute.

In November 1758 the *Scots Magazine* published the "Death of Marshall Keith," an elegy of sixty-six lines mourning the loss of the Jacobite soldier, later Prussian field marshal. James Keith had been shot dead on 14 October 1758 at the Battle of Hochkirch while leading for the third time a cavalry charge against the enemy. He and his brother George were descendants of a noble family who had held the hereditary office of Great Marischal of Scotland since the twelfth century. James, who was considered a military genius by Frederick the Great, had been involved in the Jacobite uprisings of 1715 and 1719, and was forced to flee with his brother to the Continent where he soldiered in the armies of Russia, Spain, and Prussia. His name, famous throughout Scotland, called up memories of more rebellious and high-spirited times. Macpherson, who would in two years write an ode celebrating the return of George Keith to his homeland, was content in the elegy with plaintive effusions soaked in sentiment. He may have sincerely wished to capture the nation's sense of loss, but instead what he offers must be regarded as a misguided attempt to cater to the vitiated tastes of the Edinburgh aristocracy. The poet seems only to demonstrate his acute perception of popular taste in an atmosphere thick with the sentimental poems of William Shenstone and Thomas Gray. Though writing on his favorite subject, the martial spirit, Macpherson seems trapped by ill-chosen words and unskillfully inverted phrasing:

> Hungaria gives the tribute of the eye,
> and ruthless Russia melts into a sigh:
> They mourn his fate, who felt his sword before;
> And all the hero in the foe deplore.
>
> (2:587)

Of Macpherson's next two poems little need be said. They reflect the strong influence of late neoclassical sentimentality that would persist until the poet found a less imitative, more congenial voice in *Ossian*. In the elegies "On the Death of a Young Lady" (May 1759) and "To the Memory of an Officer Killed Before Quebec" (October 1759) there is a disappointing lack of genuine feeling, stanza after stanza seeming "only empty noise." As a technician Macpherson had made improvements in the handling of these English verse forms, but no real promise of a literary career can be found here.

The final poem of his apprenticeship, "The Earl Marischal's Welcome to His Native Country" (September 1760), made its appearance three months after the publication of the *Fragments of Ancient Poetry* and was largely forgotten in the excitement surrounding the translations. It is a strict Pindaric ode in the manner of Gray's "The Bard" (1757), celebrating the expected return of the Jacobite George Keith to Scotland after an exile of nearly fifty years.[13] After his escape from Scotland the Lord Marischal had become a trusted diplomat in the service of Frederick the Great, and only in 1759, as a reward for valuable service, did the British government pardon him and allow him his estates.

The language of the poem is dignified, restrained, and imaginative, at least when the narrator speaks of Scotland. In an undramatic way Macpherson has made an excellent choice in the verse form. Since the Pindaric ode was a popular vehicle for enthusiastic religious and patriotic poetry, he employed its characteristics by focusing the rise and fall of emotional power on the critical issues: lost freedoms and love of country. He seems to grasp Gray's method of concise narrative technique and swift transition. As in the more effective stanzas in his short epics, Macpherson is responsive to the strife of battle, its vivid, shocking action. It may be extravagant to suggest that, having discovered that his greatest strength lay in the traditions of his native land, here in this last ode he found himself as a poet. Nonetheless, the last stanza suggests the fire and enthusiasm of which Macpherson would later prove himself more capable:

> Thus as he spoke, each hoary sire
> Fights o'er again his ancient wars;
> Each youth burns with a hero's fire,
> And triumphs in his future scars;
> O'er bloody fields each thinks he rides,
> The thunder of the battle guides. . .
> And hears applauding legions hail
> Him with the shouts of victory.
> (2:600)[14]

The Scottish Gaelic Tradition

When Macpherson met John Home in the autumn of 1759 at Moffat, he had made only minimal progress toward becoming a successful poet. But in his discussions with Home about the Highlands, the Celts, and their poetry, he came to realize that another experiment might prove fruitful. As Home would testify later to the Highland Society, he encouraged Macpherson to translate the best of the several pieces of ancient poetry he had in his possession. Home, a Lowland Scot, who knew nothing of Gaelic, thus encouraged Macpherson so that he himself might "be able to form some opinion of the genius and character of Gaelic poetry."[15]

We know that Macpherson had a working knowledge of Gaelic since it was the vernacular of his district; and he had some Gaelic originals with him, though his handling of these fragments was thoroughly promiscuous. To say he embroidered and distorted would only begin to acknowledge his irresponsibility in the matter. Macpherson's use of bardic material varies continuously, at some points only a passing reference, at others close attention to the ballad fragment in question. The result of this method is an intermingling of several different cultures.

In order to illustrate further Macpherson's manner of working, we must first confront the living and continuous tradition of Gaelic language and literature. Macpherson, in constructing his elaborate strategy, relied heavily on his countrymen's partiality for the Gaelic folklore—the tales and poems—of the Highlands.

Scottish Gaelic is a dialect of a primary language group within Celtic, the Goidelic; the others include Irish Gaelic and Manx (Isle of Man). The traditional explanation for the appearance of this form of speech in Scotland is that a small band of older Celtic peoples, the Dalriadic, came over from their homeland in the north of Ireland to the Argyll coast in the fourth century A.D. Very few examples of the early written language exist, with the exception of *The Book of Deir,* a volume from the monastery at Deer (Aberdeenshire). The annotations to this Latin text and its other memoranda are in the native dialect of the Irish monks. These inscriptions date from the ninth century, with other entries from the eleventh and twelfth centuries in a vernacular that became Scottish Gaelic. No instance of distinctly Scottish writing survives for the next four hundred years.

At the end of the fifteenth century the Lordship of the Isles, the dominant political unit of the Highlands, was dissolved by James IV, who wished to unite Scotland under his rule and prevent a further separation between the two cultures. This act was to have far-reaching consequences. The power of the Irish bards, their control of the language, was effectively undermined, and the native Scots thus reverted to their own dialect, in time producing a valid literary language. James himself encouraged the movement. He learned a little Gaelic and, in other ways as well, demonstrated an active enthusiasm for a national culture. Though the influence of the Irish bards still remained strong, the Scots began discarding the Irish orthography and various word-forms.

The growing strength of Scottish Gaelic is superbly demonstrated in *The Book of the Dean of Lismore,* compiled between 1512 and 1526 by Sir James Macgregor, Dean of Lismore, and his brother Duncan. This priceless literary record of sixty professional bards and amateur poets consists of 311 quarto pages written in phonetic Gaelic. Of its eleven thousand lines of verse, twenty-five hundred are in "the genuine

Ossian style"; these make up twenty-eight short, detached ballads that are believed to be the more ancient part of the collection. Most scholars agree that Macpherson returned from his travels to the northwest Highlands and islands in 1760 with these materials, and that he left them with his London publishers for public inspection at a later date. Of the Lismore collection, the Celtic scholar Magnus MacLean comments, "How it came into his hands or where it lay for the 300 years that elapsed between the Dean's time and the beginning of the last century is not known."[16]

Before the eighteenth century, the golden period of Gaelic poetry, there were two other manuscripts of importance to the literature of the Highlands and, ultimately, to Macpherson. The *Red* and *Black Books of Clanranald,* commonplace books begun in the fourteenth century by the hereditary bards of the Clanranald chiefs, the Macvurichs, are family histories of the Clan Macdonald, along with the record of the exploits of the Earl of Montrose in the 1640s and various Gaelic poems. During the Highland Society's investigation into the origin of Macpherson's *Ossian,* the rumor was that the poet had written both the Fingal and Temora epics from the Clanranald volumes, which were handed to him by a descendant of the last bard. Fascinating though the materials in the *Red* and the *Black* are to any scholar or admirer of Celtic culture, they cannot have served as Macpherson's originals. The translation and editing of these Gaelic texts were to prove daunting even to later scholars; this highly complicated and time-consuming task Macpherson could not have accomplished himself. Furthermore, the books contain no Ossianic fragments. As J. S. Smart notes, "We seek there in vain for so much as a line of *Fingal.*"[17]

The Ossianic Cycle

As we have seen, Scottish Gaelic literature offers little before the Celtic revival in the second half of the eighteenth century. And because of the ascendancy of Ireland in language and literature, Scotland had to depend on Ireland for the rich heritage of Celtic myths and folk tales. In the Gaelic manuscripts found in Scotland and Ireland, as well as in the manuscripts taken to the Continent by monks fleeing the Norse invasions, scholars have discovered a remarkable saga literature. In these tales, dating from the pre-Christian era through the middle of the third century A.D., we find the name Ossian (Oisein) and begin to understand its place in Celtic literature.

Before the arrival of Christian missionaries in Ireland and Scotland,

Celtic myths and tales were transmitted through a well-organized oral tradition. The professional literary man in Ireland was the *fili,* whose role in the tribe seems to have been threefold: as storyteller; as judge, including legislator and lawyer; and as poet. He had a pivotal influence in the development of society, but by the seventh century Ireland was undergoing a profound change in its societal traditions. Celtic scholars believe that the society had split into two groups, a nobility above tradition and a popular class which was beneath it. This division tended to destroy the power of the *fili* over his people; consequently, ancient literature was being forgotten. Christianity had much to do at first with suppressing such pagan institutions as the *fili.*

But the schools of oral poetry began flourishing again with fresh initiatives for learning from the monasteries and churches throughout Ireland. By the eighth and ninth centuries learned Irish monks who had excellent backgrounds in traditional native learning were working among the people. They produced the first written records of a vernacular literature and preserved such myths and legends as were still available to them with accuracy and care.

The written literature of Ireland is composed mainly of stories arranged in three cycles: the Mythological and the two Heroic cycles of Ulster and Leinster-Munster. The oldest of these, the Mythological cycle, provides a history of the gods and of successive invasions of the country. The major work in which these stories now are found is O'Cleary's *Leabhar Gabhala,* or *Book of Invasions,* 1630. Among the numerous narratives of the collection is the famous "Three Sorrows of Story-Telling," which has been identified as prehistoric.

The Ulster cycle, also known as the Cuchulain or Red-Branch cycle, is the best-known and most attractive work of the Middle Irish period (1100–1500). The ninety-six tales of the collection revolve about the exploits of the Celtic warrior champion Cuchulain, and of Conchobar, King of Ulster who join to oppose the rest of Ireland in a great war— all for the sake of a magnificent, supernatural bull. In the cycle's chief epic, the *Táin Bó Cúailgne* or the *Cattle-raid of Cooley,* the bearing, strength, courage, and pride of the two warriors create an atmosphere of memorable energy and passion. All the stories in the cycle are related thematically to the birth, fortune, and ultimate victory in life and death of Cuchulain. These medieval romances attractively employ dramatic force and humor. Arthurian courtliness has no place in these barbaric tales, however, parallels with the Arthurian legends may occasionally be discussed. MacLean calls the cycle "profuse, fantastic, minute, boldly original, tedious . . . [with] an atmosphere entirely different from anything modern."[18] Ironically, these adjectives were often the same used by eighteenth-century critics in describing Macpherson's "discovery."

The Leinster-Munster or Southern cycle, more frequently known as the Fenian or Ossianic cycle, gained predominance among the Irish and ultimately among all Gaelic speakers. The dating of these tales is uncertain; however, most scholars accept the middle of the third century A.D. as an initial reference point. This date seems appropriate to only a small number of the complete stories, for research has revealed that most were written in or after the twelfth century. The major characters of the cycle are Finn MacCumhail, a typical Celtic hero, who traces his descent from a hunter god and is capable of foretelling the future; his son, Oisein or Ossian; and their band of warriors, the Fianna. Characteristic of them all is a love of freedom, with wild romps through the forests pursuing game and long feasts celebrating the pleasures of comradeship. As warriors, the Fianna are a tough, tenacious foe who haughtily defy death and are bound in allegiance to a demanding code of service and discipline. Each warrior must take a fierce joy in battle yet be gracious to his enemies; also, he must have learned the *Twelve Books of Poetry* and compose verse. The tales of Finn and the Fianna are told by Ossian, who became as influential a poet in Gaelic culture as Homer was to the Greek.

The Ulster cycle is written in a rhythmic prose with long declamatory passages that for their tone frequently evoke comparison with the Old Testament. The Ossian cycle, made up of short ballads, is contained in such sources as the *Book of the Dun Cow*, the *Book of Leinster,* and the *Yellow Book of Lecan*. Derick Thomson found that "from the very early times . . . motifs from the Cuchulain cycle were incorporated in the Ossianic stories, and to a large extent the Ossianic cycle took the place of the Cuchulain cycle in popular tradition."[19] Macpherson apparently recognized that in Scotland the term "Ossianic" was applied loosely to both the Ulster and Fenian cycles, and he employed that ambiguity to strengthen his conviction that the Ossianic cycle was Scottish, not Irish, in origin. His personal aloofness from the Irish came from a deep-rooted belief in the degeneracy of their ballad sources. From the first, he accused Irish historians and ballad scholars of perpetrating a hoax; his extensive prefaces and lengthy notes demanded that readers recognize his authentic Ossian and reject the late and spurious works of Irish poets who had borrowed Ossian's name for their "wicked arts."

The ballad form remained constant into the eighteenth century; its earliest manifestation in the cycle, as mentioned earlier, is the six-teenth-century *Book of the Dean of Lismore,* found in Scotland. But the Dean's *Book* was not the only Ossianic material known to exist prior to Macpherson's second and last epic, *Temora,* in 1763. Derick Thomson's seminal work, *The Gaelic Sources of Macpherson's Ossian* (1952), is important largely for its detailed comparison of Mac-pherson's text with the authentic Gaelic ballads. Macpherson, as Thomson and others have noted, was the inheritor of an oral tradition in the Highlands that was, in fact, timeless. Thus many of these native ballads remained current in Macpherson's day and were probably known to him. In addition, Thomson cites these written sources: the Dean's *Book,* in which four ballads resemble the poet's text; the 1748 Turner manuscript with its fourteen Ossianic poems, two appearing to have been sources; a collection of Ossianic ballads by Jerome Stone, four of which Macpherson took as sources (Stone had also translated a Gaelic ballad for the *Scots Magazine* in January 1756 which Macpherson had undoubtedly read); the Archibald Fletcher collection of ballads written down during the 1750s, which provided Macpherson with seven sources; a 1755 compilation of six Ossianic ballads by the Rev-erend Donald MacNicol, who in 1779 would publish *Remarks* on John-son's trip to Scotland in 1773; and an extensive collection of Ossianic poetry by the Reverend James Maclagan, who corresponded with Mac-pherson and sent him possibly ten ballads. Because two later eigh-teenth-century collections, one by Duncan Kennedy (1774–80) and the other by John Gillies (1786), contain Ossianic ballads close to the poet's text in at least five important instances, it seems likely that Macpherson saw them in another form at an earlier date.[20]

First Fame: *Fragments of Ancient Poetry* (1760)

On 2 October 1759 the Reverend Alexander Carlyle of Inveresk, known to his friends as "Jupiter," traveled to Moffat with the express purpose of seeing his ingenious colleague, the dramatist John Home. Carlyle had met the young man in 1756 when David Hume had asked the minister's support in helping Home produce his new tragedy, *Douglas.* The literary aspects of this project excited Carlyle. When he arrived at Home's lodgings near the theater, he found the room peopled with the greatest literary men of the Scottish Enlightenment. Hugh Blair, Adam Ferguson, David Hume, and William Robertson had all agreed to take minor parts for this rehearsal. Close by stood an appreciative audience, men of rank and sophistication—Lord Elibank, Lord Kames, Lord Monboddo, and the clergymen William Home and John Steele—whose very presence would insure the success of the play.

Three years later Carlyle unsuspectingly arrived at Moffat at another propitious moment to find an excited Home proclaiming the discovery of a new poetical genius. Home spent the entire day describing Macpherson and his translations to the astonished minister, who agreed that as soon as possible this precious manuscript should be presented to the world. The dramatist had taken great pleasure in the fragment known as "the Death of Oscar," a piece Macpherson had concocted from various ballad sources and his own imagination.[21] With this translation and others, Home made rapid preparation to return to Edinburgh and seek out the liberal-minded clergyman Hugh Blair. It is pleasant to think that, just as David Hume and his coterie had acted as patrons and advocates for the young playwright, John Home was now returning the favor done him by the Edinburgh literary community by his advocacy of the untried, ambitious James Macpherson.

Blair, a vain yet highly intelligent man, responded favorably to Home's vivacity and to his enthusiasm for these "genuine remains of Scottish poetry." He soon invited Macpherson to his home in order to hear more about his discoveries; he was fascinated by the coincidence of their appearance just when he was writing his lectures on the sublime and the nature of poetry. Blair, who spoke highly of this Gaelic poetry to his friends in the Select Society (as did Home), believed that Macpherson should translate the other pieces in his possession and allow him to circulate them to those literati who could do the poet and the nation the most good. Blair felt, and others would shortly agree with him, that he could trust this young Highlander to find those "greater and more considerable poems in the same strain" he had mentioned to him and to Home. For more than ten years Blair's friends had explored the north for Highland poetry, yet with little success; thus they could hardly ignore Macpherson's arrival, especially "with the inspiring thought of a national epic, worthy of Homer, spurring them on."[22]

Blair's first duty, as he saw it, was to determine whether or not his and Home's response to these translations was correct. By circulating the manuscripts of what were later published as Fragment 11 and "The Six Bards," a descriptive poem, he hoped to advance the principle of the Select Society, which was "to bring about a renaissance of Scottish letters . . . and enjoy the feast of reason." In doing so, he chose among

its membership for his first respondent a thirty-three-year-old Scots-
man and lawyer of noble family, Sir David Dalrymple, later Lord
Hailes, who not only possessed a sensitivity for literary and antiquarian
pursuits, but also maintained an extensive correspondence with a
highly visible group of English men of letters, particularly his fellow
Etonians Horace Walpole and Thomas Gray.

In January 1760 Dalrymple sent the manuscripts to Walpole, who
wrote back in the next week (3 February 1760) with cautious amuse-
ment, commenting that the poetry contained "natural images and nat-
ural sentiment elevated." Walpole apparently agreed to Dalrymple's
request to send the poems to Gray for his reaction. Gray, showing more
specific interest, found the poems charming and asked Walpole (April
1760) to gather more information about the originals, the author(s)
and their historic period, and about whether or not more Erse poems
existed in Scotland. In a few days Walpole wrote Dalrymple in order
"to satisfy the curiosity" of Gray, whose infectious enthusiasm had
alerted more than one English reader to the poems: "But seriously he,
Mr. Mason, my Lord Lyttelton and one or two more whose taste the
world allows, are in love with your Erse elegies: I cannot say in general
they are so much admired—but Mr. Gray alone is worth satisfying."[23]

The weeks between April and the publication of the *Fragments* in
early June were fairly choked with correspondence on this matter. To
put matters briefly, Gray remained the most active in pursuit of Os-
sian. Unable to await further word from Walpole's correspondent, he
wrote to Macpherson requesting Gaelic "originals" with translations,
which he was sent in May. In the meantime, Gray began his own
circulation of the poems to friends Richard Stonehewer, William Ma-
son, Dr. John Clerke, and Thomas Warton. The letters from Mac-
pherson were intriguing less for the answers they supplied to Gray's
questions than for the new questions and doubts they raised about the
Highlander and his sources. Gray was immediately on his guard, sus-
pecting that "the whole external evidence would make one believe
these fragments . . . counterfeit."[24] Whatever his doubts, they were
lost in his fervent desire to prove a long-held belief that English poetry
was deeply indebted to Celtic literature. Gray's "extasie with their in-
finite beauty" made certain that the publication of the *Fragments* would
be perhaps the most fervently awaited literary event in England since
Johnson's publication of the *Dictionary* five years earlier.

The first edition of the *Fragments of Ancient Poetry* was placed on sale by Edinburgh booksellers on the morning of 14 June 1760. The thin volume of seventy pages, containing fifteen prose poems of varying length introduced by Hugh Blair in a nine-hundred-word preface, was published by the eminent Scottish house of Gavin Hamilton and John Balfour, the firm that had printed the popular classic, Hume's *History of England* (1754–62)[25] Macpherson's biographer, among others, suggests that the poet was reluctant to publish these unauthenticated works but could not resist the "great potentate," Blair, who was eager to prove his support for the literature of Scotland. Blair did write later to the *Ossian* investigators that he "repeatedly importuned" the poet for publication; however, Macpherson had every intention of publishing and only expressed a genteel hesitancy so as not to appear self-seeking. Most important, Thomas Gray, who had spurred on Macpherson and Blair, was not to be disappointed.

The preface, though brief, tantalizes the reader with assurances of the authenticity of the fragments, while alerting him to the "spirit and strain" of the pieces.[26] Blair writes less as a critic than as a reporter who had interviewed a source for the facts of a particular story. As the preface unfolds, Blair deliberately reveals that his dependence on Macpherson to account for the origins of the poems leaves Macpherson free to shape a reader's response. First Macpherson deftly blunts the uncertain reaction of Christian readers to pagan poetry by explaining that these pieces were of a pre-Christian era when marvelous heroes who traced their descent from Druidic gods walked the land. In this way, Macpherson caught and played to the mid-century's fascination with Celtic mythology; his description of Ossian is equally calculated. This "principal personage" he shows as scornful of any religion that might interfere in the deeds of men. Though Macpherson had not yet named Ossian as the author of the fragments, as a character Ossian does act as a central symbol of a once-proud people who remember "the illustrious actions" of their ancestors. This hint of nationalism and sentiment is unmistakable in Blair's early paragraphs.

Second, the preface notes provocatively that these "fragments" are but pieces of a great, and as yet undiscovered, epic. As John Dunn points out, "Macpherson was shifting from the reluctant 'translator' of a few 'fragments' to the projector of a full-length epic 'if enough encouragement were given.' "[27] Blair explains further that the epic may exist in bits and pieces in various ancient manuscripts, as well as be preserved (though unrecognized as such) in tales still transmitted orally. This revelation of the possible existence of a Celtic epic in the Highlands is, of course, the most dramatic moment in the preface. The disclosure not only raises readers' expectations to new heights, it sounds a clarion for further and more intensive investigation. What literate Scotsman (or Englishman) could refuse so clear a challenge?

Blair, at the last, emphasizes the scrupulous attention the translator has paid to the originals. He notes especially Macpherson's concern for preserving the simple beauty of Gaelic thought, his sensitivity to the cadence and length of Gaelic versification, and his desire to do nothing that violates the spirit of the verse. Blair thus assures whatever detractors may be among the poet's readers that they may have faith in Macpherson's literary integrity. It is as a skilled rhetorician that Blair returns to the likelihood of further discoveries and promises that, if Macpherson is encouraged, an epic might be recovered that would "serve to throw considerable light upon the Scottish and Irish antiquities" (2:383–84).

Blair made no evaluation of the literary merit of the poems, leaving such judgment to the public. His reticence was taken as an implied tribute to contemporary taste in literary matters, though, of course, it would protect him from public embarrassment should readers deem the poems a failure. His caution proved unnecessary, however, for the public's trumpeting of the fragments began almost immediately.

One reason for such an enthusiastic reception was the appearance of two selections in the *Gentleman's Magazine* for June 1760. Later in the year, the *Annual Register* published Edmund Burke's review of Macpherson's book, which contained a selection of three fragments, two of them, Fragments 5 and 12, the same as had been published in the *Gentleman's Magazine*. Burke also printed Fragment 6.

Fragment 5

Not only did Fragment 5 give the general reading public its first glimpse into "Highland antiquities," but it also clearly conveyed the tone and effect of the remaining fragments. The poem employs long prose cadences punctuated with extensive parenthetical or descriptive phrases. Though the subject is heroic, the diction is vigorous and rugged rather than majestic and lofty. Macpherson breaks with traditional concepts of style, but his "measured prose" with its shorter native words makes each sentence striking and prevents the sentiment from becoming tedious.

Autumn is dark on the mountains; grey mist rests on the hills. The whirlwind is heard on the heath. Dark rolls the river through the narrow plain. A tree stands alone on the hill, and marks the grave of Connal. (2:390)

Fragment 5 begins with a highly emotional description of a foreboding landscape. The melancholy of the scene parallels the bards' recounting of the death of Connal (the Victorious, as he is known in the Ulster cycle). The major themes appear swiftly: the ironic relationship between love and death, the pathetic death of the hero at the moment of victory, the primitive and unspoiled wildness of nature.

As a song of love and death, the fragment has a superficial resemblance to its ballad sources, but the entire atmosphere has been altered from the original. The dominant note of the poem is unshakable grief. Connal, whose friendship with Cuchulain was renowned in Gaelic literature, is killed accidentally by his lover, Crimora, in the heat of battle. Inconsolable, she dies of grief, and the pair are buried together on a hill above the battlefield. Only the bard is left to recall the splendor of the past ("The wind sighs through the grass; and their memory rushes on my mind").

Macpherson combines in this thirty-five-line prose poem the essential qualities of Ossianic poetry. He pursues in tandem the states of love and war. Almost as an afterthought, he then introduces the hunt, a *locus classicus* in Celtic legend as well as in his own early poetry ("At times are seen here the ghosts of the deceased, when the musing hunter alone stalks slowly over the heath"). Displaying a characteristic lack of restraint, he responds exuberantly to the sublime effects of the wildness and strangeness of nature.

In his *Annual Register* review Edmund Burke, who had three years earlier published *A Philosophical Enquiry into the Origin of our Ideas of the Sublime and Beautiful,* reacted with pleasure to this validation of his aesthetic principles: the poems, he said, "are animated with a wild, passionate and pathetic spirit."[28] Later, Burke would qualify such praise, but in 1760 he was quite disposed to join those who would laud the poems' tempestuous nature, their evocation of feeling.

All Scotland, as David Hume reported, flowed with excitement over the natural refinement of this bard who recalled the wars of Fingal.[29] Readers found a similarity of theme, mood, and tone in all the fragments where events of overwhelming vastness tested the courage of the individual in battle and explored the depths of his love for another human being. The narrator's intense nostalgia for the past effectively distanced the reader from the more immediate horror of defeat and death. He could thus give way to sentiment, to a mass of impressions; his imagination need have no curb. And in Edinburgh, the literati—equally taken with the work—asked themselves what they might do to assist Macpherson further.

Of the Select Society, Lord Elibank, Lord Kames, and David Hume, all offered advice. Hugh Blair took charge of arranging a subscription dinner. Hume suggested a guinea or two be collected from each of the Faculty of Advocates, as well as from the solicitors at the Court of Session, since Macpherson, never retiring when his own interest was at stake, had written to Blair complaining that without funding he could not attempt to recover "our epics." In a letter of July 1760 Blair asked Sir David Dalrymple to take temporary charge and lend his name and prestige to the project. Dalrymple did his work well, apparently convinced by his own impression of the *Fragments* and by Macpherson's insistent letter, which Blair had enclosed in the correspondence. While Macpherson appears to have been sincerely committed to further research on the epic, his letter affords a rare glimpse of the astonishing audacity of which he was capable. Nonetheless, Dalrymple with his usual precision compiled a list of forty persons, James Boswell among them, who in total contributed more than twenty guineas. At Parliament House Robert Chalmers collected sixty pounds, and it is believed that Mrs. Elizabeth Montagu, the fabulously wealthy patroness of the arts and "Queen of the Blues," sent £100.[30]

At the dinner itself, Macpherson was feted in the grand style, surrounded as he was by the most illustrious literary, legal, and religious figures of Edinburgh. Lord Elibank, who presented the poet to the assembled guests, assured Macpherson of their total intellectual and financial commitment. Blair was delighted with such a successful affair; years later he recalled how Macpherson, brimming with pleasure and confidence, followed him to the door seeking a final word: "That hitherto he had imagined they were merely romantic ideas which I held out to him, but he now saw them likely to be realized, and should endeavor to acquit himself, so as to give satisfaction to all his friends."[31] Three weeks later, in August 1760, Macpherson had readied himself, promising as he went again into the north country "to seize on every opportunity" to restore "these remains of genius" to Scotland.

Chapter Three
Poems of Ossian:
Fingal to "Berrathon"

The spectacular natural beauty of the Grampian Hills and the northwest Highlands held little interest for James Macpherson as he journeyed through his native districts in the late summer of 1760. This time he had not left Edinburgh a desperate and uncertain man with only the bleak prospect of a village schoolmaster's post before him. Instead, the twenty-three-year-old poet had departed the capital a celebrated figure, translator of a remarkable series of fragments that held out to Scotsmen and Celtophiles alike a vision of an exotic, majestic past.

His six-week literary journey took him through the northwest section of Inverness-shire and out to the Isle of Skye, and then to the Outer Hebrides. He returned to his home in Ruthven in October but felt the need for a subsequent trip to the southwest along the Argyllshire coast and across to the Island of Mull. As Macpherson wrote in the preface to *Fingal,* he traveled here "to recover what remained of the works of the old bards, especially those of Ossian, . . . who was the best, . . . to lay [the epic] before the reader, as I have found it" (1:1xii).

Evidence exists to validate his success in finding Gaelic fragments of ballads and of other tattered manuscripts; he transcribed as well some oral recitations of Ossianic legend that he gathered from various residents. In just a few weeks Macpherson had collected nearly forty-five hundred words of authentic Gaelic poetry and had received promises from a number of his collaborators for further deliveries of material. Before returning to Edinburgh he visited his Badenoch district to secure the assistance of two Gaelic scholars, Lachlan Macpherson of Strathmashie and the Reverend Andrew Gallie, in collating the poems and translating the more difficult passages.

By mid-January 1761 Macpherson was living in Edinburgh in the same house as Blair, immediately below Blair's lodgings. During this period Blair visited him often and found him feverishly translating the

Gaelic poems into English: "He gave me accounts from time to time how he proceeded and used frequently at dinner to read or repeat to me parts of what he had that day translated."[1] Since Blair knew no Gaelic, there was little chance he could determine on his own what specific work Macpherson was accomplishing, though the doctor's friends who had reviewed a portion of the material found the poet's version "exact and faithful" to the originals. Macpherson seemed a diligent young scholar who gave every appearance of integrity.

Within four months he had completed the nearly nineteen-thousand-word epic. In the early spring of 1761 Macpherson, with his friend the solicitor Robert Chalmers, traveled to London, where Blair believed the Earl of Bute would use his influence to ensure the best circumstances for the publication of the manuscript. Bute was well disposed towards Macpherson. His private secretary, John Home, of whom he was fond, had warmly praised the poet. And Bute, as chancellor of Marischal College in Aberdeen, was keen to further the interests of former students who came to London seeking their fortune.[2]

Fingal: An Ancient Epic Poem was published by Becket and deHondt in quarto volumes on 1 December 1761 in London and eighteen days later in Edinburgh. The work included a preface, a dissertation on the era of the poems Ossian, and, following the epic itself, a group of miscellaneous pieces loosely connected to the history of Fingal. Confident in the knowledge that he had done as much as his skill and imagination would permit, Macpherson had even solicited the approval of his earliest supporters, Horace Walpole and Thomas Gray, before going to press.

Months earlier, Macpherson had sought out Walpole and given him the manuscript of book 1 of *Fingal* for his criticism. Walpole advised him "to have the names prefixed to the speeches, as in a play—It is too obscure without some such aid." Adopting this suggestion, the poet seemed pleased by what he assumed was Walpole's acceptance of the authenticity of the poems.[3] Probably Gray was also consulted during the same period, but whether he gave any advice is uncertain. In the weeks following publication, however, both Walpole and Gray were expressing to friends their admiration for the poems, as well as suspicion about their authenticity. Public opinion would reflect this dichotomy for years to come.

Fingal was written to conform to a theory of the sublime as a thing of the spirit rather than a product of technique. Thus the epic would seem more the work of the venerable bard Ossian. Macpherson implies at every point that his responsibility as a "translator" had been made doubly difficult by the obscurity of the language and the majestic though primitive simplicity of the original. In the preface he establishes his connection with the works of Ossian, pointing out, in general, the difficulties in rescuing the work of the old bards. He assures the reader of the reliability of Fingal's story, which "is so little interlarded with fable, that one cannot help thinking it the genuine history . . . valuable for the light [it] throws on the ancient state of Scotland and Ireland" (1:lxiii). He goes to some length to establish for Fingal a Scottish nationality, implying that historical misinterpretations have produced an unfortunate confusion. The folk legends of Ireland and Scotland, he says, share many of the same characters and adventures; however, the Irish bards have mistakenly assigned material to Ossian that is clearly their own and have introduced anachronisms that "destroy the authority of the bards with respect to Fingal." Macpherson, though knowing the truth of Finn's Irish heritage, had no intention of acknowledging it; he preferred a true Scottish hero who "spoke for all patriotic Scotsmen in expressing their hope that indigenous values would be sustained and alien ones expelled." Beyond this justification on patriotic grounds, Macpherson found the Irish Fenian ballads unsuitable as a basis for an epic of his people. As a translator of rude Irish lyrics, he would not much advance his reputation; as translator of Ossian, he might rank with Pope and Dryden, who had translated the classical epic poets.[4] His position on this matter provided his detractors with a ready-made argument for disavowing the poem's authenticity; a number of them thought it the best evidence that no Gaelic originals existed for the epic.

Macpherson develops his Scottish claim in an elaborate "Dissertation concerning the antiquity of the poems of Ossian." The premise of this formal essay is that a single and consistent historical framework was, in fact, available for explaining the settlement of the Highlands and the bardic tradition of the Celts. He believes that Scotland was founded by Britons from the south who had originally traveled from Gaul and that "some adventurers" from Britain were the earliest settlers of Ireland. The absence of religious allusion in the poems is traceable, according to Macpherson, to "a civil war . . . which soon ended in almost total extinction of the religious order of the Druids." This explanation conveniently clears up a troubling difference between, for example, Homer and Ossian: unlike Homer, Ossian never allows gods to intervene in the affairs of men since their doing so, he says, would

"derogate from their fame," and because writers "in the Gaelic lan-
guage seldom mention religion in profane poetry."[5] Macpherson thus
offers an ingenious justification of why Fingal could have defeated Ro-
man legions, rescued Cuchulain, and conquered a fleet of Viking raid-
ers without divine assistance.

The dissertation also reviews the variety of methods by which an
oral tradition flourished in Scotland. "The care they [the early Scots]
took to have the poems taught to their children, the uninterrupted
custom of repeating them upon certain occasions, and the happy mea-
sure of the verse, served to preserve them for a long time uncor-
rupted."[6] The poems of Ossian, Macpherson argued, reawaken
ancestral memories and recall primordial states; they preserve modes of
expression believed lost; they serve as a genuine historical record of
ancient Scotland; and they vindicate the beauty and variety of "the
Celtic tongue."

Though full of literary and historical falsehood, the sheer bravura of
such claims compels a perverse admiration because it creates an atmo-
sphere "of an abiding spiritual presence, of a waning, a perishing
World, and of the mystery and incommunicable destiny of Man"[7]—all
of them necessary if the poems were to be convincing.

Fingal: The Story

Fingal recounts an episode in the Irish struggle to exist as an inde-
pendent nation. In her weakest moment when Cormac, Ireland's king,
is in his minority, Swaran, King of Lochlin (Scandinavia) and the most
fearsome warrior of the North, invades the country with a vast army.
Cuchulain, guardian to the king and commander of the Irish forces,
decides to fight against the advice of his subordinates, although he
knows that his armies are no match for the Vikings. He hopes for
assistance, however, from Fingal, King of Morven (Scotland's north-
west Highlands), to whom he dispatches an emissary. Meanwhile, his
gallant action and lack of concern for his own welfare slow Swaran's
advance, but inevitably Cuchulain is defeated in the first battle near
Tura, a castle on the coast of Ulster. The consequences of the defeat are
soon felt. The Norsemen now appear to have the upper hand in the
war and Cuchulain joins Connal, another Irish hero, in a desperate
action to withstand their final attack. In the heat of battle Fingal's
ships appear on the horizon, and Swaran is forced to halt his pursuit of

the Irish and prepare for the Scottish landings. The Irish, despite their loss of honor, decide against further combat and leave the field to Fingal, whose personal prowess and determined army immediately score substantial gains against the Vikings. With Fingal is his son Ossian who observes the action closely so that he may later recount the events, while Ossian's own son Oscar gains a reputation in battle as a savage warrior. By the end of the fourth day the Scots have destroyed the Norsemen except for a small band of warriors under Swaran, whom Fingal meets in single combat and takes prisoner. With the invaders defeated, Fingal holds a celebration where "the song of peace" is sung; Ullin, the Scots bard, reminds the king of his earlier love for Agandecca, Swaran's sister, and Fingal releases Swaran who promises never to return to Ireland. The nobility of Fingal's actions does much to relieve the bitterness of Swaran's defeat. On the sixth day, while hunting, Fingal discovers the embarrassed Cuchulain, whom he consoles with the prophecy that "hereafter thou shalt be victorious." The epic ends with the joy of victory for the allied forces and Fingal's return to his native Scotland.

The central story is based on two main Gaelic ballads, the "Garbh mac Stairn" and "Magnus," and is enlivened by numerous episodes in which other Irish, Scots, and Norse heroes play their parts. Most poetic among these digressions is "Ossian's Courtship," in book 4, where the poet recounts his romance with the now-dead Evirallin. The episode ends with the supernatural appearance of Evirallin, who warns the sleeping Ossian to rescue their son Oscar before his patrol is overwhelmed by Lochlin warriors. In several places in the poem the bards play significant roles: Cuchulain's bard, Carril, introduces an important passage in book 3, "Fingal's Visit to Norway," that provides crucial information for later developments in the narrative; in book 3 also, Fingal's bard, Ullin, sings songs that prompt his chief to recite the episode known as the "Maid of Craca" during an interlude between two days of battle. Such passages make *Fingal* a work of conscious artistic purpose. At points the central action seems to be not advanced but simply interrupted, yet Macpherson maintains a sensitive balance among the various structures in his narrative without damaging in any essential way the drama of the story.

Whether or not *Fingal* was really an epic poem was debated at great length by reviewers for the major journals in the weeks following its publication. The reviewer for the *Critical Review* not only thought the

poem an epic but judged it superior—to both the *Iliad* and the *Aeneid*!
Accepting at face value Macpherson's statement of *Fingal*'s origins, he
attributed the poem's defects to the time of its composition, the third
century, and questioned the appropriateness of rejecting it as an epic
by applying Aristotelian epic standards: "The poet has a natural right
to chuse [sic] the manner in which it shall be presented."[8] On the other
hand, the reviewer for the *Monthly Review*, using Aristotle too, insisted
that *Fingal* was not an epic but a work of history, and he judged it a
failure as history because Ossian could write of men neither realistically
nor accurately; in particular, the critic said, Ossian provides insuffi-
cient motivation for men's actions.

Edmund Burke's review in the *Annual Register*, which appeared a few
weeks later, was more evenhanded. Whether or not *Fingal* was history,
Burke argued, had no bearing on one's judgment of the poetry: "The
poet selects, arranges, and finally creates an essentially new world."[9]
The work was an admirably inventive epic but it had numerous faults,
explicable perhaps by the barbaric environment of its composition. For
Burke the *Iliad* remained a poem of epic perfection with which no other
poem could stand comparison; for him the very resemblance between
the two suggested the possibility that Ossian was a fraud. The *Annual
Register* was thus the first to state in print what others had thought.
Burke, however, did not pursue his suspicion. In fact, he made allow-
ances for the poem's weaknesses as an epic.

Hugh Blair wrote with greater confidence of *Fingal*'s epic qualities:
in his *Critical Dissertation on the Poems of Ossian,* published in 1763, he
went so far as to claim that the poem possessed "all the essential req-
uisites of a true and regular epic." Referring to the criticism leveled at
Fingal, Blair pointed out that Aristotle had copied his rules from Ho-
mer, and that Homer and Ossian had studied nature. "No wonder that
among all three, there should be such agreement and conformity."[10]
This early friend of *Ossian* argued that the moral of the poem is "not
inferior to that of any other poet"; furthermore, "the unity of [its] epic
action," Blair asserted, "is so strictly preserved . . . [that] it must be
perceived by every reader." In "the whole of *Fingal,*" Blair concluded,
"there reigns . . . grandeur of sentiment, style and imagery."[11]

Macpherson's desire from the beginning was to convince influential
figures of the existence of a Scottish epic. Although many readers dis-
agreed, at the very least he forced his critics to ponder the resemblances
between *Fingal* and the ancient epics.

The Method of *Fingal*

To shore up the authenticity and high purpose of his epic, Macpherson followed conventions set in the *Iliad*. If he could convince readers that they were in some way already familiar with the poetry in which Fingal's story was rendered, then he might establish credibility for the works of Ossian. Long after some critics had rejected Ossian's fables as fraudulent, innumerable readers continued to regard the bard as a reliable poet capable of refined sentiment and manners. As comparisons were developed between Homer and Ossian, scholars in England and particularly Scotland began increasingly to emphasize the historical circumstances of the epics' composition. "The patriotic Scotch characterized Ossian as refined and moral, while Homer for the first time appeared impassioned, crude, and barbaric, of small value to anyone except the historian."[12]

The historical approach of such primitivists as James Beattie and Henry Home (Lord Kames) offered less opportunity for disagreement about the relative merits of the two. They argued that though the *Iliad* and *Fingal* might not meet at every point, "the grand essentials" were clearly revealed, thus proving that both epics arose during a time when man was closer to nature, less subject to the corrupt influences of society. When the Greek bard differed from his Celtic counterpart, it was because of the differences between their countries. Otherwise, both Homer and Ossian wrote poetry that was natural or instinctive, not cultivated; they were original geniuses.

Later, in the introductory essays to *Temora,* Macpherson would expand further upon Ossian's genius, building his case in large part upon this heroic ethos developed earlier by other Scots. *Fingal,* to many readers, resembled the *Iliad,* at least superficially, because its author had applied the rules of the genre with surprising craftsmanship. He deviated from the classical model only for nationalistic reasons.

Macpherson's use of a number of traditional epic features is noteworthy. The hero, Fingal, is an adventurer whose exploits and fame achieve national importance—an ever-triumphant fighter who leads his devoted warriors against tyranny and in defense of his allies. The setting is vast, magnificent, and terrible: dark rolling waves, ethereally silent hills, lonely isles, heaths. The action consists primarily in deeds of great valor; just six are depicted. Such intense concentration is achieved, however, against a background of intermittent warfare between the Vikings and Fingal; "the Scot" and two kings of Norway, Starno and Swaran, engage in innumerable battles. Macpherson wisely forgoes this seemingly unending war, and focuses instead on these few days when Fingal saves Ireland and rescues its greatest hero. Supernatural forces are managed with consummate skill. Macpherson employs ghosts as functional beings who seem genuinely interested in the action and intervene frequently. The epic is in the high style; tone and language are elevated, while at the same time diction is both vigorous and simple. Macpherson's "measured prose" exhibits, as Hugh Blair observed, "justness, force, and sublimity." The style as a whole reaches toward what Diderot was later to call "l'energie de nature."[13]

Epic conventions otherwise serve Macpherson's purpose. The narrative, for example, opens in medias res with the action then unfolding in logical progression; Blair would argue that "not only is unity of subject maintained, but that of time and place also."[14] Fingal and Swaran engage in single combat, the destinies of both their countries dependent on the outcome. There are catalogs of warriors and numerous warrior speeches prompting various of the poem's episodes.

Fingal: Book 4

Book 4 of Fingal is indicative of the epic as a whole. It displays the grandeur of Ossian's heroes, the intensity of the environment, and the sublimity of the language in a manner characteristic of the entire poem. Critics have found that book 4 most successfully conforms to Macpherson's intentions; to Ossian's defenders, the book revealed the bard's virtues in their perfection.

The fourth book begins on the third night of the battle. The bard Ossian is speaking to "the maid of the voice of love," Malvina, his daughter-in-law, companion, and muse whom he seems to conjure up by incantation. In the opening paragraph Macpherson establishes the characteristic tone of the work and defines the role Ossian must play:

> Often hast thou heard my song; often
> given the tear of beauty. Dost thou come to
> the wars of thy people? to hear the actions
> of Oscar? When shall I cease to mourn, by
> the streams of resounding Cona? My years
> have passed away in battle. My age is
> darkened with grief!
>
> (1:122)

Ossian, worn by age and experience, laments the passing of time and the loss of comrades. The transience of life—"the inevitable coming of decay and death"—expressed this movingly suggests the theme. The emphasis on sentiment, everywhere apparently throughout the poem and nowhere clearer than in such exclamatory interjections as here, forces the reader to concern himself less with the narrative than with the evolution and turn of feelings. Though a pathetic figure, Ossian nonetheless embodies the responsibility of the ancient bard. As an observer and commentator on the wars of Fingal, he sings not only the prowess of his people but also their virtue and strength. Macpherson echoes, in this instance, a resounding Homeric theme: the insignificance of man when he relies on brute strength alone. Ossian, though he can be mournful or even frustrated, never ceases to value above all else man's courage, intelligence, and energy.

Fingal and his men are described as rejecting traditional limits; they oppose the inevitable with unwavering fortitude. Their tragedy is that they are doomed to failure and frustration but remain unable or unwilling to alter their behavior. Ossian alone is left to recall in melancholy terms the lives of these heroes: their consciousness of honor, the unhappiness of love, the sufferings, the horrors, and the superstitions. Macpherson endows Ossian's poetry with an introspective awareness of frustration and despair and a passionate affirmation of man's will to resist.

Ossian interrupts the narrative with the story of his courtship of Evirallin, the daughter of the Irish chieftain Branno. The episode heightens the nostalgic motif introduced earlier when Ossian recalls his days as a young warrior. Loved by a maid who had rejected all her countrymen, the poet-warrior came to claim her but found a band of former suitors blocking his path. "Above us on the hill appeared the people of stately Cormac. . . . The heath flamed wide with their arms" (1:123). Ossian, drawing his sword, extolled the virtues of each of the opposing warriors as well as those of his own men. The combat, though furious, ended suddenly with Ossian beheading his enemy and displaying his prize to all ("Five times I shook it by the lock. The friends of Cormac fled"). In recalling this event, Ossian immerses himself in a lament for the past and for the lost vigor of his youth. His self-pity carries the scene through to the end in a haze of sentimental associations. The bard's attitude reveals Macpherson's technique of never presenting material even of the smallest significance without emotionalizing it. His intentions as a poet had been made transparent in the

Fragments, and he holds to his purpose in *Fingal*: associate ideas with objects as closely as possible, thus implying that the one can be substituted for the other or for the whole.[15]

The retrospective serves as a preface to the main action of the present, where Evirallin's ghost emerges from a cloud before the bard imploring him to save Oscar, their valiant son. Once the warning is given, the ghost disappears without interfering further. Ossian then rescues his son and frightens off the Lochliners, who are terrified by "the distant thunder" of the bard's voice singing war songs. The passage makes clear Macpherson's indebtedness to classical tradition; he may recall, specifically, Pope's translation of the *Iliad,* "where the voice of Achilles frightens the Trojans from the body of Patroclus."[16]

As the father and son take comfort in each other's safety, Macpherson enhances the sublimity of the scene by introducing "all the images of Trouble, and Terror, and Darkness."[17] He connects the wild, exotic aspects of nature with the nobility of these figures in a manner that summons the reader to join in a profound experience. This "impression of sublimity" should cause astonishment and shock; readers are to be uplifted, morally elevated. Macpherson's description of the night and the enemy is characteristic:

> They watched the terrors of the night.
> Our swords have conquered some. But as the
> winds of night pour the ocean, over the
> white sands of Mora, so dark advance the
> sons of Lochlin, over Lena's rustling heath!
> The ghosts of night shriek afar: I have seen
> the meteors of death.
>   (1:126)

The haunting presence of nature and the solemnity with which these warriors view this scene seem both terrible and irresistible. The images and language are chosen for their ornateness, hyperbole, and violence—all paraphernalia of Ossianic poetry.[18] Evidence of what critics refer to as "the cult of nature" here surfaces: the night, winds, ocean, white sands, rustling heath, and meteors. Throughout the poem such enthusiastic renderings of external nature recur in profusion, specifically where it suits Macpherson's purpose to emphasize nature's contrasts and combination of moods.

His narrative intention is to construct a well-ordered chaos. His model is the highly structured, classical epic onto which he grafts a pagan wildness. On hearing of the Lochliners' preparations for a new attack, for example, Ossian awakens the sleeping Fingal, who has been dreaming of the dead Agandecca, daughter of Starno and sister of his present enemy, Swaran. Years before Starno had devised a plan to overcome Lochlin's foe by deceiving Fingal into believing he wanted peace between their nations. The Norse king would pretend to seal his offer with the hand of Princess Agandecca, but, instead, Starno would kill the unsuspecting Fingal. Before this treachery could be carried out, however, Agandecca fell in love with Fingal and revealed the plot to him. In a rage, Starno then killed his daughter. Macpherson tells this part of the story in book 3, so that in book 4 Agandecca can return as a ghost who, at the climatic moment, provides the reader with proof of Fingal's sensitive and noble nature: he is a man who has loved and been loved by the enemies of his people. As Ossian also recounts, "she mourned the sons of her people, that were to fall by the hand of Fingal" (1:128). The ghost thus prophesies Fingal's ultimate defeat of Swaran. Fingal rises from his sleep restored and defiant, willing to face any odds, certain of his destiny as savior of his nation. He is resplendent here as an incarnation of the will to resist tyranny.

Next, in book 4, occurs the central action of the epic: the final battle between the invader and the protector. Macpherson lingers over the battle scenes, drawing out in loving detail each significant element, including (of course) the muster of the heroes. This he describes elaborately and with manifest pleasure, building a mood that further glorifies Fingal. The hero-king calls to his men, "Come to battle . . . ye children of echoing Selma! Come to the death of thousands" (1:130). He offers them the godlike gift of eternal fame through death on the battlefield.

Fingal's decision to appoint Gaul the battlefield commander is a gesture of his magnanimity: "He shall lead my battle; that his fame may rise in song!" By this act, Fingal thus ennobles Gaul, the son of a politically powerful comrade, and encourages the other young officers to glorious deeds which may bring them also to the notice of the bards. No greater honor could have been offered these young men who devoted their lives to securing fame by combat.

Macpherson misses no chance to illustrate the noble character of his hero. Fingal's departure from the immediate area of the impending battle to a prominent hill overlooking the field is a master stroke. It permits him to leave the field a magnificent and preeminent figure,

untouched by the ravages of war, an ideal to be worshipped by his
followers. Macpherson, knowing the value the Greeks placed upon the
heroic, casts Fingal in a comparable mold. By emphasizing Fingal's
connection to the natural world and stressing both his physical prowess
and mental acumen, the poet strengthens his poem dramatically.

> Now, like a dark and stormy cloud,
> edged round with the red lightning of heaven;
> flying westward from the morning's beam, the
> king of Selma [Fingal] removed.
>   (1:131–32)

Fingal becomes at this moment the essence of romantic individualism,
"the incarnation of the aristocratic spirit, a being above those he pro-
tects, a leader and savior from outside."[19]

As the moment for battle approaches, Ossian's son, Oscar, in a sud-
den rush of youthful exuberance or foolishness, demands that his father
also leave the field. Clearly he has not understood why Fingal has de-
parted, mistaking it as a self-serving decision by an old man unwilling
to sacrifice his few remaining years. In a pungent and charming ex-
change between father and son Ossian tells the eager boy: "Raise, Os-
car, rather raise my tomb. I will not yield the war to thee. The first
and bloodiest in the strife, my arm shall teach thee how to fight"
(1:133). The eternal conflict between the younger and the older gen-
erations is explored here with a refreshing honesty and vigor.

Ossian recalls the battle in language that reveals the bloodshed and
ferocity of the warriors. Using such fixed epithets as "lightly-bound-
ing," "chief of the pointed arms of death" (for Gaul), and "the king of
generous shells" (for Fingal), he describes a form of combat where de-
ception and treachery have little place, the ethos of warfare defined
instead by a gallant directness. The fanatical zeal of the Celtic warrior
is evident as the Scots rout one flank of the Viking army:

> We pursued and slew. As stones that
> bound from rock to rock; as axes in echoing
> woods; as thunder rolls from hill to hill,
> in dismal broken peals; so blow succeeded to
> blow, and death to death, from the hand of
> Oscar and mine.
>   (1:134–35)

Ossian employs epic simile in a conscious imitation of Homer; his comparisons of martial, as well as other, subjects are elaborate and ornate. Blair points out that Ossian exceeds Homer in the number of such similes and that his "are without exception taken from objects of dignity, which cannot be said for all those which Homer employs."[20] Though Blair's pronouncements must be viewed cautiously, the poem does, indeed, rely heavily upon similes, especially in moments of desperation such as the height of battle. Swaran, overwhelmed on one flank, concentrates his remaining forces on shattering the corps led by Gaul, believing the Scot's death will weaken Fingal's power in the eyes of his men. Sensing the rage of the Norsemen and the exhaustion of Gaul's infantry, Fingal sends his chief bard Ullin to the young commander to remind him of his duty:

> Cut down the foe; let no white sail
> bound round dark Inistore. Be thine arm
> like thunder. Thine eyes like fire, thy
> heart of solid rock. Whirl round thy sword
> as a meteor at night; lift thy shield like
> the flame of death. Son of the chief of
> generous steeds, cut down foe. Destroy!
>   (1:136)

The staccato pattern of these similes illustrates Macpherson's use of natural objects for arousing the strongest emotions. The sublimity of nature is associated with images of pain and destruction. Ullin's war song reverberates with what Burke described in *The Sublime and Beautiful* as apprehensions of terror: "no passion so effectually robs the mind of all its powers of acting and reasoning as fear." The bard calls upon the spiritless commander to conduct himself in a ferocious manner. Fingal knows that Ullin must turn Gaul into an object of terror whom his opponents will associate with danger, pain, and death. By comparing Gaul to peril and distress, Ullin invests him with power. "Whilst we remain in the presence of whatever is supposed to have the power of inflicting either" pain or death, according to Burke, "it is impossible to be perfectly free from terror."[21] Macpherson's skill as a craftsman here is undeniable, although one modern critic finds him guilty of occasional "lapses of good judgment and taste."[22] Without defending the various absurdities that will likely surface in any detailed analysis of the poem, we may observe that the strength of the piece arises from

its cohesion: poetic process and emotional fulfillment are one; and if
Macpherson sustains this unity—as he does—he has attained the prin-
cipal goal of the bard.

The remainder of book 4 centers on Fingal's dramatic return to the
fight. His return is, of course, to be predicted, but the inevitability of
his reappearance does not diminish its powerful effect. Fingal's amia-
bility and benevolence, both to his own men and later to his defeated
enemies, have no place in the role he now assumes. When the hero-
king descends the hill to join the battle, he displays a savage ferocity
all the more consuming for his recognition of Swaran's dominance of
Gaul. Fingal's concern is not just for his friends and countrymen: he
leaves the hill because the Norse king has attempted to frustrate his
own continuing quest for fame. As always, what matters in such a
conflict is honor; Fingal's honor is synonymous with his manhood, his
soul. The quest for fame seems paramount in his actions, though his
soldiers, instead of questioning it, find his spirit irresistible. Fingal
holds to a heroic standard of conduct, a pattern of behavior that re-
mains impossible for the common man to follow—hence all the more
admirable. The sight of their leader in the battle line inspires and
commands his men to greater sacrifice. Ossian marks the event by
using natural phenomena symbolically in order to sharpen the contrast
between the opposing kings. Swaran becomes darkness itself. When
Fingal calls his men about him, he, "like a beam from heaven, shone
in the midst of his people." All of nature in concert assists the king in
organizing his forces for the final assault: "Raise my standards on high;
spread them on Lena's wind. . . . Ye sons of the roaring streams . . .
be near the king of Morven!" Fingal emerges as a complex figure: a
superhuman warrior in battle, a father-king to his nation, a sensitive
lover of Agandecca, and, finally, a peacemaker who establishes the new
order. Swaran "is not only a monolithic figure, but he and his force
have, so to speak, been hewn from one stone."[23] The Viking serves as
the perfect foil for Fingal, the real hero.

Macpherson, even in the early poetry, revels in the description of
combat. He exhibits a flair for military tactics, and his Fingal displays
a professional's skill as a strategist and battlefield tactician.

> Behold . . . how Lochlin divides on Lena!
> they stand like broken clouds on a hill; or
> an half-consumed grove of oaks. . . . Let every
> chief among the friends of Fingal take a

dark troop of those that frown so high: Nor
let a son of the echoing groves bound on the
waves of Inistore!

(1:140–41)

He assigns each troop leader an area of the battlefield while requiring
each of his officers to kill his opposing commander. Fingal entrusts his
ultimate victory to the capacity of each commander to survive the true
test of a warrior: individual combat with an equal. The responsibility
of the Caledonian chieftains is immense; all realize, however, that no
matter how successful they may be, the battle will not be decided until
Fingal kills or captures Swaran by his own hand.

In his recall of these events Ossian shifts frequently from one ex-
treme to another, from melancholy to exultation, idealism to despair.
As in the beginning of the poem, he calls out to Malvina, his only
solace now in old age, to hear and understand his disillusionment. On
one level the victory over the Vikings has afforded a magnificent ex-
ample of good men acting righteously to destroy tyranny. To a man
like Ossian, however, such a victory has greater significance. He sees
in Fingal's triumph an opportunity for harmony, for a revitalization of
the ethos of his ancestors, of a time when the world of nature and the
world of man were more closely linked. Howard Mumford Jones calls
such men romantic sufferers who "by their very suffering [are] throw-
backs to a healthier life on earth and prophets of a radiant age to
come."[24] Ossian has gained experience and wisdom through suffering;
he sings proudly of his people's accomplishments but mourns the death
of his companions. Intensely aware of being alone, he is forced through
a long life to recall the majesty and grandeur of the past. Capture of
this world now forever lost can only be achieved poetically—and then
but fleetingly; he piles image upon image, usually from nature, until
they tend to coalesce into a single sensation or entity in our imagina-
tion. Thus we give up the specific for the vague and obscure, the ob-
jective for the subjective; our response is to the whole of Ossian's world
rather than to any particular part. Sublimity is here achieved not
through reason but sentiment.[25]

Last of the important figures to reappear is the Irish hero Cuchulain,
who Macpherson insists is a native of the Isle of Skye and a Scot; he
reenters the narrative at the conclusion of book 4. He had retreated in
shame to the cave of Tura after his defeat in book 3: "he feared the face
of Fingal, who was wont to greet him from the fields of renown" (100).

Macpherson's alteration of his character has always been a shock to those familiar with the heroic Celtic legends. As the most famous of a circle of Irish heroes, the son of a god born under miraculous circumstances, Cuchulain had been accepted as an authentic hero. Irish myth makes much of his pride and honor, his unyielding fierceness, his unwillingness to run from an adversary. Ossian presents a wholly different warrior, a hero defined by another ethos than this; sentiment guides his actions, freeing him, in a sense, from the bonds of the Irish myth.

In the first book of *Fingal* Cuchulain remains satisfactorily heroic. He is a courageous warrior, a respected and inspirational commander, and a proud, if not overconfident, man. He refuses Swaran's terms of surrender in book 2, openly defying the Viking to defeat him; but, with the arrival of Fingal in book 3, he loses face because Swaran has turned away from single combat with him to meet the Caledonians. It is commonly thought that Swaran does not consider Cuchulain his equal and that, when he turns away, he is seeking a worthier opponent in Fingal. Cuchulain thus hides in shame, for his defiance has proven hollow. There are, however, problems with this view. Swaran respects the Irish hero far more than this interpretation permits, or he would not have felt it necessary to attempt to annihilate him and his men. When Swaran turns back to the shore, he acts as any astute military commander would who recognizes the danger of having a powerful force attacking at the rear while his main forces are otherwise engaged. As a sea raider with extensive experience in amphibious landings, he also knows the vulnerability of infantry during the transition from ship to shore. Swaran's immediate turnabout to face Fingal's approaching army has very little to do with whether or not he respects Cuchulain. The Viking has simply chosen to ignore the weaker force for the stronger; his intelligence as a military commander is here definitive, not heedless ferocity.

Macpherson is, however, interested in more than simply a display of Swaran's tactical skill. He emphasizes the perverse bond between Fingal and the Viking: "Wrath burns on his [Swaran's] dark-brown face: his eyes roll in the fire of his valour. Fingal beheld the son of Starno: he remembered Agandecca" (1:103). Swaran has personal reasons for wishing Fingal dead and his influence in the North ended. Cuchulain knows nothing of these reasons and assumes the worst, wallows in self-pity, and pathetically looks for a chance to redeem himself when the battle is nearly won.

Cuchulain's dilemma marks a turning point in the development of book 4. Given his profound sense of heroic responsibility and duty, all the more deeply felt for his shameful defeat, Cuchulain would seem to have no choice now but to commit suicide or withdraw forever from the company of honorable men. Macpherson's resolution of this conflict remains one of the more interesting aspects of the poem; Cuchulain rejects heroic idealism and allows himself, instead, to be guided by his emotions, instincts, and passions. He is converted from a classically defiant hero-god into a tender-minded man whose laments for the deaths of his friends overcome his own self-concern.

In the last lines of book 4 Cuchulain grasps at his lost honor but is prevented from rushing into the battle by his devoted friend Connal, who reminds him to "Seek not a part of the fame of the king; himself is like the storm" (1:147). Connal implied that the two men—Cuchulain and Fingal—are no longer alike; Cuchulain need no longer reach for the same goals. Immediately, Cuchulain says to Carril, "Go, greet the king of Morven . . . be thy voice sweet in his ear to praise the king of Selma! Give him the sword of Caithbat. Cuchulain is not worthy. . . . Never more shall I be renowned. . . . I am a beam that has shown; a mist that has fled away. . . . I will never return to thee, thou sun-beam of my soul!" (1:147–48). By not minimizing Cuchulain's agony Macpherson creates a fuller, more mature man; Cuchulain is not only worthy of Fingal's regard, he is as noble as his rescuer. The gran-deur of Fingal's heroism is contrasted with Cuchulain's quieter sympathy and benevolence; the soul of the one and the heart of the other. Fingal, in Sir Walter Scott's words, "has all the strength and bravery of Achilles, with the courtesy, sentiment, and high breeding of Sir Charles Grandison."[26] He is also exempt from ambition, envy, and a desire for personal fame. Cuchulain, burdened with shame, dejection, and fear at the loss of his fame, cannot escape the tomblike cave to which he has fled until, at the end of the poem, the omnipotent Fingal draws him out and gives him hope. Thus Macpherson again demonstrates Fingal's high moral and intellectual nature, his desire to promote the welfare of good men. Nevertheless, the conclusion of book 4 more accurately reflects the mood of the poem. Cuchulain, sensing the change in his nature, mourns the loss of what was and fears the uncertain possibilities of the future. His transformation signals an indulgent emotionalism, a sanction of sentimental mortality, and a belief in a universal sympathy between nature and man: all themes identifiably

Macpherson's own, as well as those of his time generally. Thus Cuchulain's appeal; thus the enthusiastic reception of *Fingal* and of the Ossianic poems as a whole.

"Comala: A Dramatic Poem"

Published in 1761, in the same volume as *Fingal,* "Comala" begins a collection of what Macpherson refers to as "Several other Poems composed by Ossian the Son of Fingal." The collection consists of fifteen poems of varying length and quality derived from ballad sources or composed by Macpherson in imitation of some favorite pieces. Macpherson retains the essential qualities of Ossianic poetry, as determined in the *Fragments* and *Fingal,* where "all is elegance, refinement, and sensibility." His talent for natural painting is displayed as effectively in these works as in the epic, and his versification and "animated" style hold to the established pattern. Though interesting, even at times provocative, the poems are important primarily as supporting evidence of heroic greatness, and of the authenticity of *Fingal.*

"Comala" has been called a Celtic drama with chorus, a dramatic rehearsal for solemn occasions, a dramatic poem of the Roman Emperor Caracalla's campaign, and "an ambitious imitation of the *Song of Solomon.*" None of these descriptions, however, is adequate in itself. The notion of a Celtic drama with a Greek-like chorus reciting prologue and epilogue, as well as occasional commentary between the acts, seems ridiculous; yet Macpherson has given a Celtic story certain dramatic characteristics, including a chorus, though with Celtic characters. In its Gaelic form "Comala" was, according to Macpherson, perhaps presented "before the chiefs upon solemn occasions." But the solemnity of "Comala" has no Gaelic origin; instead, it simply derives from Macpherson's pervasive theme of the "joy of grief": the bards' joy in rehearsing the stories of dead heroes and their lovers.[27] A less easily explained problem surfaces in the analysis of the poem's subject. Earlier, many readers of *Fingal* who knew the history of Great Britain had found it absurd that Fingal assisted a first-century Cuchulain against the attacks of eighth-century Vikings. Now in "Comala," Fingal's campaign against the third-century Roman Emperor Caracalla appears just as improbable. Macpherson's haphazard chronology brought him his severest criticism from those who took the poet at his word that Ossian was retelling the history of their island. In addition, Laing accused

Macpherson of failing utterly to capture the essence of the *Song of Solomon,* which he believed he had slavishly imitated. Before answering this charge, we should review the poem. Comala is a princess of the Orkney Islands who is betrothed to Fingal and follows him disguised as a young warrior on his campaign against Caracul (Caracalla), "king of the world." She is accompanied, as Fingal's fiancée, by her maids of honor, Melilcoma and Dersagrena, who also function as a chorus. They speak first, setting the tone and providing exposition. These "daughters of Morni" interpret signs in nature—a deer running away from a stream, light as if from a meteor "play[ing] round his branching horns," and ghosts peering down from the clouds—to mean that Fingal has been killed in battle. Hidallan, Fingal's rival for Comala, arrives as a herald from the king to announce a great victory over the Romans. Seeing a chance to overcome his rival, he tells a lie that confirms the chorus's suspicions: "The nations are scattered on their hills! They shall hear the voice of the king no more" (1:221). Heartbroken, Comala pours forth her devotion to Fingal and her hatred of his Roman murderer, her most poignant moment coming when she contemplates what might have been:

> I might have hoped a little while his
> return; I might have thought I saw him on
> the distant rock;. . . the wind of the hill
> might have been the sound of his horn in
> mine ear. O that I were on the banks of
> Carun! that my tears might be warm on his
> cheek!
>
> (1:221)

Convinced by Hidallan's false report, Comala falls into such a deep depression that she is unable to make the desired response when Fingal returns in triumph and calls to her. Frightened and certain that Fingal is his own ghost, she implores death to "take me to the cave of thy rest." In an exchange typical of the hero's strength Fingal summons her twice from the coma to "come to the cave of my rest. The storm is past, the sun is on our fields" (1:224). From this climax the poem moves rapidly and, not surprisingly, to Comala's death. It concludes with a celebration of her nobility and beauty, Hidallan's confession and his exile, and Fingal's lamentation for love. The bards sing, "See! meteors gleam around the maid!," thus reminding the reader of the maid's prophecy concerning the signs of death.

Contrary to Laing's view, Macpherson's dependence on the *Song of Solomon* is not servile. More important, however, than whether Ossian was as sublime as the Bible is the degree to which the language, rhythms, imagery, and moral principles of that work influenced Macpherson's writings. He found the prophetic and lyrical parts of the Old and New Testaments highly suggestive as he worked with his ballad sources. It may not be too much to connect his attitude toward the Bible with that of Wordsworth, who acknowledged in the Preface to the *Poems of 1815* that he found it "the grand store-house of enthusiastic and meditative Imagination."[28] "Comala" evokes comparison with the *Song of Solomon* especially in its ecstatic realization of earthly love, its idyllic atmosphere and often opulent language, its frequent repetition, and purely secular character. The weakness of the poem lies in Macpherson's unwillingness to subordinate Fingal's military character to the sensuous possibilities of this love experience. Fingal's devotion to war leaves no real opportunity for love to influence him for any length of time. Macpherson refuses to complicate the character of his hero.[29]

"The War of Caros"

"The War of Caros," along with "Comala" and "Colna-dona," reviews a series of battles with the Romans extending over three generations. "The War of Caros" narrates the life of Ossian's boldest son, Oscar, who at an early age becomes an important tribal chieftain and war lord. Fingal, whose spiritual presence the Celts find inescapable, makes no actual appearance in the poem.

In unadorned verse Ossian recalls his son's adventure for the sympathetic Malvina. Joy in grief is once again the theme as the tale is prompted by the appearance of Oscar's ghost on the slopes of Ardven. The father takes pleasure in recalling his son's fame, though at various points Ossian, overcome with emotion, interrupts the tale with cries of sadness for the passing of Oscar "the Terrible."

Caros is Macpherson's name for Carausius, a Belgian of humble origins who rose to be a commander of the Roman navy and governor of Britain and Northern Gaul from 287 to 293 A.D. Well known to historians as tough, resolute, ambitious, and unscrupulous, Carausius after arriving in Britain declared himself emperor by defeating the then-Emperor Maximian in a sea battle. As an adventurer and an effective ruler, he would seem to have had few contemporary equals; accordingly, he is a suitable figure for testing Oscar's mettle. Ossian calls Caros "king of ships," an epithet which suggests his power and position. Caros, his fleet anchored in the bay, has brought a large party ashore, where he established them behind a "gathered heap" or wall of stone. Oscar, infuriated by the arrogance of the Romans, sends his bard, Ryno, to issue a challenge:

> Tell to Caros that I long for battle;
> that my bow is weary of the chace of Cona.
> Tell him the mighty are not here; and that my
> arm is young.
>
> (1:235)

In the meantime, Oscar summons his own troops, positioning them where they can do the most damage if the Romans should leave their defensive perimeter and camp. Though he is still, as he was in *Fingal*, headstrong, naive, stubborn, brave, and handsome, Oscar's assumption of a leader's role endows him with a nobility heretofore denied him.

When Caros refuses the challenge, Oscar makes camp along the banks of Carun, where Comala died, and from where the now-dead Hidallan was banished. Ryno, who senses the arrival of their ghosts, relates (at Oscar's urging) the pathetic episode of Hidallan's return to his family. This exiled warrior has received little solace from his father, who rejects his son's excuses for leaving the battlefield and insists that a warrior's actions must lead either to glory or death. When Hidallan seems confused—"where shall I reach for fame to gladden the soul of Lamor"—the father calls for his sword and slays him. With the death of the heir the family ends: "the valley is silent, and the people shun the place of Lamor" (1:241). This parable about duty and honor, and the consequences of ignoring both, prompts Oscar to commune with the ghosts of his fathers on Ardven.

At night Caros crosses the stream and nearly surrounds Oscar's forces while they sleep. Oscar, who has had an epiphany on the mountain— "he foresaw the fall of his race"—discovers the approaching enemy, sounds the alarm, and faces their charge alone. He wavers for a moment overcome by terror, but his ancestral tradition of courage and determination persuade him to remain "growing in his place, like a flood

in a narrow vale" (247). Ossian mourns as the vision of this magnificent
fighter and leader fades from his mind.

"The War of Inis-thona"

Macpherson's next poem in the same volume resulted from his
overhearing a piece of an Ossianic ballad during his Highland excur-
sion in 1761. With his usual aplomb the poet suggested that this
fragment was a portion of a "great work" by Ossian now lost, though
the traditions of the Highland people, he said, had managed to pre-
serve the general narrative of the original and some of its episodes. In
fact, Macpherson wrote, "there are some now living, who, in their
youth, have heard the whole repeated" (1:255). As Thomson and others
have shown, it was quite possible for Macpherson to have recorded
fragments of authentic ballads, especially from people who remem-
bered the legends of the heroes of the Fianna. But the implausibility
of a precise structural relationship between a particular fragment and
the epic from which it derived, as Macpherson here claims, is evidence
enough of his complicated plan for deceiving the literary world.

From an artistic point of view "Inis-thona" is of minor importance.
It is an occasional piece, celebrating another victory by Oscar in his
persistent search for personal glory. Macpherson's characteristic vigor
of expression and his neatly woven narrative are its greatest strengths.
In the middle section, for example, is a provocative scene of lust, mur-
der, kidnapping, and revenge. Oscar, who has asked leave of Fingal
and Ossian to fight in the battle of Inis-thona (Iceland), finds the island
king (Annir) deep in mourning at the murder of his two sons and
kidnapping of his only daughter by Cormalo, "chief of ten thousand
spears." Cormalo, proud and ruthless, had come to Annir's court to
participate in a tournament; when he lost to the elder prince, he killed
him as well as his younger brother in revenge. In the meantime, the
young princess "was seized in his love" and "they fled over the desert."
This scene, foreshadowing Ann Radcliffe, blurs the distinction be-
tween the obvious lust of the two lovers and the brutality of a relation-
ship in which the daughter is not permitted to see her family. The
chivalrous Oscar immediately assembles his men and promises Annir
revenge for the sins of Cormalo, and the poem concludes in the usual
Ossianic fashion, with the murderer dead, the daughter returned, and
Oscar celebrated by Fingal and the bards.

"The Battle of Lora"

In the next Ossian poem of the *Fingal* volume, "The Battle of Lora," Macpherson returns for his inspiration to the *Book of the Dean* and possibly other collections of Ossianic ballads. All versions refer to the legendary eleventh-century battle of Ventry where Finn is pitted against one of the numerous Norwegian Viking chiefs who attacked Ireland. As Thomson has shown, Macpherson probably used this battle as a framework for "Lora" and, in working with the ballad sources, added at least five significant changes, all of them following a pattern established in *Fingal*.[30]

The original ballad version is addressed to St. Patrick, who had asked a question of the bard. But Macpherson, given his historical framework, could not permit a Christian figure to surface, and he opens the poem with Ossian addressing a Culdee, "son of the distant land, who dwellest in the secret cell." Ossian asks the Culdee to look across the Scottish plain at the tombs of dead heroes, where in one desolate spot lies the body of Erragon, "king of ships! chief of distant Sora" (Scandinavia). He provokes the Culdee's curiosity with questions reminiscent of—no matter his pagan setting—the Old Testament: "How is the mighty low" and "how hast thou fallen on our mountains?" Answers are quickly provided as Ossian recalls Fingal's triumphant return from Ireland and the great feast held in honor of the Caledonians who died there. Two of Fingal's finest warriors, Aldo and Maronnan, who were not invited to the royal banquet, become enraged at this apparent discourtesy and immediately set sail for Sora. Using a feast as an occasion for initiating conflict or bringing peace was a favorite Macpherson device to be found at two or three significant points in the *Fingal* narrative. Characters meet and discuss the great victories of the past, the traditions of their fathers, their own willingness to face death or peace. In "Lora" the feast is also a symbol of the reconciliation of all Fingal's heroes. When the two warriors leave to join the enemy, they have failed an unspoken test of their loyalty and fall victim to pride and arrogance. Based on what we know of his character, Fingal must be held blameless for the loss of his men; it is they who lacked faith in him.

Learning of their rejection of Fingal, Erragon accepts them as soldiers and trusts them as men of honor, a foolhardiness that causes him to lose his wife Lorma to the young, rakish Aldo. Macpherson diminishes Erragon in stature by deftly contrasting him with the astute Fin-

gal. The Scandinavian king appears a frustrated, almost ridiculous
figure in love, who must pursue his wife and her lover back to Scot-
land. With his honor in tatters Erragon can only restore his sense of
pride on the battlefield. Fingal seems to understand his plight and,
instead of condemning him, gives him his chance for redemption.
   Although brief, the episode in which Aldo abducts Erragon's wife
provides an opportunity for Fingal to underscore the importance of
personal honor. Aldo's violation of the laws of the house, of hospitality,
and of the marriage bonds threatens the rule of law in Sora, and, be-
cause he is a member of Fingal's family, it brings dishonor on the whole
race. His disgrace can be passed on to the young and the unborn,
eroding the very basis of the society. Fingal speaks as the father-king
to a son who has dishonored his people:

> Also, of the heart of pride! shall I
> defend thee from the rage of Sora's injured
> king? Who will now receive my people into
> their halls? Who will give the feast of
> strangers, since Aldo, of the little soul,
> has dishonoured my name in Sora? Go to thy
> hills, thou feeble hand. Go; hide thee in thy
> caves.
>   (1:278–79)

   The king knows that for a warrior honor and fame remain the only
concerns in life. Because personal honor and public duty are so closely
intertwined, Fingal must fight Erragon. He banishes Aldo, but that
act does not release him from having to attempt to erase a shameful
act. Macpherson again has gone beyond the limitations of the ballads
in raising questions of ethical conduct. No new alternatives to war are
given; none are necessary when men willingly die in seeking eternal
fame for themselves, their ancestors, and descendents.
   Macpherson has accomplished much of what he intended to do. The
actual battle occupies only fourteen lines; the section immediately pre-
ceding he reserves for Ossian's description of Fingal's cunning as he
attempts to gain time for the return of his chiefs (who are away hunt-
ing) by sending his daughter to Erragon with various delaying tactics.
When Fingal can no longer wait, he moves forward and in the crucial
moment of the ensuing battle the "young heroes" appear; Erragon is
killed by Gaul but not before executing the transgressor Aldo. Since

his main interest in the piece is elsewhere, Macpherson collapses the nine days given to the battle in his sources into one day, emphasizing sentiment over swordplay.

The only figure who thus far remains unaffected is Lorma, who awaits the return of Aldo. His ghost appears to lead her to her lover's corpse. In a sentimental statement quite unlike anything in the ballads, Macpherson has Lorma lament Aldo's death and then succumb herself from an excess of grief. As Sir Walter Scott wrote in his review of Laing's *Edition of Macpherson,* "in the original ballad [for this poem] there is no splendid scenery, no sentimental exclamation, no romantic effusion of tenderness of sensibility; it is a matter-of-fact statement. . . ; the venerable Ossian tells his story to St. Patrick in the style of a half-pay officer describing his campaigns to a country parson."[31] Scott was making his case against Macpherson as translator of Gaelic originals, but his comment suggests that, despite an unconvincing narrative, Macpherson had succeeded in adapting his sources to suit his own purpose.

"Conlath and Cuthona"

P. H. Waddell, in *Ossian and the Clyde* (1875), described "Conlath and Cuthona," another of the *Fingal* poems, as "a romance of crime and cruelty, originating in the lawless love of a stranger of the coast of Arran, carried out on the coast of Cantyre, and punished on the rocks of Sanda."[32] Conlath is the young, vigorous brother of Gaul, who had led Fingal's warriors against Swaran in Ireland. He is much like the headstrong Celtic warrior portrayed throughout the Ossian poems: proud, generous, passionate, fierce, and unswerving in devotion to tribal custom. Cuthona, who lives on a distant island and is betrothed to Conlath, meets the requirements of an Ossianic maid: beautiful, spirited, sensitive, and compassionate. She would be the perfect companion in war or peace: a symbol of devotion to her warrior husband.

The conflict that upsets this relationship arrives in the form of Toscar, an Irish friend of Conlath, who is hospitably received by the Scots. As he returns home with his men, Toscar spies Cuthona, the "huntress of the desert isle," rapes and kidnaps her as a prize of his journey. Inevitably, Conlath hears of this outrage and gives chase, catching up with Toscar, who in a storm has taken refuge in a cave on a small island. Before Conlath reaches them, Cuthona convinces Toscar of the wrong he has done; he agrees that "Cuthona shall return to her peace; to the towers of generous Conlath." In a romantic flourish Macpherson ends the narrative with a furious sword fight in which the two antagonists are joined by their followers. All the combatants die "at the cave of Thona." Cuthona, surrounded by the dead, mourns the loss of Conlath and her own senseless death, which she has forseen in a vision.

An ill-conceived structure, in addition to "its dramatic abruptness and occasional involution," weakens the effect of the poem. Ossian is told this tale by Conlath's ghost, who sits on a dim cloud before the band of Celtic warriors. As he greets Conlath's ghost, Ossian hears the ghosts of Toscar, his countryman Fercuth, and in the distance Cuthona, which come to urge him to tell their people how glorious was the last battle. Macpherson's note makes clear that Fingal has buried Toscar and Fercuth on the island, "but forgot to send a bard to sing the funeral song over their tombs" (1:295). Without the elegy and the bards' recollection of their deeds at royal banquets, these dead heroes will suffer an eternity of horrors.

The complex artificiality of "Conlath and Cuthona" precludes any feeling one might have for the sufferings of the main characters. If what has occurred can be called a feudal atrocity, as Waddell suggests, one is nonetheless tempted to view it with indifference, an inevitable response, in fact; Ossian himself sees the offense imperfectly and with no awareness of its implications. What seems noteworthy about the tale is not its amalgam of chivalry, battle, and elegy, but the uncharacteristic incoherence of Ossian's aesthetic vision. The bard eagerly grasps a chance to dismiss the ghosts from his view, as if marking the unimportance of the tale. In this one poem Macpherson treats his own material in the shallow, superficial way that, ironically, his bard dismisses the poem itself.

"Carthon"

Of the smaller pieces in the 1762 collection "Carthon" has elicited an exceptional amount of contradictory criticism. Celtic scholars cite it as an illustration of Macpherson's ruthless treatment of his sources. Other critics, leveling a charge of plagiarism against the poet, find the concluding Address of the Sun a perfect example of Macpherson's flagrant borrowing from the Bible and Milton. Other critics and sponsors see "Carthon" as "a highly finished piece," an uncommon poem surpassing even the epic *Fingal*. Those most vehement in their attacks, in fact, are not always uniformly critical: the poem, or at least the Address to the Sun, "is the best thing in the whole series [and] still retains a certain splendor."[33] Such contrary opinions foreshadow those following the publication of the last group of Ossianic poems the next year. What seems remarkable is that a relatively short, even elementary, poetic exercise could produce this diversity of comment.

"Carthon" is no more skillful or splendid than many of the extended passages in *Fingal*. The poet here sustains the same unhurried, unassertive manner characteristic of his work. Using an effective array of metaphor, compound sentences, and a sublime melancholic atmosphere, Macpherson delights in producing his own brand of verbal nuance—"a tale of the times of old! The deeds of days of other years!"

The introduction is deliberately imprecise. Ossian describes a natural scene as he typically does: not as one might actually observe it but as one might feel it:

> The murmur of thy streams, O Lora,
> brings back the memory of the past. The
> sound of thy woods, Garmallar, is lovely in
> mine ear.
>
> (1:311)

The bard's vision unfolds in characteristic fashion, the whole prompted by the appearance of an unidentified ghost. Inspired by the spirit, Ossian sees Fingal returning triumphantly from the wars and celebrating with a magnificent feast. Fingal asks to have Clessammor, his father's old friend, join him:

> Tell . . . the tale of thy youthful days.
> . . . Mournful are thy thoughts, alone, on the
> banks of the roaring Lora. Let us hear the
> sorrow of thy youth, and the darkness of thy days!
>
> (1:315–16)

Clessammor's story reveals a period when a few daring men traveled, hunted, raided, and loved without any thought of the consequences. In one such journey to Balclutha, Clessammor falls in love with Moina, who is also loved by "the son of a stranger." The two men fight; Fingal's friend kills the stranger but is forced to flee the province. Moina is left crying on the shore and soon dies of her grief. Clessammor, who never returns, tells Fingal he knows she is dead because he has "seen her ghost . . she was like the new moon, seen through the gathered mist" (1:318).

The narrative pauses for Fingal's song of mourning for Moina. In firm control of every detail Macpherson provides additional evidence of his hero's compassion and genius, both in warfare and the arts. Later, Blair would assure readers that the song "is inferior to no passage in the whole book," Yet, at best, Fingal's song serves merely as an effective transition to the main action of the poem. Clessammor's story and the song of grief become extravagances rather than essential parts of Macpherson's interpretation of a well-known folk legend.

At the heart of "Carthon" is a famous theme of heroic myth: a father unknowingly killing his son in combat. The tragic meeting of father and son, adapted from an ancient Indo-European myth extant in the ballads of the Ulster cycle, gave Macpherson a further opportunity for sentimental amplification. He extended the unity of tone in Ossian— Wain calls it "monotonous lachrymosity."

The ballad story has Cuchulain begetting a son, Conloch, by a woman he must leave before the infant is born. He gives her a token so that the son may come to him when he is grown and thus be recognized. Conloch, after he becomes a man, arrives in Ireland to search for his father. His own pride causes the tragedy, for even when he suspects that Cuchulain is his father, he refuses to identify himself. Cuchulain, thinking Conloch a mortal enemy, kills him. Conloch, near death, at the last reveals himself to his distraught father, who cries out while he holds the boy in his arms: "Here is my son for you, men of Ulster." The ballad, as Thomson points out, "is told with economy and restraint in the best ballad style."[34]

The emotional reserve of this Irish legend evokes comparison with that of, for example, the Germanic *Lay of Hildebrand,* the Persian *Book of Kings* episode of Sohrab and Rustum, and the Russian Kiev cycle legend of Ilya Murometch, in each of which is found the motif of the battle between father and son; it is not likely, however, that Macpherson knew these works. Yet it is an ancient theme that the poet here attempts. Perhaps having written an epic that many felt rivaled the *Iliad* and the *Aeneid,* Macpherson felt himself able to handle "Carthon" with relative ease.[35]

The arrival of Carthon's small fleet marks the beginning of the climactic stage of the poem's development. When Carthon refuses Fingal's invitation to dinner at the royal banquet tables, he chooses war over peace, and his fate is sealed by Fingal's symbolic reference to him as "the son of the stranger," the same epithet Clessammor uses for the man he killed in Balclutha. The horrors of the past, it appears, will be repeated here with even more tragic results.

Macpherson tampers freely with the ballad story. At least one critic believes that he "could seldom resist the temptation to prettify the result still further in the direction of 18th-century taste."[36] His frequent changes, however, are mostly in details; in intention the piece remains true to the ancient myth, in which details commonly vary, often radically, from country to country.

One significant change from the Irish ballad occurs in the dialogue between father and son. Clessammor's sense of self-esteem is as easily threatened as Carthon's. When the young man inquires why an old warrior comes to battle him, Clessammor is no longer capable of restraint:

> Why dost thou wound my soul . . . Age does
> not tremble on my hand; I can still lift the
> sword. . . . I never fled: exalt thy pointed spear.
>   (1:337)

The father, unlike the original Cuchulain, pours forth all his feelings. This surprised late eighteenth-century readers, who expected emotional outbursts from arrogant youths but not from mature heroes. Macpherson is, however, attempting in Clessammor a new hero, one who cannot be measured by a standard that attributes greater character to the person who holds something of himself in reserve. The battle between Clessammor and Carthon is really not a battle at all but an agreement to rely upon feelings as guides to truth and conduct.

The death of Carthon causes the father such excessive grief that his own death seems a relief. They are buried together on the "plain of the rock," and Ossian reports that the ghost of Moina has been seen keeping watch at the tomb. In a final address to the sun Ossian laments their passing and the loss of beauty and youth.

> O thou that rollest above, round as the
> shield of my fathers! Whence are thy beams,
> O sun! thy everlasting light? . . . But thou
> art perhaps, like me for a season, thy years
> will have an end. Thou shalt sleep in the
> clouds, careless of the voice of the
> morning. Exult then, O sun, in the strength
> of thy youth! Age is dark and
> unlovely . . . the traveller shrinks in the midst of his journey.
>   (1:342–43, 346–47)

This passage became famous because Macpherson had the mistaken impression that by calling attention in a note to Ossian's resemblance here to Milton he would add dignity and importance to his work. Laing turned the similarity against him, however, alleging hundreds of parallels between other established works and *Ossian*. When Macpherson likened the "Carthon" passage to Satan's address to the sun in book 4 of *Paradise Lost,* Laing submitted additional evidence that brought the authorship into greater doubt. Scholars have shown that nearly four-fifths of Laing's attributions are either wrong or farfetched, and R. D. Havens suggests that "in view of Milton's extraordinary vogue, it would be strange if the Ossianic epics did not take some phrases from *Paradise Lost.*"[37] Macpherson had studied Milton, and "in the grip of an imaginative impulse," he may have drawn upon that epic but not in a vital way.

"Carthon" ends with Ossian's tragic soliloquy on the majesty of youth with its glories and the horrors of old age and eventual death. The bard speaks frankly with himself, and permits us a clear view of his own motives. The permanency of the sun in nature has no rival; man must ultimately submit: he cannot battle a universe of ever-re-newed vitality and win.

"The Death of Cuthullin"

The narrative of Cuchulain's death serves two notable functions in the *Poems of Ossian.*[38] It is the linchpin that connects the two major epics, *Fingal* and *Temora,* and it is a symbol of the indomitability as well as the fragility of the Scottish heroic spirit. As mentioned earlier, Macpherson had no regard for Cuchulain's traditional Irish origins and promoted the hero as a son of rugged Skye. His primary concern was as always to move the reader, emotionally, to appeal to his finest sensibilities. The hero, who seeks eternal fame and faces courageously the fate prophesied for him, has an inescapable fascination.

At the conclusion of *Fingal* Cuchulain had resumed his place as regent of Ireland, with all his rights and powers restored to him by the generous King of Morven. After the events described in "The Death of Cuthullin," Irish affairs become chaotic and the young Irish King Cormac is assassinated. "Darthula," the poem next in the sequence, prompts further doubts about the survival of Irish sovereignty. Macpherson creates a need, then, for a literary sequel that will answer these questions. In *Temora* Fingal returns in order to reestablish the Irish royal house, to secure its proper role in the society.

As early as 1760 Macpherson had mentioned to Blair the existence
of two epics on the exploits of Fingal as revealed by the bard Ossian.
His difficulty after *Fingal,* however, was in deciding upon a motive for
involving Fingal in a second expedition to Ireland. He resolves the
problem in part by assuming his favorite role of scholar-investigator
and concluding that the Cuchulain poem is merely an episode in an
ancient epic of which the greater part is lost. A partial motivation is
present, however, in Fingal's desire to return to Ireland not only to
restore order to the community but also to consecrate those principles
for which Cuchulain died. As Ossian says:

> . . . my soul grows in danger, and
> rejoices in the noise of steel . . . But my
> name is renowned! my fame in the song of
> the bards. The youth will say in secret, "O
> let me die as Cuchulain died."
>   (1:364,68)

Ossian is startled from his reverie by the song of Bragela, wife of Cu-
chulain, who waits patiently for his return to Skye. The bard, sensing
her desperation and sorrow, encourages Bragela to sleep and dream of
her hero. With this introduction Ossian, by using his power and Bra-
gela's love, deduces the facts of Cuchulain's final days.

The tale itself follows a familiar pattern with an invading force ar-
riving to challenge the status quo. Both forces are led by noble, pow-
erful figures with, however, one significant distinction between them.
The invader Torlath seeks war, demanding nothing less than total ca-
pitulation; the other, Cuchulain, believes the peace can still be pre-
served, as "the sword rests not by the side of Cuchulain," though he
admits in the same breath "my soul delights in war."

Surrounded by his hundred bards, Cuchulain calls to the enemy's
bard to sit and hear the song of joy. Even when his offer of conciliation
is rejected, Cuchulain remains even-tempered, calmly self-assured in
the face of threats and bombast. His equanimity seems most attractive
when he agrees repeatedly with Torlath's bard that his master is indeed
brave. Blair may have been more correct than he knew when he said
that "Cuchulain is a hero of the highest class; daring, magnanimous,
exquisitely sensible to honor."[39] Nonetheless, in *Fingal* Cuchulain
seems inferior to the main hero, and for this reason Blair implies that
he deserves better treatment. As if anticipating such criticism, Mac-
pherson enhances Cuchulain's personal worthiness in this last battle.

As the bards sing of the deeds of old, Cuchulain is visited by the
ghosts of dead warriors who seem to beckon him away from the fight.
With the insight and shrewdness of a superior leader, he turns the
ghosts back with words of such praise that they are forced to recall
their own glorious deeds in battle. It is, indeed, the relationship be-
tween the ghosts, who establish the seriousness of the event, and the
soldiers, who will fight the battle, that increasingly becomes the back-
drop for Cuchulain's character. Displaying a talent peculiar to Fingal,
Cuchulain unites both the supernatural and natural world into a more
potent force.

Macpherson maintains some continuity with Cuchulain's early char-
acter by having him call for peace, adopt a tone of conciliation, and
encourage the bards to sing mournful songs. The change that is sharply
marked in Cuchulain is the strength of his intelligence. For example,
he can in the same statement admonish a warrior for not standing by
him and restore the man's self-respect by assigning him a more impor-
tant role as guardian and advisor to the King. The hero, though always
aware of his duty, appears in "The Death of Cuthullin" capable of or-
dering his emotions by the force of reason, particularly during periods
of greatest stress. Macpherson here seems more willing that Cuchulain
die nobly rather than as a weeping sentimentalist, a significant shift
from his fawning obsequiousness at the conclusion of *Fingal*. Although
the poem, in its predictability, resembles a number of the other shorter
poems, it captures with vigor and skill many of the qualities that make
Cuchulain, in the Celtic epic *Táin Bó Cúailgne* (*Cattle Raid of Cooley*),
one of the great figures of Indo-European heroic legend.

"Dar-thula"

In "Dar-thula" Macpherson has cleverly taken from the Ulster cycle
a thirteenth-century story having both Irish and Scottish connections;
altered the names, setting, and tone; and used it to supplement his
tale of the events following the tragic loss of Cuchulain. The poem
alludes frequently to a greater war fought by Fingal against the usurper
Cairbar. As the poem concludes, Cairbar issues a challenge:

> My battle would have roared on Morven,
> had not the winds met Dar-thula. Fingal
> himself would have been low, and sorrow
> dwelling in Selma!
>
> (1:406)

Ossian recounts the tragedy of Dar-thula, the daughter of the noble Colla, as it was told to him by the Irish bards when Fingal "came to green Erin to fight with car-borne Cairbar" (1:407). The poem tells the story of three warrior brothers, Nathos, Althos, and Ardan, who have been fighting Cairbar, murderer of Cormac, the Irish king. Cairbar, who has steadily grown in power, discourages the brothers' army from further battle. Nathos flees into Ulster seeking passage back to Scotland. Dar-thula sees the young fighter, falls in love, and joins him on board ship. Unfortunately the ship is driven by a storm back to shore and lands near Cairbar's encampment. The usurper, who wants to possess Dar-thula, as well as secure the destruction of the three Scots, shows his lack of nobility by insulting his enemies. The brothers and Dar-thula, true to their noble natures, face the usurper's entire army in what is certain death. Finally overpowered, the brothers are killed, and the grieving Dar-thula commits suicide on her dead lover's corpse.

"Dar-thula" has evoked two contradictory evaluations. Hugh Blair finds "assembled almost all the tender images that can touch the heart of man. . . . The story is regular, dramatic, interesting to the last. He who can read it without emotion may congratulate himself, if he pleases, upon being completely armed against sympathetic sorrow."[40] The contemporary Gaelic scholar Derick Thomson, however, writes that "the fine clear colours of the original are gone. . . . In this telling the tale has lost its tragedy, its pathos, its dignity, and practically all its meaning."[41] The divergence in these two points of view would be surprising had we not seen exactly the same dichotomy in the analyses of *Fingal*.

To Blair, "Dar-thula" appears regular, even sublime. The poem's introductory address to the moon has the essential qualities of Macpherson's best verse: striking epithets, effusive joy in nature, and the strange mixture of pleasure and pain to be found in recalling the glories of the past. The focus upon regularity implies a balanced narrative structure, as well as a delight in the poem's symmetry of emotional entanglements. By an effective use of dramatic structure Macpherson transcends the rules, Blair believes, and "prepares the mind for that train of affecting events that is to follow."

For Thomson, on the other hand, "Dar-thula" represents a thorough rejection of the original in favor of "impoverished pattern-making." The clarity and sharp focus in the Ulster story of the *Tragical Death of the Sons of Usnech, or the Life and Death of Deidre* are pushed aside for a confusing tale of despairing love and passionate regret.

In the Irish story, according to the prophecy, the beautiful Deidre's rejection of Conchobar's marriage proposal will precipitate a tragedy. Deidre instead falls in love with Conchobor's warrior, Naisi, one of Usnech's three sons, and escapes with him to Scotland, where they live for many years. To end their exile, a group of Ulster warriors secure a promise of amnesty if they return to Ireland, but when they land, Conchobar treacherously kills Naisi and his brothers, and makes Deidre his property. Unwilling to accept such a fate, Deidre commits suicide by dashing her head against a stone.

The basis of Thomson's argument becomes clearer here. The characters are vigorous and simple, quite unlike the sensitive creatures in the perishing world of Macpherson. The tone of the original is both melancholy and joyous, reflecting a full appreciation of nature and a love of life. Unlike its Celtic source, "Dar-thula" has a pathetic dignity. For Celtophiles, this difference may be intolerable, yet Macpherson always vehemently insisted he was correcting corrupt ballads, restoring Celtic literature to its rightful place, and reshaping the mythology of a doomed Celticism into a spiritual bequest.[42]

The poem is designed, as I see it, to perpetuate the memory of youth and its finest qualities: love, friendship, bravery, and sense of purpose. Macpherson takes care to have the speaker present himself as isolated from both the past and the future. The connection, if one can be made to exist, is in the songs Ossian sings about these heroic youths. As in earlier works, the poem comforts the reader by undergirding the present with an evocation of the past. The main point, however, is allowed to stand: hero worship is much preferred to any loss of glory for a nation. The true subject of the song is not Ossian's memorializing of past heroes, but fame itself.

"Carric-Thura"

"Carric-Thura" has created some minor critical interest because of its opening address to the sun. Macpherson opened the better-known "Carthon" in the same way, and at one point the Ossianic debate focused upon this similarity without further discussing either work. "Carric-Thura," accordingly, was made to seem the equal of "Carthon," though the evidence was slim for such a critical estimate. Under closer scrutiny, however, "Carric-Thura" is more revealing of Macpherson's poetic gifts, at least in dealing with the Ossianic theme.

The central purpose of the poem is to illustrate the sublime power of Fingal. Ossian describes his father's actions against supernatural powers capable of arousing the greatest dread and terror; Fingal must fight the spirit of Lora, a supposed disguise for Odin, the supreme Norse god. Fingal also rescues his defenseless allies from the ravages of invaders from the North. Both these ventures he accomplishes without bloodshed; such is Fingal's capacity for evoking fear in his enemies, who are astonished by his superior nature and horrified into insensibility. Blair speaks of the poem's sublime dignity, especially in its demonstration of chivalry. However, when Fingal spares Frothal's life, he withholds his sword not simply as a result of some attachment to the chivalric code, but because, as an omnipotent god, he has no need to kill a human being to prove his divinity. Macpherson's intention was not to create some hero of medieval romance, as Blair suggests; instead, Fingal is more nearly an embodiment of what Burke describes as the nonrational power in the sublime.

What may have prompted Blair's interpretation is the perplexing structure of "Carric-Thura." It has a loose three-part division arranged about the movements of Fingal. The king returns from an expedition against the Romans; he goes to war again to rescue Cathulla, under attack at Carric-Thura (roughly translated as the Towers of Carrick) from the King of Sora, Frothal; and he concludes the war with the usual feasting and singing. Among the events of these sections Macpherson has woven various fragments (1,2,4,5) that were published earlier in the 1760 collection and are not consistent with the rest.

The Shilric and Vinvela episode (Fragment 1), which is introduced by Ullin at the invitation of Fingal, creates, for example, a disturbing, artificial sense of disorder in the narrative. Macpherson prolongs the disjunction by inserting the other fragments at the appropriate moments. In each instance, the fragment upsets the traditional movement of the story; however, it gradually becomes clear that Macpherson's purpose is to sustain the aura of mystery and fantasy in the poem. Ossian's haphazard, often disjointed manner of recalling the past undermines all orderly, logical plotting of time and action. The reader cannot depend upon just the facts of who fought whom and where in order to understand the poem. Instead, he must feel his way by sensing the emotional atmosphere of the piece.

Macpherson here alters the traditional balance of proportion and order while keeping to his original plan. His purpose remains the creation of a magnificent cultural hero in Fingal. He also appeals to the curious emotional qualities in the joy of grief.[43] Fingal invokes the bard

"to strike the harp . . . let me hear the song," and prefaces his request
with "pleasant is the joy of grief." Ossian's recollection once again bears
out the aesthetic pleasure to be had in contemplating things now for-
ever lost. The reason such stories may prove valuable to the listener is
suggested by Ossian's double question: "Who can reach the source of
thy race, . . . who recount thy fathers?" (442). In defining the contri-
bution his people have made to the British Isles, Ossian recounts Fin-
gal's defense against the Norse invaders. Macpherson through Ossian
can point to the inherent honor and martial spirit of the Scots, while
demonstrating the poetic genius of the nation.

The one remaining aspect of "Carric-Thura" deserving of interest is
"the spirit of Loda." Macpherson, with his usual cunning, associates
the spirit with Odin, the supreme Viking god, a complex, demonic,
sadistic figure.[44] As Fingal approaches the Orkneys to visit Cathulla,
he sees a distress fire burning from the battlements of Carric-Thura
and his way blocked by the supernatural spirit of Loda. Ferocious and
treacherous, Loda at first threatens death, then advances—"he came to
his place in his terrors, and shook his dusky spear" (1:426). Fingal,
who fears neither man nor god, warns him to leave—with no effect;
finally, they meet, and the king destroys the ghostly form.

Earlier, in "The Death of Cuthullin," Macpherson compares Cuchu-
lain to Loda, who appears as a frightening force in order to strengthen
the martial image of the Irish hero. His use of Loda is quite different
in "Carric-Thura." Fingal's killing of a spirit linked to the supreme
Odin makes him one with the divine figure. By association Fingal
ironically takes on one of Odin's chief attributes: the god of skalds or
bards who governs the mystic ecstasy. This elevation of the King of
Morven is comparable to the creation of cult figures in the Greek
world. Macpherson has fashioned not only a brave man in Fingal but
also, through Ossian's paean to his dead father, a figure displaying the
highest martial spirit. It is this idealization that the reader is encour-
aged to admire in the poems.

"The Songs of Selma"

Macpherson would have been gratified to read the preface to *The
Sufferings of Young Werther,* Johann Wolfgang Goethe's 1774 sentimen-
tal novel of frustrated love. Speaking of his hero, Goethe stated, "you
cannot withhold your admiration or your love from his spirit and char-
acter, nor your tears from his fate."[45] In one sentence the German ro-

manticist summarized the effects of the Ossian poems. Years later
Goethe would criticize his hero's affection for Ossian as the sign of a
deluded mind; however, the long quotation from Ossian at the climac-
tic point in *Werther* did much to increase the vogue of the poems.
When the desperate young Werther read a translation of "The Songs
of Selma" to the beautiful Lotte, Goethe was suggesting the close af-
finity between the theme of the novel and the noble lamentations of
Ossian. The bard's songs capture exactly Werther's profound misery at
the end of the work, the delicacy of conscience that causes his eventual
suicide. In a more general way Ossian's connection to the central theme
of Goethe's work is defined as "the destruction of an extreme idealist
by his contact with inexorable reality."[46] Werther is a romantic sufferer
alienated by reality; he longs for the idealism of the past when nature
dominated man's existence in the world.

"The Songs of Selma" (1762) immerse one in the melancholy, form-
less world left to the bards after the deaths of the great heroes. These
infrequent stoics cling dearly to their memories of dead warriors and
their grief-stricken lovers; and as often as the dead warriors refuse to
reveal the secret of existence, the bards in a contrary spirit break forth
into uninterrupted wailing, offering all their wisdom to the listener.

His imagination having transported him to the feast of Selma, held
at an earlier time in Lora, the banqueting hall of Fingal, Ossian sings
three songs in the poem. The bard begins his poignant recollection of
the feast and the songs he heard there with an invocation to the evening
star:

> Star of descending night! fair is thy
> light in the west! thou liftest thy unshorn
> head from thy cloud: thy steps are stately
> on thy hill. . . . What dost thou behold, fair
> light?
>
> (1:451–52)

Ossian then sings the opening verses of Minona's lament for Colma,
who suffered the double tragedy of losing her lover Salgar and her
brother Morar. Ironically, the maid waits forever in vain for their return
because the two men have slain one another in battle. The second song
is sung by the bard Ullin in concert with Ossian as an elegy for the
dead Morar. It takes the form of an eclogue, the principal speakers
being Ryno and Alpin, two unlikely shepherds. Because of Morar's
fame in battle, the bards promise that "future times shall hear of

[him]," thus offering hope of an eternal life through their art. This song of mourning ends with a picture of the aged, grieving father, the last of a family whose members are now all dead.

The third song is a rather complex amalgam of tragedies, centering on the deaths of Armin's children. Armin, who sings the piece, is the chief of Gorma and a poet. His lament traces the kidnapping of his daughter Daura by Erath, a traitor, who is soon captured by her brother, Arindal. At the moment of victory Arindal is killed by Armar, Daura's beloved, who has mistaken him for Erath. As if the depths of sorrow have not been reached, Macpherson has Arindal and Daura's boat break up in heavy seas. When Armar tries to rescue her, he drowns; she reaches the shore but dies from grief. In the meantime, Armin, who is powerless to stop these horrors, is forced to listen to the dying moans of his daughter.

The excessive emotionalism and unswerving focus on destruction in this poem would serve Goethe well. He intended in the last few pages of *Werther* to insure the credibility of his hero's suffering. These songs provide the necessary intensity for the novel's death symbolism. As Schiller would later write of Werther, "his dreams alone are reality, while his experiences are mere barriers." Macpherson has attempted to enhance the reader's aesthetic delight by having Ossian escape reality through the dream and yet emerge into the outside world with total recall of "the tales of other times."

"Calthon and Colmal"

"Calthon and Colmal" has evoked little reaction from its readers. Hugh Blair, Macpherson's most generous critic, offers only a short, positive comment on the poem.[47] Macpherson had (we may suppose) little enough inspiration for the piece, which had as its source an old Irish ballad about a blood feud between two rival families. His theme is a familiar one: love's triumph over villainy and death. The poem differs from others resembling it, however, in its accumulation of atrocities. Macpherson allows his villain Dunthalmo full rein in perpetrating a savagery unparalleled in Ossian.

The bard invokes the son of the rock (Macpherson's cryptic reference to St. Patrick) to listen to his song of the two sons of Rathmor, Calthon and Colmar. As youths they were taken into the house of Dunthalmo, who had murdered their father in a violent rage; foolishly he had hoped the boys would become the sons he never had. As they grow to be young men, the brothers can think only of avenging their father's murder, and Dunthalmo, fearing their power, imprisons them in twin caves. The narrative makes an abrupt turn when Ossian reveals that Colmal, daughter of Dunthalmo, loves Calthon and has cleverly engineered his escape through the ruse of dressing as a warrior and appealing to his practical military sense:

> Let us fly to the king of Morven, he
> will come with war. His arm is stretched
> forth to the unhappy; the lightning of his
> sword is round the weak. Arise, thou son
> of Rathmor; the shadows will fly away.
> Arise, or thy steps may be seen, and thou
> must fall in youth!
>
> (1:478)

She persuades Calthon to leave Colmar, who is too well guarded, and seek instead Fingal's help in ridding themselves of Dunthalmo. As always, Fingal receives the weak graciously, at once agreeing that their cause is right. He sends Ossian with three hundred volunteers to rescue Colmar and subdue Dunthalmo. Reacting with brutal indignation, Dunthalmo executes the captive Colmar in full view of his brother and his rescuers. Ossian with no choice charges into battle with his men, kills the rogue chieftain, and destroys his army. In the meantime Ossian discovers that the young rescuer of Calthon is, in fact, the woman Colmal; he reunites the two and the kingdom is restored to order.

Three aspects of the poem deserve further notice: Fingal's statement on the education of princes, the portrait of the Gothic villain in Dunthalmo, and the triumph of love as orchestrated by Ossian. Macpherson, as in the earlier poems, continues his examination of Fingal's wisdom and Ossian's magnanimity. His cunning, evil Dunthalmo, immersed in a blood lust, bears comparison with Horace Walpole's Manfred in *The Castle of Otranto* (1764) and Ann Radcliffe's Schedoni in *The Italian* (1797).

Fingal's rousing speech in support of Dunthalmo's victims inspires his men to action. However, Ossian is destined to lead this raid against the villain, for Fingal sees in it an opportunity for him to demonstrate his leadership and his kingly potential:

> "Son of my strength," began the king,
> "take thou the spear of Fingal. Go to

> Teutha's rushing stream, and save the
> car-borne Colmar. Let thy fame return before
> thee like a pleasant gale; that my soul may
> rejoice over my son, who renews the renown
> of our father."
>
> (1:479)

His comment strikes the now-familiar themes of honor, recognition, and tradition. But in his final words Fingal reaches beyond these soldierly commitments to the essence of royal virtue. The father defines for his son the character that will cause a people to embrace their king:

> "Ossian! be thou a storm in war; but
> mild when the foe is low! It was thus my
> fame arose, O my son; be thou like Selma's
> chief. When the haughty come to my halls,
> my eyes behold them not. But my arm is
> stretched forth to the unhappy. My sword
> defends the weak."
>
> (1:479)

Macpherson has once again stated his requirements of royalty and enhanced the cult of his hero.

Dunthalmo's savagery seems a product of uncontrollable hubris, the arrogance that defies the wrath of the gods, and Fingal, representative of godlike virtue on earth, must punish him. Dunthalmo, whom Macpherson describes in his note to the poem as "infamous for his cruelty and ambition," is a man of violent extremes, assuming that whatever he is, nature is also, abusing power for the sheer pleasure of it. Never far from our sight or mind is his indifference to human life; each new murder seems more savage than the last. He is stripped of honor by the time he deprives the defenseless Colmar of his right to a dignified warrior's death:

> They brought Colmar to Teutha's bank,
> bound with a thousand thongs. . . . Dunthalmo
> came with his spear, and pierced the hero's
> side: he rolled on the bank in his blood. We
> heard his broken sighs.
>
> (1:482)

The poet suggests the horror of this act by having Colmar die a lowly captive without a sword in his hand; the tyrant's bloody deed condemns him to the worst of fates: to be an outcast. When Ossian destroys Dunthalmo, he punishes a transgressor in the name of Fingal while restoring order to the community. Significantly, the calm that Ossian establishes by military might is symbolized by the love of the couple who have struggled against tyranny and the threat of death. Ossian's bringing the couple together and his willingness to honor their love above all else, including his victory, create an effective conclusion for the piece. With admirable consistency Macpherson maintains a delicate balance between Ossian's two natures: the warrior and the artist. The bard in the early lines exhibits the thoroughgoing militarism of a hardened warrior who continually seeks adventure. When Colmal reveals herself, in the final moments of the poem, Ossian's dominant nature also emerges. His deep-seated sensibility guides his response to the couple, each of whom represents an opposing political camp:

> But when I heard the name of the maid,
> my crowding tears rushed down. I blessed
> the lovely beam of youth, and bade the
> battle move!
>
> (1:485)

Ossian sympathizes with these two youths, vicariously sharing in their joy and sorrow; he proves capable of understanding their complex situation. To say that he easily solves their difficulties and the nation's would be an understatement. The essence of the poem is not political accomplishment but an emotional test of faith. Colmal has sacrificed her name, rank, and position for love, which guides her conduct. Her feelings for Calthon are translated into truth and right action. Ossian simply acknowledges her sacrifice and then sanctions their love as the highest form of human integrity. He can do no less than award them control of the kingdom. Macpherson has again joined his moral bard to an action that makes an institution of humanity's inherent goodness. Though aberrant behavior will occur to test this goodness, in the final analysis Macpherson believes that men and women of Ossian's kind will not only counter its vicious effects but will prevail.

"Lathmon"

In "Lathmon" may be seen the traditional Ossian pattern of tone, images, and mood. The poem's similarity to that of so many others in the canon may be its strength, for Macpherson can thus assume a reader is already well acquainted with both Fingal's character and Ossian's sense of defeat even in victory.

The resemblance here between the Lathmon story and other Ossianic narratives arises primarily from Fingal, the dominant figure. Once again, the King of Morven demonstrates his courage as well as his deep sense of duty and obligation to the state. As the best and most representative warrior-product of his nation and culture, Fingal in dramatic fashion defeats the lesser opponent, the English prince Lathmon, who in his absence has attempted by devious means to attack and capture the kingdom. Fingal's strong personality serves also as motivation in the subplot involving his two young companions, Ossian and Gaul. Emphasizing their development as warriors, Macpherson takes pains to examine the psyches of these two young men as they are about to go into battle:

> "Son of Fingal," he [Gaul] said, "why burns
> the soul of Gaul? My heart beats high. My
> steps are disordered; my hand trembles on
> my sword."
>
> "Son of Morni," I [Ossian] replied, "my soul
> delights in war. . . . But what if the foe
> should prevail; can I behold the eyes of the
> king!"
>   (1:500–501)

His psychological probing adds another dimension to the poem; the reader's previously shaped sense of Fingal's courage points up an exquisite tension in the work. Will the sons possess the zeal and talents of their fathers? An even more important issue is whether the sons, in their extreme ambition and desire for fame, can translate their successes on the battlefield into a wise, compassionate peace. Ultimately, Macpherson makes clear that sensitivity, intuition, generosity are the proper measurements of a warrior's maturity. Fingal's sending Lathmon home unharmed after his failed invasion serves as an admirable model for these youthful warriors, who must learn diplomacy as well as warfare.

"Lathmon" revives a central figure in Macpherson's verse: the dynamic skillful fighter whose tactical imagination may verge upon genius, but who must, nevertheless, employ compromise and compassion if he is to insure his people's survival. While Macpherson develops his theories on the nature of men intimately involved in war and peace, he does not undermine the irony that his speaker, Ossian, is the last of his race. Precisely because Fingal and his warriors no longer live among us, their actions and beliefs become all the more poignant and significant.

Blair often makes the point that the sublime is, to a great degree, coincident with magnanimity and generosity of sentiment. "Lathmon" fulfills this principle of the sublime rather well, especially in its emphasis on valor. Fingal, Ossian, and Gaul demonstrate courage and loyalty on numerous occasions without being cruel to or insulting either the enemy or their own troops. Always aggressive on the battlefield, they never neglect an opportunity to close rapidly with the enemy. Though incredibly brave in their eagerness to take the offensive or counterattack, whenever possible these Scots will choose generosity rather than force in overcoming their enemies. Macpherson treats sentiment as a mark of supreme valor. The poem's final lines well suggest the effect of such conduct on the enemy:

> Lathmon beheld the son of Morni [Gaul]. The tear
> started from his eye. He threw the sword of his
> fathers on [the] earth, and spoke the words of the
> brave. "Why should Lathmon fight against the first
> of men? Your souls are beams from heaven; your
> swords the flames of death!"
>
> (1:511)

Such valor so affected Napoleon, an ardent admirer of the Ossian poems, that in his *Maxims* he wrote, "in matters of government, justice means force as well as virtue." Observing the statesmanship of Fingal, his favorite hero, the emperor must have taken a distinct pleasure in seeing the English prince Lathmon taught an unforgettable lesson in international politics.

"Oithona"

"Lathmon" and "Oithona" are companion pieces. The narrative of
"Oithona" extends that of "Lathmon." The two have similar characters
and scenes, but Oithona, daughter of Nuath, Lathmon's father, appears
for the first time in the second poem. She represents a contrasting
figure to those powerful women in Irish literature who, like Queen
Medb in the *Táin,* thirsted for power over their husbands and country.
Oithona meekly assumes her subordinate role to men, and only when
her lover is threatened does she disguise herself as a man and join him
in battle.

Women in *Ossian* are not highly individualized; they accept the so-
cial status of their men; their importance is clearest in the home, where
they have trained their sons in some of the military arts. Macpherson
at various points disguises women in armor, using them as foils to his
heroic men. Often, especially in scenes that turn upon sentiment, pro-
priety, or tenderness, women serve as the motivation for men to assert
these virtues.

In hopes of clarifying the link between the two poems, Macpherson
adds a footnote to "Oithona" revealing that Fingal has ordered Gaul to
escort young Lathmon back to his lands, where Nuath and his family
generously receive him. In the spirit of these poems, Gaul is soon
attracted to Oithona, quickly forgetting their nationalistic differences.
The actual poem begins with Gaul returning to Oithona's castle after
having had to leave his new love to return to the wars of Fingal. He
finds no warm hearth. In a dream the distraught figure of Oithona
appears to him; she has been kidnapped, ravished, and imprisoned by
a raider. Immediately upon awakening, Gaul sails to the desert island
on the heath, where Oithona, hidden in a cave, has been revealed to
him in his dream. Soon, on the heath, he confronts her kidnapper and
kills him. Returning to the cave, he discovers a mortally wounded
youth whom he soon recognizes as Oithona.

Readers of Ossian will find in the narrative a familiar pattern. Fre-
quently the poet separates lovers when marriage is imminent, only to
reunite them after some violent event tests severely or even subverts
the honor of one of the two. Artificial and often forced as dramatic
tension of this kind is, "Oithona" does contain sufficient plausible ac-
tion to maintain the reader's interest. Throughout, Macpherson draws
upon themes associated with all Celtic poetry: women of unsullied vir-
tue who, by the force of their own martial courage, have withstood

every insult to their honor; men who, no matter how brave, are none-theless affected by the dark melancholy spirit of the scene; a bard whose recollection of disaster is shaped by a strange enjoyment. Music and poetry are played off against each other as Macpherson celebrates the extraordinary sacrifices of his protagonists; the dominant chord is appropriately sentimental.

In 1768 when Francois Barthélemon, orchestra leader at the London opera, composed the music for an opera at the Theatre Royal based upon the story of Oithona, he found in the poem a series of primary passions. Love, death, heroism, patriotism, and simple piety—"Oithona" imbues each with dramatic intensity; all proved readily exploitable, especially given the late eighteenth-century taste for emotional music. His central theme was the appeal to the feeling heart by a portrayal of virtue in distress. Barthélemon understood precisely Macpherson's intentions.

"Croma" and "Berrathon"

The final two poems of the collection are connected by the pervading influence of Ossian's faithful companion and poetic soul mate, Malvina. In the early poem Malvina laments the death of her lover, Ossian's son Oscar, preparing the way for her own death in "Berrathon." "Berrathon," which because it depicts Ossian's death has been called his Dying Hymn, marks the end of an exceedingly long history of the early wars of Fingal.

"Croma" is set in Ireland, where Ossian has led an expedition under orders from Fingal to relieve the kingdom of Crothar from the vicious assaults of the Viking raider Rothmar. Before Ossian can arrive, Crothar's inexperienced son, Fovargormo, foolishly attacks the superbly trained Norsemen; the Irish army is annihilated and the prince is killed. While Rothmar enjoys his victory, Ossian, having received Crothar's blessing, launches an immediate attack and in short order defeats him.

The story, characters, and themes of "Croma" are familiar; only the reason why Ossian felt it necessary to relate the tale at this particular moment has fresh significance. The poem had begun with Malvina's desperate call to her lover Oscar, who she now knows has died in battle. Her grief, terrible to a degree, prompts Ossian to introduce his own tale of battle and sorrow. The bard, who remains acutely sensitive to pain and danger, understands the importance of distancing the grief-stricken from an immediate contemplation of death. Macpherson had used this motif before in the poems, but it had not taken this particular form until now. The joy of grief is played as a refrain throughout "Croma," emphasizing Macpherson's increased dependence on the concept for establishing a special atmosphere.[48]

Ossian's nostalgic recollection of his youthful exploits so engages Malvina that she can put aside her pain for the moment. He recalls an earlier time when as a young, vigorous warrior he punished vice and praised virtue. He remembers the brave Irish lad, Fovargormo, whose spirit resembled that of his own son, the now-dead Oscar. The fact that both warriors died young, probably before their greatest accomplishments, in no way detracts from the bard's rendering of their story. "Happy are they who die in youth, when their renown is heard" (1:548–49). Indeed, the theme is recurrent in the Ossianic poems.

The most attractive feature of "Croma" is the tender-minded portrayal of Malvina and its attendant theme of dying young. In other poems Macpherson managed such nostalgic sorrow in a vague, impulsive fashion. "Croma" brings a more disciplined, conscious ordering to it. Thus the validity of melancholy—within prescribed circumstances—is affirmed. For Ossian, dying young is always preferable to the lingering death of the old who "wither away by degrees." Young men killed in battle while fighting courageously have the best opportunity for lasting fame: "Their memory shall be honoured in song; the young tear of the virgin will fall" (1:549). Later when Samuel Johnson would comment on the composition of the Ossian poems, saying that a writer might "abandon his mind" to this effect, he suggests his basic distrust of Macpherson's method. The key to rejecting Johnson's remark is one's faith in Macpherson's artistry. Although the view is widely accepted that Macpherson's melancholy was formless and inarticulate, in fact he provides an artful structure to which a sensitive reader is expected to respond in a predictable fashion. A reader might respond to the emotion of the poem, Macpherson would argue, as it heightened awareness and deepened or extended the experience of life. Youthful death and the related concept of the joy of grief were for Macpherson emblematic of the precarious nature of man's condition.

"Berrathon" aroused similar feelings by glorifying the primitive and sanctioning sympathetic benevolence. Macpherson embraces the pleasure of tragedy in the poem, thus establishing for the volume that exquisite despondency that Hugh Blair later called a "luxury of woe." With melancholy feeding upon melancholy, Ossian mournfully reviews the passage of time, the death of beauty, and the triumphs of long-dead heroes. Unlike Aristotelian tragedy, Macpherson's tragedy evokes compassion and pity but not fear, innocent misfortune but not poetic justice.[49] Sadness and melancholy mark the opening section. Ossian here speaks of a kind of naturalism:

> "Why dost thou awake me, O gale," it [a flower] seems to say, "I
> am covered with the drops of heaven? The time of my
> fading is near, the blast that shall scatter my leaves.
> Tomorrow shall the traveller come; he that saw me in my
> beauty shall come. His eyes will search the field, but
> they will not find me?"
>
> (1:556)

The transience of human life is poignantly realized through the metaphor of a thistle flower covered with the evening's dew and blooming in the autumn air. Macpherson explores with a sure hand the bond between nature and man's soul. The inevitable process from birth to maturity to decay and death as symbolized by the flower represents a truth about the relative position of man in the universe. It is Ossian's recollection of the past that lends meaning to his present existence. The past is retold with a minimum of analysis; the emphasis is on what Wordsworth would call the "calm oblivious tendencies of Nature."

Macpherson's faith in the power of nature is the central reason why he has Ossian recount the deeds of Fingal. The bard adduces the majesty and glory of the past because then Fingal triumphed, Fingal whose distinguished reign was "the happy effect of following nature . . . : wisdom without reflection." The wars of Fingal issue from a concept of a state based upon emotion, not reason; benevolence, not realpolitik. Nonetheless, Macpherson's understanding of nature reveals no unusual contradictions between the neoclassicists' and romanticists' views of the term. In "Berrathon," as in many of the other poems, human nature in any Fingalian sense represents order and regularity: both the manner in which Fingal's sons respond to the attacks on innocents, and the warrior's pursuit of fame. The same poem, however, also anticipates the romantic emphasis upon human nature as primitive and individualistic. Insofar as he reveled in the wilder, disordered aspects of nature as a background to human emotion, Macpherson joins ranks with an earlier poet like Thomson, and, I think, deserves the praise Johnson gave the latter poet: he has "a mind that at once comprehends the vast, and attends to the minute."[50]

The death of Malvina, which occupies the second major section of the work, evokes an emotional outpouring that calls forward not only the living but the ghosts of the dead heroes. Ossian's shock at her death, along with the sincere grief he feels, seems to shake him out of a death-in-life state. His response, which is reassuring, depends on observing clearly and reporting the supernatural scene:

> I asked about Malvina, but they [the trees of the hill, i.e., Nature]
> answered not. They turned their faces away:
> thin darkness covered their beauty. They
> were like stars, on a rainy hill, by night,
> each looking faintly through the mist.
>
>   (1:557–58)

The darkness becomes a source of spiritual insight for the bard, leading to his recollection of the early battle at Berrathon. Associating emotions with past events is recurrent in Macpherson's poetry. Ideas and objects of gloom, ghosts, and death produce "agreeable sensations" that, in Monk's phrase, "turn the soul in upon itself" creating a vast, uniform emotional response of pathetic solemnity.

Macpherson so values deliberate sensationalism that he is constitutionally incapable of describing the most straightforward scene without first arousing what the critic John Dennis had called "the delightful Horror, the terrible Joy" of the immensity of external objects:

> Night came down on the ocean. The
> winds departed on their wings. Gold and pale
> is the moon. The red stars lift their heads
> on high. Our course is slow along the coast
> of Berrathon. The white waves tumble on the
> rocks. . . . But thy [Fingal's] steps are on the winds of
> the desert. The storms are darkening in thy hand.
> Thou takest the sun in thy wrath, and
> hidest him in thy clouds. . . . The sun laughs
> in his blue fields.
>
>   (1:562–63, 573)

Literally, all the passage says is that the sun has set and darkness approaches. Here are combined the ruling principles of the sublime: infiniteness, power, wildness, obscurity. The danger inherent in the scene arises not from the fact of Ossian's fleet sailing to Berrathon to rescue a maiden. Rather it is the deeper, more wrenching fear occasioned by man's journey across the unbounded vastness of an ocean that produces the desired effect. The danger is altogether grander than the description of the battle which follows. For sheer emotional magnitude, not even warfare can match the contest between man and nature.

When Ossian draws his sword and slays the villain Uthal, the scene remains concrete, even predictable. The sublimity occurs in those scenes before and after the planned series of incidents in the plot. Typically, Macpherson abruptly turns away from the military engagement in order to linger among the various half-lights produced by the battle. Ossian's death is foreshadowed, but not confirmed:

> There is a murmur in the heath! the
> stormy winds abate! I hear the voice of
> Fingal. . . . "Come, Ossian, come away," he
> says, "come, fly with thy fathers on
> clouds." I come, I come, thou king of men!
> The life of Ossian fails. . . . Beside the
> stone of Mora I shall fall asleep. The
> winds whistling in my grey hair, shall not
> awaken me. Depart on thy wings, O wind:
> thou canst not disturb the rest of the
> bard. The night is long, but his eyes are
> heavy. Depart, thou rustling blast.
>
> (1:574–75)

The passage offers no clear evidence, nothing precise, only mysterious murmurings of the wind evoking "that invisible world into which the aged Bard believes himself now ready to enter." The mood arouses a feeling of disorder, a sense of darkness that invests the scene in melancholy uncertainty. Macpherson accomplishes what to some critics would be unorthodox: he allows truth to emerge from emotion and overcome all other considerations. "Berrathon" serves as an appropriate conclusion to the *Fingal* volume that, for all its faults, stunningly anticipates the coming age in poetry and painting.

Chapter Four
Temora: the Second Epic

Beginning in December 1761 and for the next sixteen months, Macpherson basked in the applause of London society. *Fingal* had marked him as an author of rising reputation, whose revelations concerning primitive society had shaken the London literary circle from their complacency. Supremely confident, with his insecurities buried beneath numerous accolades, Macpherson had received visits from such a luminary as Thomas Gray and attended elegant receptions in his honor at the luxurious home of his early patroness, Mrs. Elizabeth Montagu, in Hill Street, Berkeley Square. During these months, relying upon only one ballad source and his own instincts, Macpherson wrote a new work that would make permanent his membership in the elite fraternity of successful men of letters. In March 1763 his publishers issued *Temora, an Ancient Epic Poem,* in eight books.

Earlier, in "Dar-thula" and "The Death of Cuthullin," Macpherson had introduced the notion of a final expedition by Fingal to Ireland, and with characteristic aggressiveness had annexed the first book of *Temora* to *Fingal* in 1761. The opponents now are the usurper Cairbar and his brother Cathmor, who had murdered Cormac, the young Irish king, at the royal palace of Temora in Ulster. Fingal has decided to subdue the rebels for both personal and political reasons, since the dead Cormac was the grandson of Fingal's grandfather Trenmor. Though the lineage is illogical, Macpherson admitted no absurdity; instead, he took pains to make plausible each aspect of the story. The curious nature of this ancestry went unmentioned in the first epic, a surprising oversight, since Fingal had rescued Cormac earlier from the Vikings. In keeping with his method Macpherson cast aside historical restraint in order to satisfy his fictional purposes. By introducing a dominant emotional motive based upon family interest, the poet reduced the political significance of restoring the rightful heir to the Irish throne. Cairbar's murder of an innocent and his total disregard for the law remained notably provocative acts; however, what enraged the Scots had its roots in a more fundamental issue. The usurper's implied contempt for Fingal's role as the hero-god of his people and his challenge to the king's mysterious power demanded a swift response. *Temora* reflected more overtly than *Fingal* Macpherson's own proud, passionate nature, mirrored in his characterization of Fingal. Moderation and clemency had been characteristics of Fingal, but in the second epic they would compete with less amiable states of mind.

The public was more responsive to Fingal's shift in attitude than Macpherson, in the preface to *Temora,* had anticipated. There he attacked the lack of taste, judgment, or candor of those readers who had been suspicious of *Fingal's* authenticity. Damning his critics, Macpherson scorned all insinuations about his translations, even going so far as to profess indifference to the attacks he now fully expected to receive with the appearance of *Temora.* In sharp rebuttal, he charged that "an incredulity of this kind is natural to persons who confine all merit to their own age and country. These are . . . the weakest, . . . the most ignorant of the people."[1] Thus Macpherson in his harshest voice attempted to discredit his detractors. But as would happen with his later historical writings, his perverse attack would merely give further ammunition to his critics, who promptly used it against him.

Macpherson's explanations about his research for *Temora* could hardly have been more damaging. He admitted to having only ballad sources for book 1, and, as he told it, the remaining sections came to his hand in a "very imperfect and confused" condition. Through the help of friends who mailed him fragments, he said, he assembled and translated the epic in London. Beyond these astonishing revelations, the poet conceded that he entitled the work and arranged the material in its present form. Nothing short of an open admission that he had composed the epic out of whole cloth could have caused him as much trouble as such comments. Why he chose to play the "free and easy" scholar can only be guessed. Thomson suggests that he "had become more careless in his methods, and at the same time more confident in his own ability to produce an epic." Smart describes an overconfident poet who "was alone in the field . . . the first translator of Gaelic poetry"—in other words he was blinded by arrogance.[2] Whatever his reasons, Macpherson alone did more in his prefaces and personal correspondence to sharpen suspicions than, in fact, the poetry itself aroused.

Reviewers for the *Monthly Review* and the *Critical Review* did not ignore Macpherson's challenge to their judgment. The former journal asked pointedly, "Would our Editor Macpherson insinuate, that the

Celtic Bards, and Scandinavian Scalders, have an exclusive title to ad-
miration?"[3] This reviewer spoke for many who found *Temora*'s preface
extraordinarily pretentious and arrogant. The *Critical Review* was more
temperate in its analysis of the poem: "It will be sufficient to remark
on this occasion, that *Temora*, is strongly marked with all the charac-
teristics of the former poem, and undoubtedly the production of the
same author."[4] Though apparently finding high literary merit in both
poems, the reviewer preferred to discuss their authenticity. His chief
evidence for thinking them authentic was that contemporary Scots
knew many of the poems already. This argument, of course, did little
to answer the questions of Ossian's detractors. Having given assurances
to *Temora*'s readers, he retreats in his final paragraph to a more neutral
position. As Stewart suggests in "Ossian in the Polished Age," most
critics concentrated on developing more ingenious (and less desirable)
arguments for authenticity without seriously analyzing the work's lit-
erary merit. This emphasis would ultimately be detrimental to the
reputation of the Ossianic poems, as well as to Macpherson's credibility
as a man of letters.

In 1763 Hugh Blair was preparing a second edition of his *Disserta-
tion,* to include a ten-page discussion of *Temora.* Satisfied by the in-
quiries he had made at the request of a nervous David Hume, Blair
had no doubt that Macpherson's translations were authentic. More spe-
cifically, he had discovered that "*Temora* had perhaps less fire than the
other epic poem; but in return it has more variety, more tenderness,
and more magnificence."[5] As the doyen of Ossian critics, Blair was in
a triumphant mood. Whatever direction the critical discussion would
take in the future, his criticism could not be ignored by either side.

Temora: The Story

Temora recounts the last stage of a great civil war in Ireland between
two powerful tribes, the Firbolg and the Irish descendants of the
Caledonian race. The Caledonian Irish control the throne of Ireland
until Cairbar, prince of Atha in Connaught, who acceded to his present
rank by murdering his father, again strikes treacherously, killing Cor-
mac, the young king of Ireland. Cormac, as mentioned earlier, is a
kinsman of Fingal, King of Morven, who has by the strength of his
armies kept the young man on the throne.

The epic opens with the invasion of the Caledonian army, which
comes to dethrone Cairbar and punish the rebels for disturbing the

lawful peace of Ireland. On the morning of the first day, as Fingal's army approaches the castle of Temora in Ulster, Cairbar, troubled by this turn of events, ignores the advice of his officers, who counsel immediate attack, and instead plans a feast and entertainment for Oscar, Ossian's son. Through this ruse, Cairbar can delay the arrival of Fingal's troops by seeming to honor Oscar and thus provide more time for his brother Cathmor's troops to join his main army. If a balance of troops can be achieved between the two opposing armies, Cairbar feels certain he can defeat Fingal. Complacent in his arrogance and foolish pride, he falls instead into a quarrel with Oscar, who has never declined a fight; both men are mortally wounded. Fingal, warned by the clash of arms, finds his grandson dead and loses his taste for the battle.

The next day and a half of action occupies books 2 through 5. Macpherson offers a considerable variety of episodes, including a recollection of Fingal's first marriage and the arrival of Cathmor's beloved Sulmalla dressed as a warrior. Though the progress of the conflict slows as a result of these interruptions, Macpherson does manage to describe two battles. In episodes that enliven the narrative he allows other Scottish and Irish heroes to play their parts in the main action: Gaul and Fillan, Fingal's son, assume command of the Caledonians and fight bravely, though losing Connel at the hands of Foldath, the Irish commander. In the second battle Fillan becomes commander when Gaul is wounded, kills Foldath, and nearly overwhelms the Irish army.

As book 6 begins, the Irish have retreated in disorder; nonetheless, the conflict rages unabated. Macpherson, who never loses his gift for describing warfare, implies that the battle may be in some doubt. On the afternoon of the third day Cathmor rallies his weakened forces, attacks the Scots with new vigor, and in single combat kills Fillan. Ossian arrives too late to prevent this tragedy; the Irish under Cathmor appear to have the upper hand: they push back the Scots in spite of brave resistance. When Fillan's ghost appears before the mourning Fingal, it awakens the warlike spirit of the king, who immediately assumes command of his army. He is now prepared to take personal revenge and throws himself into the battle, never relenting until he has killed Cathmor. The epic ends after the surrender of the Irish, with Fingal relinquishing his command to Ossian, who sees that a legal peace is restored and a legitimate new king placed on the Irish throne.

Blair wrote that "the events are less crowded in *Temora* than in *Fingal*; actions and characters are more particularly displayed; we are let into the transactions of both hosts; and informed of the adventures of

the night as well as of the day."[6] This criticism seems just, particularly
with reference to episodes that explore the quality of feeling inherent
in the opposing heroes. Love and friendship still define the best sort of
men whether they are engaged in war or at peace. Fingal's love, ten-
derness, and sensitivity go far toward accounting for the first epic's
appeal. *Temora* demands no less of Fingal, yet Macpherson has achieved
some balance by creating an opposing hero, Cathmor, with comparable
benevolence. The scene of Cathmor and Sulmalla in book 7 offers an
excellent perspective on the poet's grasp of the sublime. The hero pro-
claims his fearlessness and courage: "the time of danger, O maid, is the
season of my soul" (2:207). Sulmalla suffers the deepest anxiety for her
love's safety. Her emotional state nearly overwhelms her reason and
threatens to do the same to Cathmor. But in a passage that shows the
healthful effects of love on the warrior, Macpherson turns an over-
indulgence in emotion into a virtue:

> Often did she look, on the hero, when he was
> folded in his thoughts. But she shrunk from
> his eyes, and turned her lone steps away.
> Battles rose, like a tempest, and drove the
> mist from his soul. He beheld, with joy, her
> steps in the hall, and the white rising
> of her hands on the harp.
>
> (2:210)

His recognition of his own erotic passion charges the Irish hero with a
fervor for combat. Dejection at being separated from Sulmalla creates
a deep gloom that can only be relieved (as Burke had said) by "great
bodily labour."

The episodes in *Temora* seem more closely integrated with the main
action than in *Fingal*. Blair asserts that "the poet's art is not yet ex-
hausted"; however, it is also true that the poet indulges in lavish out-
bursts of Ossianic bombast which, excessively repetitive as they are,
extend the work by two books. Yet Macpherson effectively maintains
a harmony between the passions of his characters and the gloomy back-
drop of their activities. The primitivist appeal of the material has lost
none of its terror, awful grandeur, or potential for astonishment.

In the short arguments before books 7 and 8 Macpherson presents a
case for distinguishing between the two, based on the contrast between
the pathetic and the sublime. The earlier book offered images more

"soft and affecting" that contrast with "the more grand and terrible images" of the latter. Macpherson's own assessment here has been largely accepted; if anything, critics have enhanced his emphasis.

In *Temora* Macpherson capitalizes upon his success with *Fingal*. He now feels no compunction at structuring the reader's response, not only to the general work, but also to each division within the poem. Those readers who had found *Fingal,* with its exquisite sentiments, an unalloyed delight had ample reason now for praising *Temora.* The dispassionate reader or the unreconstructed skeptic, on the other hand, discovered in Macpherson's scheme of history, which held together the disparate elements of the epic, further evidence damaging to the poet's reputation.

Temora: Book 1

Near the end of the eighteenth century a writer for the influential *European Magazine* confronted the spectacle of the poems of Ossian with an astonishment bordering on incoherence.[7] The profusion of heroes, battles, streams tumbling, and storms raging, as in the following quotation from *Temora,* had thoroughly unsettled him:

> Trees shake their dusky heads
> in the breeze. Grey torrents pour
> their noisy streams. Two green hills,
> with aged oaks, surround a narrow
> plain. The blue course of a stream is
> there. On its banks stood Cairbar of
> Atha. His spear supports the king:
> the red eye of his fear is sad. Cormac
> rises in his soul, with all his ghastly
> wounds. The grey form of the youth
> appears in darkness. Blood pours
> from his airy sides.
> (2:11–12)

The opening book of *Temora* well sustains the Ossianic spirit. As if coming full circle, Macpherson draws upon his first success—the fragment of the Death of Oscar—for the central motivation of the book. Oscar's meeting with the villain Cairbar and their eventual death precipitate the action. Although Fingal's outrage at the murder of Cormac has brought him to Ireland, eventually he experiences a deeper, per-

sonal sadness at the loss of his grandson Oscar. Macpherson enlarges
and ennobles Fingal's heartfelt sorrow by having this young man de-
stroyed early in the poem. The major characters are introduced, their
attitudes as they react to the deaths of Cairbar and Oscar, delineated.
Here at the outset Macpherson's themes and moods are anticipated:
honor, loyalty, death and fame, noble exploits, leadership and fate,
melancholy, "touches of the tender and pathetic." The themes are clas-
sical in origin; the mood ranges from noble defiance to pathos, from
despair to a morbidly joyous acceptance evocative of what later critics
would associate with Goethe's Werther or Schiller's Karl Moor.

Macpherson's mania for exploiting the same material, especially the
Gaelic sources in his possession, surfaces in book 1, which well enough
suggests his literary technique. Once a satisfactory exposition and a
suitable conflict were established, he would invest freely—embroider-
ing episodes, digressions, expansions of plot, and the like. With au-
thentic ballads for the prelude, the work, Macpherson must have
thought, enjoyed a solid footing. Once free of his ballad sources, he
cannot repress his own language and mood; thus *Temora* is in one re-
spect a more spontaneous work. Disappointingly, however, the epic
suffers as a result. Derick Thomson, a thorough student of Macpher-
son's method, deems "*Temora* as a whole a much more vague and bod-
iless production than *Fingal* had been."[8] He finds the long sections
following the first book—nearly twenty-six thousand words—notice-
ably weaker in spirit and less coherent, suggesting a barrenness at the
heart of the poem. Had Macpherson made a diligent search for further
original materials instead of borrowing and adapting the findings of
some early Irish historians, he might well have precluded the severest
comments of his critics.

Admittedly, his total dependence on the motivations implicit in the
first epic did much to diminish the second; however, one cannot ignore
one of *Temora*'s unmistakable strengths for the emerging romantic phi-
losophers: an intertwining of natural scenery with the melancholic
events of the human tragedy. In typical Ossianic fashion the poem is
imbued with sentiment; long-dead heroes and empires are honored,
their nobility heightened by the dramatic background of nature:

> The setting sun was yellow on Dora. Grey
> evening began to descend. Temora's woods
> shook with the blast of the inconstant
> wind. A cloud gathered in the west. A
> red star looked from behind its edge. I

> stood in the wood alone. . . . My soul
> was sad.
>
> (2:35–36)

Like a musical accompaniment, nature underscores human thoughts and actions, an imaginative sympathy thus created between motivation and scene, states of mind and natural settings.

Myra Reynolds, referring to *Temora* in *The Treatment of Nature in English Poetry*, cites three uses of nature by Macpherson: nature as a setting for human action or emotion, the frequent dependence upon similes where nature aids in defining a certain abstraction or character trait, and the all-too-familiar reliance on the apostrophe for evoking an emotional response when the poet manages "a beautiful external description together with an underlying analogy to the thought of the poem."[9] Life in the Ossian poems is played out on a colossal stage with magnificent scenery, glorious costumes, and an irresistible sadness.

In reading the final epic, one finds evidence again for William Blake's high regard for the Ossian poems. Here is the poet's imagination in full bloom emerging through nature, sensing the organic unity of the whole. The call seems not for man to return to the idyllic simplicity of precivilized nature, but instead for him to learn from the struggles of his predecessors who lived in concert with the fierceness of the external world. Wordsworth, who would have us see primarily with the eye the organic relationship of man and nature, found Ossian wanting, especially in the narrow range of its imagery. Although fashionably contemptuous in his public statements, he came in time to share Macpherson's view of the natural goodness of man and the universality of individual freedom and equality as expressed in both Ossianic epics.

Macpherson lost some of his popular support with the publication of the monotonous *Temora*, though his sense of purpose remained clear. He again flew in the face of conventional literary thought. By appropriating a familiar and respected genre of a past age, by infusing ancient epic with the passionate individualism of a new era, he hoped to achieve lasting recognition.[10]

"Cathlin of Clutha"

The first poem following *Temora* in the 1763 volume is a short lay of nine hundred words examining the same themes as the earlier work and relating a familiar pattern of characters and action. Macpherson writes his poetic prose with brief, syntactically independent lines consisting of descriptive phrases, assonance, alliteration, and internal rhyme. He extends various lines with similes and apostrophes:

> In the rushy desert were my steps. He fled in
> the season of night. Give thine aid to Cathlin
> to revenge his father. I sought thee not as a
> beam, in a land of clouds. Thou, like the sun,
> art known, king of echoing Selma!
>
> (2:271)

In this most characteristic poem one observes the short parallel sentences divided into two or more corresponding clauses of the same structure and length. The first clause offers a sentiment that in turn is balanced in the second clause with a repetition, contrast, or explanation. The cadence reflects an ear finely attuned to the measured prose of the King James Bible as well as the qualities of Gaelic originals, and the manner of its use suggests a primitive quality that most of Macpherson's contemporaries found strangely attractive.

> The night came down; we strode, in silence; each
> to his hill of ghosts: that spirits might descend,
> in our dreams, to mark us for the field. We struck
> the shield of the dead; we raised the hum of songs.
>
> (2:271)

"Cathlin of Clutha" is an episodic narrative illuminating another minor conflict in the wars of Fingal. With a dedication and appeal to Malvina, Ossian recalls how a youthful foreigner, Cathlin, had come to Selma's shores demanding Fingal's assistance in securing revenge against the raider Duthcarmor, who had killed the chief of Clutha and kidnapped his daughter Lanul. Fingal, now quite infirm, looks to his warriors, who all at once begin contending for the chance to represent their king in combat. Dependent as always on supernatural guidance, the warriors retire, "each to his hill of ghosts," to await a spiritual sign that will mark the fortunate one.

Ossian, his acute sensitivity to the spirit world as ever linked to his desire for new experiences, convinces himself that the spirits have come for him. He pauses only to acknowledge the arrival of the most aggressive of Fingal's warriors, the young Oscar, who announces that his "beating soul is high": the spirits have chosen him. With due respect for his son's volatile nature, Ossian agrees that Oscar may go if he can accompany him.

Arriving in Rathcol, Ossian sends Oscar's challenge to Duthcarmor for individual combat. Both combatants welcome the prestige that will come from such a confrontation. As one Celtic scholar reports, "the whole nation is war-mad, both high-spirited and ready for battle."[11] Macpherson heightens the drama of this imminent fight by describing Duthcarmor as "a beam of fire, marked with smoke, rushing, varied, through the bosom of night" (2:274).

The supernatural overtones of warfare play a significant part in creating the gloom that permeates the narrative. Ossian compares his son's battle charge to the appearance of ghosts "amidst the storms they raise." The indications of magic remain strong as the great bard calls upon the powers of long-dead warriors to lend their irresistible force to that of Oscar, who is reminded of his duty in the unfolding of this ritual combat. The climax of the poem occurs quickly in a series of striking apostrophes to stars, night, and tempest:

> They meet before the oak. In gleams of
> steel the dark forms are lost; such is
> the meeting of meteors, in a vale by
> night: red light is scattered round, and
> men foresee the storm! Duthcarmor is low
> in blood! The son of Ossian overcame!
> (2:277)

This sense of nature paralleling thought pervades the poem.

With the transgressor dead, Macpherson has only to reveal the whereabouts of the princess of Clutha, whom Duthcarmor had taken from the murdered king's palace. In a reversal familiar to the reader of the Ossian poems, Macpherson ignores the possibility of a simple, precise ending. Irony and a sense of fatalism, characteristic of Macpherson's work, issue in a torrent of romantic melodrama.

Oscar, rejoicing in his victory, finds Cathlin lost in melancholy and wandering the heath. The youth seems unable to respond to the welcome news of Duthcarmor's death. The reason for this curious reaction becomes clear when Cathlin reveals her true identity as a princess of Clutha. She had fallen in love with her kidnapper, but shortly her sense of duty and remorse at the loss of her father convinces her that she should escape. Now surrounded by death, Cathlin takes no pleasure in

her revenge. Ossian closes by resigning himself to the inevitable trag-
edy of life.

Though there are profound differences between true Celtic poetry
and Macpherson's "translations," scholars like Ernest Renan and Mat-
thew Arnold, as well as William Butler Yeats, recognized the essential
themes upon which both depend for their success: "a love of Nature
for herself . . . ," as Renan wrote, "accompanied by the melancholy
that man knows, when, face to face with her, he believes that he hears
her commune with him about his origin and his destiny." The Celtic
race, according to Arnold, "with their vehement reaction against the
despotism of fact, with their sensuous nature, their manifold striv-
ing . . . are the prime authors of this vein of piercing regret and
passion."

Renan and Arnold, though their speculations are flawed by racism,
provide a distinct view of Ossian; however, Yeats offers a significant
clarification: folk literature, he wrote, is immersed in "immortal
things, weighed down by the mystery of all things." Man whose life
is brief cannot match the depths of his desires; man "had been born
and must die with [his] great thirst unslaked." Macpherson embraces
both the racial assumptions inherent in Arnold and Renan and the view
held by Yeats. His are the ancient melancholic themes: "departed
hopes, lost life, the vanity of this world, and the coming of death."[12]

"Sulmalla of Lumon"

The Scottish poet, essayist, and professor of moral philosophy, James
Beattie, wrote of the characteristics a poet must possess if he aspires to
a lasting reputation. He "must not only study nature, and know the
reality of things; but must also possess . . . sensibility, to enter with
ardent emotions into every part of his subject, so as to transfuse into
his work a pathos and energy sufficient to raise corresponding emotions
in the reader."[13] Macpherson must have surely trembled with pride at
Beattie's words because he felt above all else that his work displayed
just these attributes.

Beattie was echoing Adam Smith, who, in the *Theory of Moral
Sentiments* (1759), spoke of the moral force of sympathy in one's life.
Macpherson had read Smith with great interest; perhaps Ossian's sym-
pathetic imagination, a significant aspect of his character delineation,
is Macpherson's response to Smith. In the dissertations, prefaces, and
notes to the poems Macpherson joined ranks with those poets and phi-
losophers who agreed that extreme sensibility and enthusiasm are re-

quired of a poet who wishes his audience to sympathize with his poetry. Furthermore, he held as a cardinal principle that a sympathetic reader will gain exquisite pleasure from a good poem; every section of a poem should, therefore, evoke and develop this union of feeling and imagination. His difficulty was, of course, his inability to sustain verse of such high quality. *Temora* and the accompanying shorter poems of the volume had stretched his poetic capacity to the breaking point.

"Sulmalla of Lumon" continues in obvious fashion the association of characters and settings begun in book 4 of *Temora,* when the princess was introduced as the lover of Cathmor, Fingal's valiant opponent. The story more directly reminds us of "Cathlin of Clutha," in which the lonely Cathlin, despairing of any happiness, wanders into "the distant land" of Lumon, where she soon dies. Macpherson builds the present poem upon the sorrow of Sulmalla (and our sympathy for her), who mourns the loss of her love for Cathlin, who has also suffered great despair. Her sympathy is so compelling that Sulmalla is moved to recall her own first meeting with Cathmor. The recollection affects her listeners, Ossian chief among them; his sympathetic response to the passions thus aroused stimulates his imagination, and he is moved both intellectually and emotionally. In other words, Ossian's art is essentially empathetic: his intention is to evoke a correspondent emotion—in his protagonists one to the other, and in the reader.

The poem rests on the barest of structures, its plot serving only to introduce related episodes told by the main characters. The frailty of the piece is confirmed by the fact that Macpherson can find no effective ending for it. He lamely pretends that a passage is missing and, hence, unavailable to the translator; thus "the story is imperfect." Yet, whatever his imperfections, Macpherson forged ahead; in the perceptive terms of one critic, the poet has a "secret attraction to chaos."

"Cath-Loda"

When Macpherson died in 1796 he left £1,000 and exact instructions in his will for the publication of the Gaelic originals of the *Poems of Ossian.* His executors, however, were hard pressed to complete such a task; one trustee, John Mackenzie of the Temple, London, whose sole responsibility was to organize the manuscripts, found himself unable to begin work. No collections of ancient poems or fragments of manuscripts were to be found, and the only piece of evidence that surfaced was a bit of marginalia in a first edition of the *Poems,* where Macpherson wrote that he had sent the originals of *Fingal* and eight lesser poems to Mackenzie. In death, he seems to have had every intention of continuing to assert the authenticity of his life's chief work.

"Cath-Loda," a poem in three *duans* or cantos, is one of the "translations" that Macpherson had supposedly given Mackenzie. It was the opening piece of the corrected 1773 edition of the *Poems,* where it served as an introduction to the wars of Fingal. Though Macpherson's chronology, as has been seen, is typically unreliable, we may nonetheless learn something from this placement. "Cath-Loda," "Comala," "War of Caros," "Colna-dona," and "Carric-thura" are all related in Macpherson's scheme of Ossianic geography and history. The setting of this group of poems is the western Scandinavian coast and the Orkney Islands, the archipelago of some seventy islands and islets off the northernmost tip of Scotland. The shift in these poems from the western Scottish coast and eastern Ireland seems to produce more rugged, less civilized opponents for Fingal and his warriors. In Macpherson's historical arrangement the poems review the events of the king's youth before the epic conflicts in Ireland. Battle after battle traces the crises in the hero's life as he grows to manhood, and as courage and loyalty become his dominant characteristic. Fingal, from the first, sets himself against utility and self-interest.

"Cath-Loda" is like other Ossian poems, an extended gloss on one line, "A tale of the times of old!" Ossian sketches Fingal's evolution as a hero who wins, rules, and retires. The story follows a predictable path: the hero's voyage being interrupted by some natural force (in this instance a storm at sea), he is compelled to confront an enemy determined to dishonor his name and kill him. The king must defend his integrity and punish the guilty, while never ceasing to be generous and compassionate.

With little introduction, the poem finds Fingal and his men blown off course to the east, unable to reach the Orkneys and thus forced into regrouping in hostile territory on the coast of western Norway. Unluckily, the bay where the Scots land is near the castle of Starno, King of Lochlin and father of Swaran, later Fingal's noble opponent in Ireland. Starno, who bears special enmity against all Celts, immediately joins his tribes for war. Fingal, reluctantly, calls upon his men to defend themselves.

> Around the king they rise in wrath. No
> words come forth: they seize their spears.
> Each soul is rolled into itself.
> (2:299)

The king, with youthful energy and general good sense, conducts his own intelligence-gathering in preparation for the morning battle. He discovers a captive princess imprisoned in a seaswept cave, overhears the Viking king and prince consulting the spirit Loda (Odin, the supreme Nordic god) in a forest, and fights a brief, inconclusive contest with two men who find him spying.

Canto 2 centers upon the battle on the following day. Fingal has given field command to the "dark-haired" Duth-maruno, who stuns the Viking army into retreat, but then is recalled by the king before he can secure a complete victory. Fingal's pleasure at this early repulse of Starno and Swaran plunges quickly to despair when Duth-maruno reveals that he has been wounded—mortally, he fears. Duth-maruno's death, even as he is victorious in battle, mirrors the prevailing motif of the Ossian poems—sorrow in joy, the inescapable proximity of death to life.

The final canto focuses on Fingal mourning the loss of his favorite commander, a picture in stark contrast to the two desperate Viking warriors, "wrathful," surly creatures, their dispositions "fierce and uncomplying":

> Turned from one another, they stood, like
> two oaks, which different winds had bent;
> each hangs over its own loud rill, and
> shakes its boughs in the course of blasts.
> (2:329)

The ferocity of the enemy—his iniquity—builds when Starno proposes that his son assassinate the solitary Fingal. The young prince refuses: "I shall not slay in shades. I move forth in light: the hawks rush from all their winds" (2:333). In an unusual example of uncontrolled rage, Starno nearly kills his uncompromising son before rushing screaming into the night to find Fingal. Unperturbed, the Scottish king defeats Starno, binds him to an oak, and reprimands him: "dreadful king away! Go to thy troubled dwelling, cloudy foe of the lovely! Let the stranger shun thee, thou gloomy in the hall!" (2:335). Fingal echoes a recurrent theme of the Ossian poems: such a villain can seek atonement only from his own conscience.

The contrast between the two warrior kings remains the most intriguing aspect of the poem. The young Fingal's courage when he faces an army fighting on its own soil and led by a fanatical chief marks him clearly as a leader of great promise. His compassion for friend and enemy is ennobling. Finally, he never forgets his eaglelike beginnings; throughout his reign his response to peace and war remains eminently noble and just. His opponent is quite different—often pitiless, capricious, and heartless. Blair explains the contrast in racial terms:

When the poet relates the expeditions of any of his heroes to the Scandinavian coast, or to the islands of Orkney . . . the case is altered. Those countries were inhabited by nations of the Teutonic descent, who in their manners and religious rites differed widely from the Celtae . . . this difference is clearly pointed out in the poems of Ossian.[14]

Macpherson, he argues, was intent on recapturing the effect of the pagan kings on the Christian peoples of Western Europe. The poet chronicled the energy and blood expended by the Vikings during their raids and in defense of their territory. More than this, he depicted, in Blair's words, "that ferocity of manners which distinguish those nations . . . , a peculiar savageness."

He was attracted to the Norse culture for its sensationalist qualities; it dealt out destruction, rape, plunder, and murder. By manipulating both the popular myth and the historical truth regarding the Vikings, Macpherson portrayed them as foils to Fingal and the Fianna. The Vikings' promotion of lawlessness and political disorder underscored the distinctive stability of Fingal's reign.

"Oina-Morul"

Ossian, who made no appearance in "Cath-Loda," becomes the central figure in "Oina-Morul," the shortest piece in the *Poems* except for the *Fragments*. The setting remains essentially the same, an island off the Scandinavian coast. Motivation has much in common with that of nearly all the other poems in the collection. Fingal has heard that a distant king, whom he feasted with once and considered his friend, has been attacked by a more powerful and ruthless neighbor, who desires his daughter, Oina-Morul, for a wife. The father, Mal-orchol, King of Fuärfed, refuses Ton-thormod's offer of marriage, and Ton-thormod in turn determines upon taking the girl by force and leveling the kingdom. Ossian arrives bearing Fingal's message: "our friends are not forgot in their danger, though distant is our land" (2:343).

The poem is divided into three sections: the invocation to the muse, Malvina; the fulfillment of Ossian's duty as warrior; and, finally, the arousal of sentiment in Ossian, out of which are forged new ideas and possibilities. This final section is the most interesting, largely because Macpherson suggests how the young Ossian may be maturing into a responsible, powerful bard. Once Ossian has defeated Ton-thormod, taking him prisoner, Malorchol offers him Oina-Morul as his wife. In a dream that night the girl's spirit enters Ossian's subconscious: he becomes acutely aware of the invisible life, the effects produced in the inner self by external events:

> In the hall I lay in night. Mine eyes
> were half-closed in sleep. Soft music
> came to mine ear. . . . It was the maid
> of Fuärfed wild! . . . She knew that my
> soul was a stream, that flowed at pleasant sounds.
>
> (2:345)

But in a desperate attempt to reveal the identity of her true lover, Oina-Morul paints a sympathetic picture of the defeated Ton-thormod—"his manly breast . . . heaving over his bursting soul"—suffering for the loss of his true love. In her appeal to Ossian she reveals the infinite longings inherent in every human spirit. Ossian juxtaposes the unrestrained hopes of the two lovers with the limited possibilities in a world where war and hate rule men's lives. Ossian's giving up of Oina-Morul to his enemy stands as convincing evidence of his altruism. His immediate delight in sensation evolves through experiences into a deep feeling for people and nature that culminates in reflection:

> Thou shalt not wander, by streams unknown,
> blue-eyed Oina-Morul! Within this bosom
> is a voice; it comes not to other ears:
> it bids Ossian hear the hapless, in their
> hour of woe.
>
> (2:346)

That Ossian listens to his conscience, rather than to the more rational traditions of the old world, is indicative of a cultural shift. (Macpherson seems to grasp what Wordsworth would later describe as the evolution of the thinking mind.) Ossian's recognition of Oina-Morul as an individual with choice and his determination to supplant the continual warfare between the two tribes with a lasting peace, define a significant element in his character. However, his call for a new world where spiritual and moral achievement will be regarded equally with military victory is a minor, if not undeveloped, aspect of the Ossianic figure. Macpherson never fully realizes the possibilities of these themes; their development would have to await the more powerful genius of the romantic visionaries.[15]

"Colna-Dona"

Frederick Pottle said, concerning the writing of poetry, that "the mark of the poetic imagination is to simplify: to make the manifold of sensation more meaningful by reducing it to a number of objects that can actually be contemplated."[16] "Colna-Dona," the last Ossian poem as printed in the corrected edition, offers a fair example of this principle. Macpherson has dispensed with all but the most essential aspects of his subject, Fingal and his wars. In quality as well as length the poem evokes comparison with the earliest work in the *Fragments*: fleeting and suggestive, yet resonant with sentimentality and sensibility.

The poem begins with a sentimental journey initiated by Fingal, whose desire it is to erect a stone celebrating an early victory over "the strangers" (southern Britons supported by the Romans from beyond the Wall). Fingal sends Ossian and his companion Toscar, later father of Malvina, to fulfill this dream. Though young and caught up in this, their first adventure, the boys find the battlefield and glorify their good king's deeds. The simplified opening section reflects the central motifs of the Ossian poems: the heroic code of Fingal and his warriors; the genteel wildness of the landscape, which mirrors both the primitive savagery and nobility of these people; and the heavy melancholy that pervades even the most joyous occasions.

The middle section of the poem begins with an invitation to a great feast with Carul, chief of Colamon (a neighboring district), whose brightest possession is his daughter Colna-Dona. The venerable chief recalls his meeting Fingal and though traditional enemies, the admiration and respect of the two warriors for each other. Meanwhile, Toscar is smitten by Colna-Dona, charmed by her singing and the harp:

> She came on his troubled soul, like a
> beam to the dark-heaving ocean: when

it bursts from a cloud, and brightens
the foamy side of a wave.
                                    (2:357)

Her presence unnerves, yet attracts, him; from this point on, he can think only of her welfare. The next morning as the two young men return through the woods to their ship, they are intercepted by a youthful warrior whose unexpected appearance causes Toscar immediate concern for the safety of Colna-Dona. The warrior informs him that a son of a king has kidnapped the girl, seizing "with love her soul." Toscar demands to know in what direction the two have gone, and in a fury commands the youth to give up his shield. Having succeeded in testing the love and fidelity of Toscar, the warrior reveals herself as "Colna-Dona of harps": "Her blue eyes had rolled on Toscar, and her love arose!"

With an abruptness suggestive of its fragmentary nature, the poem concludes by leaving us with the image of a beautiful maiden who rejects the security of her life in order to embark on an uncertain journey with her warrior-lover. Macpherson has relied with some frequency on women who follow their lovers into battle disguised in the armor of men: Crimora in "Carric-thura" and Colmal in "Calthon and Colmal." Their reunion, at the moment of discovery, produces a spontaneous overflow of the warmest, most benevolent feelings. Macpherson uses such luminous reconciliations, moments of the most intense pleasure, to relieve the general darkness of his poems.

The movement of "Colna-Dona," from Ossian and Toscar's ceremony on the battlefield, where "the blood of Fingal's foes hung curdled in its [the stream's] ooze," to the scenes in the "hall of harps" and the marshy wood drowned in eternal mist, where the lovers meet, suggests that the dominant chord is dark rather than light, painful even if it is simultaneously pleasurable. Macpherson's structure allows only short-lived moments of joy; these emotional periods serve as signals to the reader, who can then associate joyous emotional experiences with other significant sensations.

Macpherson had brought off the publication of a second volume of Ossian's poems quite brilliantly. With unbounded zeal and cunning he had produced a multitude of notes and extensive prefaces, which for his partisans, as for the uninitiated, would point to his scholarly care as a translator. Beyond this, his introductions and notes would serve as a smoke screen masking the poems as originals, thus preventing their discovery as forgeries. With an arrogance that would infuriate his critics he published in this second volume four hundred lines of Gaelic that he called "A Specimen of the Original of Temora," in order, he wrote to satisfy "those who doubt the authenticity of Ossian's poems." His critics were not, of course, rebutted by this ploy; in fact, the controversy would grow to unprecedented proportions before it was over. In the meantime, the poet basked in the admiration of those critics who spoke of the poems as the work of exalted genius.

Chapter Five
The Ossianic Controversy

With the publication of *Temora* Macpherson decided against writing any further poems of Ossian. His material wealth and literary fame had exceeded all expectation, but the entire experience, which had begun with the most gratifying encouragement, had now turned bitter. He had suffered under a series of critical attacks on the authenticity of the poems, and he recognized the utter impossibility of sustaining the charade while locked in a protracted public dispute. His only defense at this point lay in vehemently maintaining that he was merely a translator of ancient documents. This he would do (only occasionally telling the truth) for the remainder of his life. Curiously, the controversy now required little of Macpherson himself; nursed by greater men than he, it bloomed with remarkable fullness for nearly fifty years.[1]

The Ossianic controversy is best understood by viewing the argument in three distinct stages. The early period (1760–65) gave prominence to the critical suspicions of Horace Walpole, David Hume, and Samuel Johnson, and to the counterattack of Hugh Blair. The middle phase (1773–1783) was notable for a moral fury stirred up by Macpherson's corrected edition of the poems, Johnson's tour of the Highlands and his publication of the *Journey to the Western Islands of Scotland* (1775), Hume's critique "Of the Poems of Ossian," and Sir John Macgregor Murray's initiation of a fund to publish the Gaelic originals. The last stage (1797–1805) began when the Highland Society of Scotland appointed a commission to inquire into the nature and authenticity of the poems, and to publish its findings. To say that the matter was resolved in 1805 when the report came out would be to ignore subsequent editions, commentaries, versifications, and translations (into twelve other languages), as well as the immense influence of the poems throughout the nineteenth century, especially in Great Britain, on the Continent, and in America. In the final analysis, the controversy insured the dissemination of the poems and goes far to explain their enduring interest.

Early Stage

When Dr. Blair determined that his respected friend David Dalrymple should see the *Fragments*, he gave impetus to the first stage of the controversy. Dalrymple immediately put a few of the poems in the hands of his fellow antiquarian, Horace Walpole. In the midst of compiling the *Anecdotes of Painting in England*, Walpole, in 1760, was quite hopeful for the future of the arts in the kingdom, and the casual connection between his own *Anecdotes* and these poems may have encouraged him to speak kindly of Macpherson's work. His good sense, however, compelled him to question Blair's suggestion that the fragments were part of an epic poem: "I could wish . . . that the authenticity had been more largely stated." But with evident consideration for Blair's reputation, he said that he would take Blair's word, although "the gross of mankind . . . will demand proofs, not assertions."[2] Walpole's deference to Blair was prompted by his respect for Dalrymple and his acute awareness of the sensitivity of the Scots on the matter.

When Blair published a *Critical Dissertation on the Poems of Ossian, the Son of Fingal* in 1763, he argued that Ossian, Homer, and Aristotle enjoyed a natural affinity, the first two having been inspired by nature, and Aristotle having studied nature in Homer. He remained resolute as to the authenticity of Ossian, while conceding that men whom he respected had—some of them—begun to have their doubts.

In a conversation with Boswell and Andrew Erskine on 4 November 1762 David Hume had mentioned his change of attitude toward Macpherson, whom he now regarded as a "most curious fellow . . . full of highland Prejudices . . . [who] would have all the Nation divided into Clans, and those clans to be always fighting."[3] The philosopher surely had seen such things in the poet earlier, but evidently he could no longer allow "nationalistic prepossessions" to cloud his reason. His stand put him in opposition to the many Scots who argued that Ossian and Macpherson were Scotland's pride and had enhanced their country in the eyes of the world.

Whether Boswell, who was then preparing to set out for London, had the opportunity to speak with Blair is unclear; he certainly met with him in April 1763 in London. He would not willingly have missed an occasion to observe Blair's reaction to his report of Hume's comments. Blair, who may have come to London "to play second lion in the Ossianic circus," found the literary atmosphere unforgettable.[4] Most memorable of all was his meeting that spring with Dr. Johnson, who had earlier voiced his doubts about Ossian. When Blair confidently asked Johnson "whether he thought any man of a modern age could have written such poems?" Johnson shot back, "Yes, Sir, many men, many women, and many children."⁵ Though Blair did not deserve so rude a shock (Johnson would later acknowledge that he had not known of his connection with Macpherson), the exchange does reveal Johnson's strong feelings on the matter, as well as suggest the energy with which he would pursue it.

Shortly after Blair returned to Edinburgh and took up residence in Hume's vacant house, he began in earnest a second edition of his *Critical Dissertation,* with expanded comments on *Temora* and the lesser pieces. In the meantime, Hume, residing in London, had heard the same kind of doubts that were expressed to Blair; but, more sensitive to the charge of nationalistic prejudice than Blair, he decided that if the truth could be found it must be told before Macpherson's "absurd pride" ruined them all. Hume laid down for Blair, in persuasive fashion, the method he must use in substantiating Macpherson's claims of authenticity: "My present purpose . . . is . . . to give us proof that these poems are, I do not say so ancient as the age of Severus, but that they were not forged within these five years by James Macpherson. These proofs must not be arguments, but testimonies . . . of two kinds."⁶ Hume provided specific directions: Blair should find Gaelic scholars capable of comparing portions of *Fingal* with the ancient manuscripts of Clanranald. Finally, Blair must secure testimony from Highlanders that such poems are "vulgarly recited" there—"send for such of the bards as remain and make them rehearse their ancient poems."

Blair dutifully set about his research, yet with little enthusiasm for it. As he wrote to Hume, "it is impossible for me to entertain the smallest doubt of their being real productions. . . . Who but John Bull could entertain belief in an imposture so incredible as this?"⁷ He implied that Hume may have been swayed too easily by his English friends into believing the worst of a fellow Scot. Blair was, in fact, more worried about what Macpherson might do when he discovered his work was under investigation than he was concerned for its authenticity.

Blair, who knew his man better than Hume, was quite right in assuming that Macpherson would be enraged by such questions. Before leaving for Paris in October, Hume met with Macpherson at Blair's suggestion—it was a painful interview.

You need expect no assistance from Macpherson, who flew into a passion when
I told him of the letter I had wrote to you. . . . I have scarce ever known a
man more perverse and unamiable. He will probably depart for Florida . . .
and I would advise him to travel among the Chickisaws or Cherokees, in order
to tame him and civilize him.[8]

Truculence of this kind only fueled Hume's suspicions about Ossian,
and he persuaded Blair that he was "upon a great stage in this enquiry."
While Blair waited for conclusive proof of Ossian's authenticity to ar-
rive from his correspondents, Hume left London as secretary to the
British ambassador in France, and Macpherson soon sailed for America.
   No specific proof ever surfaced; only hearsay and vague generalities
came of the inquiry. Undaunted by what others would have thought a
failure, Blair, instead, found the testimonies he had solicited most sat-
isfactory, even appending them to the second edition of the *Disserta-
tion,* which appeared with a third edition of *Ossian* in 1765. The first
act of the controversy thus ended inconclusively with two of the prin-
cipal actors out of the country, and the third believing that his new
Dissertation had "silenced all infidelity and even scepticism . . . con-
vert[ing] even that barbarian Sam Johnson."[9]

Middle Stage

   The poems continued to gain immense favor abroad. The Diderot
circle in Paris enjoyed them; such German intellectuals as Lessing and
Herder found Ossian comparable in character to the Old Testament
prophets; and the Italian scholar Abbé Cesarotti prepared a second edi-
tion of his translation (1763). While Ossianism was fostering an eman-
cipation in continental literature and culture, the fondness for
sensibility and mournful lamentation that it engendered further an-
noyed Johnson. He remained unsympathetic primarily because he be-
lieved the poems were fraudulent historical romances, and the entire
matter a national conspiracy led by Macpherson and supported by Scots
who knew the truth. Convinced that the poems were modern produc-
tions, he demanded to see the manuscripts upon which the purported
translations were based. Giving one excuse after another, Macpher-
son—as, of course, he could not—never produced the Gaelic
manuscripts.
   In 1773 Macpherson published a fourth edition of *Ossian,* which
contained Blair's *Dissertation* and two of his own pieces describing the

history, manners, and customs of Fingal, along with numerous notes. In this corrected edition he reordered the poems chronologically "so as to form a kind of regular history of the age to which they relate." In a fairly elaborate preface he explained that the errors made by a twenty-four-year-old can now be corrected and "some exuberances in imagery may be restrained." But a veiled claim for the poems as his own work— "the writer has now resigned them for ever to their fate"—gave his critics occasion to resume their abuse.

Johnson had first mentioned a Scottish tour to Boswell in 1763, and by 1773 he had decided to investigate the question among the Gaelic-speaking Highlanders. Encouraged by Boswell's warm invitation, he arrived in Edinburgh in August 1773 for a three-month tour of Scotland. Both men would take careful notes of the journey; Boswell's observations were kept in a daily journal, and Johnson's letters to Mrs. Thrale were long and detailed. On the way to the Hebrides Johnson decided upon a plan for a short book; Boswell would later offer his journal for publication, largely in order to see if the public might be interested in a *Life of Johnson*.

The two books thus produced are different in their intentions, but complementary. Johnson's *Journey to the Western Islands of Scotland* is primarily a travel account, though notable for its sympathetic portrayal of the Highland poor. *The Journal of a Tour to the Hebrides with Samuel Johnson* (1785), Boswell's account, is important largely for the record it provides of Johnson's conversation. Johnson's interest is, frequently, man as he exists in a rugged environment in the throes of abrupt social change. Boswell, on the other hand, is more taken by the importance of daily life; typically, he depicts Johnson in situations revealing of his intellect where, often, he must respond to new and unfamiliar surroundings. Frank Brady observes that Boswell places Scotland "in uneasy opposition to Johnson as John Bull, trueborn Englishman. Boswell, guide and journalist, also acts as a mediator, coming to Scotland's defense when necessary."[10] With Scotland as "an active entity" Boswell can arrange various meetings, tours, and conversation to engage Johnson's intellect and wit, so that he may then record the results. Johnson, who embarked upon the tour in a good mood, evidently tolerated the arrangement (at least), even going so far as to read his companion's account.

Ossian is not central in either work. If Johnson's major intention in taking the trip was to research the question of the poem's authenticity, the results of his inquiries were disappointing and inadequate. In such

contempt did he hold Macpherson and his work that he seemed inca-
pable of doing much more than confirming his opinion. It must, of
course, be kept in mind that Johnson was correct in believing that
Macpherson had invented the poem: after a decade of waiting for him
to produce originals—after two epics and numerous short poems, all
kept afloat by Macpherson's insolence and Blair's credulity—Johnson
was in no mood to be apologetic for his views. Whenever he discusses
Ossian in the *Journey* he takes the combatant's role, offering no quarter
to Macpherson or the nation. He hears Gaelic (Erse) spoken and finds
it "the rude speech of a barbarous people, who had few thoughts to
express"; he announces mistakenly "that the Earse never was a written
language." Building to his main argument, he even asserts that there
is no worthwhile poetry in the whole language over a hundred years
old; "yet . . . the father of Ossian boasts of two chests more of ancient
poetry, which he suppresses, because they are too good for the En-
glish."[11] Extending his attack, he stops short of accusing all High-
landers of a conspiracy of lies, and instead settles for a general insult:
"perhaps [they] are not very scrupulous adherents to truth."[12] Not to
be misunderstood, he states his final assessment of Macpherson's work:

I believe they never existed in any other form than that which we have seen.
The editor, or author, never could show the original; nor can it be shown by
any other; to revenge reasonable incredulity, by refusing evidence, is a degree
of insolence, with which the world is not yet acquainted; and stubborn au-
dacity is the last refuge of guilt.[13]

Macpherson's method is, in fact, no match for Johnson's shrewd literary
sense: "he has doubtless inserted names that circulate in popular
stories, and may have translated some wandering ballads."[14] Johnson's
tone at this point is quite severe; he proceeds to damn Macpherson and
blame the whole country for Ossian's success: "A Scotchman must be
a very sturdy moralist, who does not love Scotland better than truth:
he will always love it better than inquiry."[15]

    After "pursuing and destroying the dragon Ossian," Johnson ends
his extensive observations on the Highlands and their sons, and con-
tinues his tour by sailing away from the Isle of Skye into a severe storm.
The Scottish weather took its revenge early.

    Boswell's *Journal,* published nine months after Johnson's death, of-
fers a more intimate and elaborate picture of the great man comment-

ing on Ossian. In Aberdeen, at a dinner with academics from Marischal College, Johnson again challenges Macpherson: "If the poems were really translated, they were certainly first written down. Let Mr. Macpherson deposit the MS in one of the colleges at Aberdeen where there are people who can judge."[16] Obviously the subject came up at Boswell's insistence and was meant to provoke an argument among the dinner guests; however, the professors did not rise to the bait. Later, in discussion with the Reverend Donald Macqueen of Kilmuir, Skye, a devotee of Ossian, Johnson was blunt, though not insulting. He wished sincerely to know Macqueen's reasons for enjoying Ossian. Although his contempt for Macpherson remained undiminished, Johnson, in Boswell's account, takes no pleasure in destroying Ossian's supporters. Instead, the tone of one discussion where Macqueen is present is playful. The two men clearly enjoy teasing Macqueen; Boswell draws him out in reach of Johnson's wit and precise questioning.

Johnson's emphasis in the *Tour* on historical investigation as a measure of an author's integrity stands in contrast to the attitudes of his Scottish hosts. The Scots literati had not met their responsibilities to Ossian or the public; they had ignored modern investigative techniques and accepted the romantic notions and nationalistic assurances of their colleagues. Johnson relied upon his experience, his common sense, and—in this instance—empirical investigation to reveal the value of a work of art, and he found Ossian wanting on all counts. Experience had taught him that literary taste may be eccentric, and that the grossest factual errors may arise from mere romantic speculation about the past. Criticism, Johnson believed, must provide a way of comparing one work with another, an established set of truths informing the whole; criticism is—or should be—an intellectual discipline. When Macqueen attempted to compare the *Iliad* with *Fingal,* Johnson could only conclude that the latter was "a mere unconnected rhapsody." It is not surprising that he returned to London more certain than ever of Macpherson's fraudulence.

Macpherson soon became aware of Johnson's comments in the *Journey,* and through an ill-considered correspondence tried to prevent him from proceeding with publication. Unable to persuade the publisher or, presumably, Johnson himself to stop the press or excise "injurious expressions," Macpherson, with the audacity that had long been his hallmark, urged Johnson to insert a disclaimer. This too was ignored. The quarrel reached its height when Macpherson sent a threatening note, to which Johnson penned his now-famous reply.

Mr. James Macpherson—I received your foolish and impudent note. Whatever insult is offered me I will do my best to repel, and what I cannot do for myself the law will do for me. I will not desist from detecting what I think a cheat, from any fear of the menaces of a Ruffian.

You want me to retract. What shall I retract? I thought your book an imposture from the beginning. I think it upon yet surer reasons an imposture still. For this opinion I give the publick my reasons which I here dare you to refute. But however I may despise you, I reverence truth, and if you can prove the genuineness of the work I will confess it. Your rage I defy, your abilities since your Homer are not so formidable, and what I have heard of your morals disposes me to pay regard not to what you shall say, but to what you can prove. You may print this if you will.

SAM: JOHNSON[17]

This magnificently severe letter spurning the threats of the younger man achieves its effect by a combination of bristling language and an abusive tone. It begins with an allusion to Macpherson's written challenge as a further example of fraudulence and impropriety from a man whose worst insult has been to perpetrate a hoax upon a gullible public. Johnson in the role of Truth's champion proclaims his courage before all men, especially one who has neglected his moral obligations to the society. The final two sentences extend the insult by driving home Macpherson's inadequacies as a writer and a gentleman.

Though Johnson carried an oak staff reportedly to protect himself from assault by the angry Macpherson, no direct contact or correspondence between them occurred after January 1775. The *Journey* and the wide reports of his verbal thrashing of Macpherson barely satisfied an impatient public, which had enjoyed their contest, unequal though it was. Macpherson, realizing how mismatched he was, retired from any further confrontation. Thus the controversy over the authenticity of the Ossian poems attained a new level of rancor and bitterness, many writers assuming an uneasy silence as a result.[18]

However, David Hume, whose friendship with Hugh Blair and early support of Ossian had caused him great concern, now felt incapable of silence. Johnson's anti-Scottish prejudices in the *Journey,* he believed, must be answered; a fellow Scot may have acted dishonestly, but an English critic could not accuse an entire nation of immorality. Hume told Boswell in March that he resented Johnson for the nature of his attack, though "he agreed with him perfectly as to Ossian." His anger was, in part, caused by Johnson's refusal to accept what Hume considered a given: the Scottish "will to believe" the poems authentic. There can be no question of immorality, he said, where a people are psychologically attuned to receive an idea no matter what the evidence against it. Hume did not publish his views, but he felt a response, even one held in the strictest confidence, was now required.

By June 1775 Hume had written "Of the Poems of Ossian," a grand summation of the facts of the case as he knew them. In a closely reasoned essay consisting of ten arguments, he assessed the likelihood that originals of the Ossian poems existed. Hume's framework for the analysis followed a well-established pattern developed earlier in his essay "Of Miracles." Now he examined the truth or falsity of the Ossian question against a theory of the possible and the impossible. Not to dismiss Blair outright, Hume wrote that his analysis of the poems remained "very respectable." Yet he admitted, finally, that no epics of the kind Macpherson claimed to have unearthed could possibly be extant. Hume then demanded that Macpherson come out from behind the mask and explain his joke to the public. Having posed this solution to the question, he would go no further: he suppressed the manuscript. The pleasure of defending Scotland's moral integrity had proved most satisfying. His friendship with Blair remained intact, and his final estimate of Macpherson, though less than fair, was to dismiss him and his works as "a ludicrous imposition."[19]

Hume's dismissal of "Ossian" Macpherson in no way reflected the attitude of other prominent Scots. As the influence of the poems grew on the Continent and Macpherson became immersed in public affairs, he felt less the abusive attacks from various quarters. This was not the case of his friends in Edinburgh, London, and even in India, many of whom had never met him but would defend him and his work with nationalistic fervor. They believed the controversy would redound favorably to Macpherson if he would but publish the Gaelic originals. Macpherson readily agreed, yet contended that his limited means would not permit this luxury. During the late 1770s and early 1780s he resisted all such appeals. This financial excuse was removed, however, when, in 1783, Sir John Macgregor Murray of Lanrick and a group of Highland gentlemen from the East India Company collected £1,000 and sent it to him in care of the Highland Society of London. Macpherson assured them of his full cooperation in publishing the originals, but nothing was to appear in his lifetime.

The second stage of the controversy ended as it had begun; again Macpherson was afforded an opportunity to admit the truth. Having

fabricated his translations nearly a quarter of a century earlier, un-
doubtedly he was now daunted by the prospect of extricating himself
from a web of such extraordinary complexity. He found it next to im-
possible to supply Gaelic verse for his English "translations." Unwill-
ing to lose the respect of his friends and supporters, however, he began
what could only have been a desperate effort to provide a Gaelic orig-
inal. So crucial were the Gaelic "sources" to his reputation that Mac-
pherson worked on them before his death, only to leave an unfinished
manuscript. He left, as well, £1,000 to John Mackenzie, secretary of
the Highland Society of London, who would prepare the Gaelic edition
for publication.

Final Stage

When Boswell announced in the *Life of Johnson* (1791) that the pub-
lic was no longer interested in the question of the authenticity of the
Ossianic poems, he spoke for many Scots who had decided that the
best course lay in bearing their embarrassment in silence. This attitude
prevailed until Macpherson's death in 1796, when the Highland So-
ciety of Scotland appointed a committee to investigate the matter. The
commission's chairman was the well-known and respected lawyer and
writer, Henry Mackenzie. As literary arbiter of Edinburgh, author of
the sentimental novel *The Man of Feeling* (1771), and Hume's former
literary page, Mackenzie seemed perfectly fitted for sending inquiries,
interviewing scores of people, and collecting all information relevant
to Macpherson's work. Under his guidance the committee was wel-
comed as the ideal vehicle for settling one of the thorniest literary
questions of the past half century. The stage appeared set for the final,
definitive phase of the controversy.

The committee adopted a research method suggested by David
Hume to Hugh Blair (Letter 215, 19 September 1763), though they
did so unknowingly. As Mackenzie would make clear in the *Report*
(1805), they were interested mainly in collecting materials and testi-
monies on "the authenticity and nature of the poems ascribed to Os-
sian, and particularly of that celebrated collection published by Mr.
James Macpherson."[20] The strategy of gathering information without
falling prey to elaborate arguments regarding authenticity or discus-
sions of the various critics seemed sensible on its face. The reality,
however, proved quite otherwise.

Using a technique long practiced by the legal community, the committee composed a set of six questions and circulated them among a number of individuals, mostly clergymen and local antiquaries, in the central Highlands, particularly the Badenoch district and the western islands. Respondents were instructed to compose each answer "in the same manner as if it were a legal question"; replies received the attention reserved for only the most significant of court documents. Mackenzie had gone so far as to secure the valuable services of Dr. Donald Smith and the Reverend Donald Mackintosh, both of whom read Gaelic, to translate the ancient manuscripts, including those from Macpherson in the collection of the Highland Society of London. From the first, the committee took their responsibilities seriously, going to some length to ensure credibility for the venture.

The requirements of the individual questions demanded the reader's fullest attention. Each inquiry posed a general concern that was followed by a series of subordinate questions. The first will serve as an example of all six:

1. Have you ever heard repeated or sung, any of the poems ascribed to Ossian, translated and published by Mr. Macpherson? By whom have you heard them so repeated, and at what time or times? Did you ever commit any of them to writing, or can you remember them so well as now to set them down? In either of these cases, be so good as to send the Gaelic original to the Committee.[21]

Requests of this kind forced the respondent to deliver highly specific answers to what he heard, knew, and could prove. The remaining questions probed his knowledge of other ancient poems that possibly were relevant, as well as his acquaintance with persons "from whom you hear any such poems."

The committee also solicited intelligence from those who may have supplied Macpherson with poems. As in everything, Mackenzie directed that no blame (if any existed) should be attached to such persons. The primary task at hand was to compare an acknowledged fact (Macpherson's poems) with whatever truth could be discovered behind it. In further questions the respondent was asked to determine "the traditional belief . . . concerning the history of Fingal and his followers" and to transmit any proverbs or accounts, if he could, in the original Gaelic. Thus the guidelines required the respondent's best efforts as a literary historian, sociologist, psychologist, and linguist. The burden on each was as great as the potential prize.

Though the requirements were exacting, the committee felt, apparently, that evidence (testimony) so delivered would constitute the most legitimate grounds for judging the case. If petty jealousies and general ignorance could be dispelled by such evidence, the Ossian question could be brought to a satisfactory end, no matter what the verdict. So the committee thought.

Reports, letters, and other documents began arriving from both Scotland and England. But difficulties soon arose that Mackenzie had not anticipated. Highland tradition regarding oral transmission differed dramatically from what Macpherson had earlier met with during his travels in the region: the poetry that had for generations served as entertainment was no longer much recited. Of equal concern to the committee was that few Highlanders were able to read and write Gaelic. Sufficient numbers spoke Gaelic; but government interference since the 1750s had discouraged writing in that language. Moreover, more than a few correspondents exhibited an obstinate prejudice favoring the authenticity of Macpherson's work. However willingly they told what they knew of the poems, their tone often suggested a reluctance to open questions that might prove detrimental to their own literary tradition—a tradition they regarded as firmly established. Clearly the Highlanders on Mackenzie's list were offended, if not by the investigation launched by their Lowland cousins, then by its implications.

After seven years Mackenzie's committee had received what it deemed sufficient materials for analysis; conclusions were drawn. An impartial report could now be written without further delay. Mackenzie organized the document into two general sections: a 155-page essay and two hundred pages of documents arranged into twenty-two separate appendices.

The documents remain impressive examples of a revival of interest in Scottish literature and culture. Beyond their direct application to the Macpherson question, these letters, affidavits, and fragments of Gaelic poetry would help open doors for those genuine Gaelic poets whose work heretofore had gone unnoticed. If the literary attitudes of Hume, Mackenzie, and other Scots literati never fully aligned them with those working in Gaelic, the *Highland Society Report* united these two diverse groups, at least superficially. This publication of letters from Blair, Ferguson, Home, and Hume, together with translations of Gaelic poetry by Jerome Stone, collections of authentic Ossianic ballads, and affidavits from Lauchlan Macvurich and Duncan Kennedy (who had gathered Ossianic poetry), stimulated modern Gaelic studies. The 1805 *Report* did not, of course, resolve the controversy. Little doubt now existed of an extensive oral tradition in the Highlands; however, no text was located that matched Macpherson's poems in title or exact meaning. Admitting that Macpherson had changed what was "too simple or too rude for a modern ear," and that he had had advantages of time and place that the committee could never duplicate, they never accused him of outright falsification. Only with minor negligence, carelessness, and presumption did they charge him. Detractors would have to wait until the late nineteenth-century researches of Gaelic scholars before the evidence could be studied knowledgeably and the truth at last "writ large" about Macpherson's *Poems of Ossian*.

The final scene of the controversy was not played until Sir Walter Scott's review of the *Highland Society Report* was published in the *Edinburgh Review* for July 1805. Writing anonymously, Scott set aside the question of authenticity as a matter now finally decided against Macpherson. He had not arrived at this decision lightly but had brought to bear his own considerable skills as a Scottish antiquarian and intimate observer of the principal events and individuals in the controversy. Rejecting the argument that the poems' importance rested on some narrow vision of Scottish patriotism and noble primitivism, Scott saw in them another significance. He found Macpherson a poet of remarkable strength who was "capable not only of making an enthusiastic impression on every mind susceptible of poetical beauty, but of giving a new tone to poetry throughout all Europe."[22] The most prominent Scottish writer of the nineteenth century had rediscovered the dynamic cultural force of Macpherson's poems and proclaimed their importance for his own work. His declaration, united with an existing tradition that the poems were a spectacular discovery, attracted major figures from the romantic movement in Britain, France, Germany, and America.

Chapter Six

The Influence of the
Ossian Poems

On Great Britain

The impact of Macpherson's *Ossian* poems is commonly described in terms of a violent, sudden upheaval, often with analogies to natural occurrences. One is told that Ossian swept like a tidal wave over all Europe or that "we can attribute . . . the popularity of *Fingal* . . . to its success in reducing 'nature' to a cloudily subjective force field."[1] One writer cannot quite decide whether to assign the influence of the poems to the natural order or to some insidious man-made force: "To this day the belief that Ossian is one of the glories of English literature, a burning planet in our sky, lingers over the Continent. . . . James Macpherson descended from his native hills and exploded a mine in the midst of Europe."[2]

Though investigating every aspect of the poems' influence lies outside the scope of this study, a brief review is possible. In England their influence can best be seen in imitations by legions of lesser poets, as well as by a number of more important poets. The nature of Ossian's impact occurs in one of two forms (or in certain instances a combination of the two): a direct absolute textual influence, whereby lines and images can be traced back to Macpherson, or a more pervasive, generalized influence, in which case the poets are kindred spirits or Macpherson-like.

Edward Snyder's *The Celtic Revival in English Literature* (1923) lists the remarkable number and variety of adaptations or imitations of Ossian produced during the last four decades of the eighteenth century. Ten dramatic/operatic works and at least three complete metrical versions of *Fingal*, including extensive pieces on *Temora,* were all well received by an apparently insatiable public.

The dynamic quality of Ossian's appeal was registered more significantly in the work of several youthful, maturing artists, first in the

1770s, though the influence continued into the 1830s. Ossianic melancholy and primitivism were not lost on the gifted, if pathetic, Thomas Chatterton, who was to fabricate the Rowley poems (1769–1777). Chatterton invented Rowley, a fifteenth-century monk and poet who had recorded the medieval splendor of Bristol in all its heroic, though provincial, character. Not only was Chatterton's response to the past like Macpherson's—a pleasurable fascination with the image of an antique world—but also his means of conveying that response: the genius of both lay in their capacity for such vivid imagining that they became, as it were, almost mediums, through and by means of whom utterly fictitious characters and events seemed real.

Born ten years after Chatterton, William Lisle Bowles began his career as a poet in direct response to Thomas Warton's sonnets about the sentiment of place; however, he imitated as well Macpherson's wild mountainous landscapes and raging seas. Bowles's sonnets reveal an excess of sentimentality and a passion for the picturesque. Though often accused of lacking real poetic force, he was praised by Coleridge, who found his response to nature genuine. Aside from their similar attitudes and approaches, Bowles and Macpherson share an ability for "harmonizing the moods of nature with those of the mind."[3]

A younger poet than Bowles who felt the Ossian attraction more deeply, Robert Southey achieved an excellent reputation in his own time based on a prodigious output of poetry and prose. Southey in any of his public references spoke disapprovingly of Macpherson, probably because, like others, he confounded artistic merit with historical veracity. John Dunn, however, points to what Southey privately believed concerning the Scottish poet: "they shared a common interest in fashioning an epic out of the beliefs and legends of remote, primitive peoples . . . [;] both experimented with verse forms that were lacking in rhyme and metrical regularity."[4] Southey's style and technique in his longer poems, *Thalaba* (1801), *Madoc* (1805), and *The Curse of Kehama* (1810), suggest his debt to Macpherson's *Ossian*.

Thomas Campbell (1777–1844), a Scottish poet of some contemporary importance, composed some of the finest martial lyrics in the language. His work resonates with a revolutionary spirit, the very passion for freedom. Similarities to Ossian are evident in Campbell's capacity for expressing "the terrible sublimity of battle." He invests his hymns "Ye Mariners of England" and "The Battle of the Baltic" with a typical Macpherson theme: the inescapable tragedy, heroism, and futility of men locked in mortal combat. His ballad "Lochiel's Warn-

ing" depends on the great Scottish touchstone, the 1745 Jacobite re-
bellion, for its power.

Another writer, Thomas Moore (1779–1852), whose poetry fills
nine volumes, rivaled the popularity of Byron with his *Irish Melodies*
(1807), the most notable of which owe something of their success to
both Percy's *Reliques of Ancient English Poetry* and to Macpherson. His
melancholy and sentimentality mark him as a kindred spirit of Ossian:
"to read Moore's poems," Wordsworth wrote, "is to feel . . . like one
who treads 'some banquethall deserted' with garlands dead and lights
extinguished."[5] Moore's superb metrical skill also brings to mind Mac-
pherson's craftsmanship and willingness to experiment.

The regard in which Ossian was held by the major British romantics
has been a topic of study in critical circles for decades. William Blake
praised Macpherson's Ossian highly, ignoring Wordsworth's disparage-
ment, and continued to admire the Scot's poetic gifts. Evidence of
Ossian's "disastrous influence," as one biographer has it, can be found
in the *Poetical Sketches* (1783), particularly the ballad "Gwin, King of
Norway" and the curious prose poems, "The Couch of Death" and
"Contemplation."[6] A more obvious influence is the appearance of an
Ossianic characteristic in *The Book of Thel* (1789), the second of the
symbolic books, where Blake uses the fourteener, his characteristic
long line, derived from Elizabethan poetry, the King James Bible, or
more likely Macpherson. Generally, nineteenth- and early twentieth-
century Blake scholars discounted any connection between the two
writers. The prejudice against merit in Ossian was in full flower, as
was an unwillingness to appreciate, even among the more open-minded
critics, Macpherson's practice of repeating images, themes, and cad-
ences. Such shortsightedness led earlier critics to disregard the liber-
ating effect, especially of Macpherson's technique, on the early Blake.
Recent critics have made a more balanced appraisal. In *Fearful Symmetry*
Northrop Frye suggests that Ossian offered Blake an alternative to the
King James Bible in his search "for a suitable form for heroic poetry."
Harold Bloom comments, in words which could well apply to Ossian,
that a poem like "The French Revolution" (1791), which "deals with
social unrest,. . . of a natural world collapsing, and human forms
being crowded from that world by an army of preternatural portents,"
called for an atypical method of exposition. Blake required a narrative
form that would support the visual image, the story, and the conflict
between the emotional and the rational states: the Ossian formula pro-
vided a proper solution to this difficulty.[7]

Ossian served as a model both for Blake's youthful expressions of adventure and revolution and for the prophetic tone of his later experimental books. Macpherson's cloud images, larger-than-life heroes and villains, and unusual, pseudo-Celtic names as well as his musicality— all attracted Blake, who transcribed and adapted them into his minor poetry. Macpherson, among other writers, gave direction and provided insight into a mythic world as Blake prepared himself for a new incarnation. With his early experimentation behind him, Blake would speak with the full authority and confidence of one who has discovered his own Word.

Macpherson's relationship to Wordsworth has often been misinterpreted. A critic prompted to be derisive of Macpherson or to question the authenticity of the Ossian poems could find support in Wordsworth's 1815 *Essay, Supplementary to the Preface* of the *Poems.* In an unsatisfying parody of Macpherson's style Wordsworth objects to the "impudent Highlander's 'spurious' " picture of nature. He finds Macpherson's description of the mountainous country "dislocated, deadened,—yet nothing distinct," and he offers in contrast his own conception of nature: "in nature everything is distinct, yet nothing defined in absolute independent singleness."[8] Wordsworth finds Macpherson unsympathetic to the idea that the purpose of the imagination is to interpenetrate things and thus create a unity, but, ironically, he cannot resist making use of the Ossianic lore, spirit, and poetic phraseology. Even a partial listing of Wordsworth's indebtedness to Ossian points to a sharp contradiction between his poetry and his criticism.

"Glen Almain" (1807), "Written in a Blank Leaf of Macpherson's Ossian" (1827), "Effusion . . ." (1827), "The Highland Broach" (1835), and four sonnets entitled "Cave of Staffa" (1835–45)—these and other poems reflect words, images, and themes in Ossian. "Glen Almain" demonstrates Wordsworth's knowledge of the legend that proposes this valley as the place of Ossian's burial. "Writen in a Blank Leaf of Macpherson's Ossian" laments the passing of primitive bards who, like Ossian, never disappoint the listener. Wordsworth calls Ossian the bond between "the blind Maeonides" and Milton. "Effusion in the Pleasure-Ground on the Banks of the Bran" dramatically recollects a visit to an apartment in the Highlands where a gardener "desired us to look at a picture of Ossian." Magically, the painting breaks apart to reveal a sublime landscape of cascading falls and "of rock that frowns and stream that roars."[9] Wordsworth never admitted openly and graciously his debt to Macpherson's *Ossian*; nevertheless, his poetry bears

witness to the influence: for him, as for Ossian, there is the language
of sun, rocks, wind, and stars.

Coleridge's response to the *Poems of Ossian* remains notable for—if
not crucial to—a fuller understanding of his period of greatest poetic
achievement. As John Dunn has shown, Coleridge's thorough ground-
ing in Ossian surfaced in three poems published from 1790 to 1793.[10]
"Anna and Harland," "Imitated from Ossian," and "The Complaint of
Ninathoma" derive their images, themes, and language from Ossian.
Beyond these specific similarities Coleridge's respect for Macpherson's
work is readily apparent: his use of a dramatic narrator, of supernatural
fancies, and of mystic experience, evokes comparison with Macpher-
son's. All are central to his three greatest poems, "The Rime of the
Ancient Mariner," "Christabel," and "Kubla Khan."

Coleridge was further influenced by Macpherson's prosodic tech-
niques, which encouraged his own experimentation. A line by line
comparison of both poets' work does not reveal exact replications; how-
ever, the general quality of versification and diction suggests Cole-
ridge's sensitivity to Macpherson's poetic skills. Coleridge's esteem for
his predecessor led him beyond mere imitation and structural adapta-
tion; he proposed an opera, in 1796, based on "Carthon," the well-
known Sohrab and Rustum poem containing the famous Address to
the Sun. Though the opera was never completed, Coleridge continued
making use of Ossian; references to him occur in political speeches and
critical essays. He felt himself a companion of Macpherson, believing
the authenticity of *Ossian* irrelevant. The usual prejudice against the
poems, of which he was certainly aware, was repressed in his efforts to
bring his own shaping imagination to bear on these utterances of the
past. In his quest for unity Coleridge took all knowledge as his prov-
ince and, in so doing, did uncommon justice to Macpherson.

The last great English poet to be much influenced by Ossian was
George Gordon, Lord Byron, most notably in Byron's early work, al-
though its effects are discernible throughout his career. The first prod-
uct of his passion for Ossian is a formal imitation, "The Death of
Calmar and Orla," published in his *Hours of Idleness* (1807), which was
reviewed sarcastically in the *Edinburgh Review* in 1808. Byron wrote to
a friend afterwards that he might have done a better piece of criticism
himself: "Instead of the remark . . . about Macpherson, I . . . could
have said, 'Alas, this imitation only proves the assertion of Dr. John-
son, that many men, women, and children, could write such poetry as
Ossian's.' "[11]

The truth is that only a poet of Byron's caliber could have captured Macpherson's style so effectively while sustaining an individual narrative technique. As he searched for his poetic voice, Byron continued to admire the characters and adventures in Ossian. If his early response to Ossian was largely superficial, underscoring Macpherson's own superficiality, he eventually sensed the magnitude of nature in Macpherson's poetry and its hold upon the poet's imagination. Like Macpherson, he projected into his poetry an acute melancholy interspersed with sudden bouts of despair. An adherent of sentimental primitivism—again like Macpherson—Byron believed that early societies survived or fell on the strength of natural leadership. In the natural organic society of an early race innate leaders were thrust forward by their own abilities.[12]

Aside from the mottoes appended to the poems celebrating the ruined Newstead Abbey in the *Hours of Idleness,* Byron extended his grasp of Ossianic characters, images, and themes in "Oscar and Alva," "Lachlin y Gair," and "When I Roved A Young Highlander." John Dunn suggests that Byron wrote these poems because "he found in Macpherson's work a mirror for his youthful melancholy."[13] The themes of fate and death, noble exploits, spontaneous passion, and fiery defiance recur throughout the volume as they would in Byron's later work. He displays an increasing interest in the important Ossianic characteristics of loyalty and duty, and seems to have been impressed by the nature of discipline and authority that prevailed among the warrior class in *Fingal* and *Temora.*

Byron understood, also, the outlaws or enemies of Fingal, noblemen who rebel against convention. *The Corsair* (1814) and its sequel *The Siege of Corinth* (1816) offer daring heroes unafraid of the repercussions of their violence. Macpherson's gloomy antagonists, Swaran (the King of Lochlin) in *Fingal* and Cairbar of *Temora,* are formidable usurpers whose designs rouse virtuous warriors and kings out of their lethargy—Fingal and his men reassert right action in a world threatened by rebellion. Byron, of course, took a different approach from Macpherson's: revolt becomes a proper response to tyranny; his rebels become heroes. Taken nonetheless by Ossian's images, moods, and methods, he read the poetry for its spiritual and poetic encouragement.

Scholars have discovered numerous Ossianic gleanings in Byron's established classics—*Childe Harold's Pilgrimage* (1812–18) and *Don Juan* (1819–35)—as well as in works whose critical reputations remain in dispute—*The Giaour* (1812) and *Manfred* (1817). One can suggest the association between *Ossian* and *Childe Harold* by pointing to the elegiac

mode explicit in both. *Childe Harold* has been called "an extended fu-
neral sermon." Byron honors the past of great empires and nations, and
in so doing recalls the despair that Ossian had made such capital of
some fifty years earlier. His sensitive appreciation of Ossian led him
naturally to such Macpherson motifs as the supernatural and the sadly
pleasing contemplation of ruins. Byron, of course, surpassed his eigh-
teenth-century forebear; yet he had the fair-mindedness to recognize
Ossian's contributions to his own development.

On Germany

Scholars generally agree that Ossian's impact on English writers, for
all the provocative evidence, remains (after argument and counterar-
gument) problematic. Ossian's influence on the European continent,
however, in particular Germany, France, and Italy, is subject to little
or no disagreement. Macpherson's poems were received in these coun-
tries with an excitement bordering on hysteria.

The complete *Poems of Ossian* appeared in a German translation by
the Jesuit J. N. C. Michael Denis in 1768–69. Living in Vienna and
himself a practicing poet with a facility for languages, Denis had begun
the translation while working from Cesarotti's Italian edition. He soon
acquired an English version and completed his edition in three vol-
umes. The popularity of the work was immense, although some re-
viewers, principally Gottfried Herder, were dismayed by Denis's choice
of classical Greek hexameters for the verse form. The critic "could not
reconcile the smooth poetry of Denis with the unpolished bard."[14] Her-
der nonetheless expressed pleasure at having available the entire work
since scholarly discussion and popular appreciation heretofore had been
hindered by the publication in German of only a few of the poems.
The Denis translation, though losing some of the spirit of the original,
stimulated an entire generation of German poets.

German literature's connection to Ossian is most conspicuous in
Friedrich Klopstock. Best known for his epic *The Messiah* (1748–73),
Klopstock, inspired by Milton, described the last days of Jesus' life in
hexameters rich with religious sentiment, melancholy, and pathos.
Klopstock's response to Ossian was immediate; as early as 1764 he had
begun to reflect Ossian's sentimentality in his odes.[15] Like other writ-
ers, Klopstock became fascinated by the shadow warriors, the gray
atmosphere, the spirits of the departed. As he fell most heavily under
the Ossianic influence, with many of the themes and motifs appearing

in his work, Klopstock decided that Ossian was German. He made no distinction between Celtic and Germanic origins: more important for him was simply Germany's need of ancient heroes. Ossian provided the means for a nation to recover its heritage, to merit the respect that ancient cultural antecedents inspire.

The effect of Klopstock's enthusiasm for Ossian was revolutionary: a number of minor poets actively cultivated the bardic influence, such that together they comprised a school—the School of the Bards. Their most recognizable characteristics were earnestness and a driving impulse toward national unity. Patriotism, virtue, nobility, and maidenly modesty predominate in their poetry. Led indirectly by Heinrich W. Gerstenberg, whose plays *Ugolino* (1767) and *Minona* (1785) bear witness to the Ossian fascination, the movement produced for the most part only servile imitations. The translator Denis wrote odes (*Die Lieder Sineds des Barden,* 1772) in imitation of Klopstock imitating Macpherson, as did another bardic poet, Karl Friedrich Kretschmann. Influenced also by Gerstenberg, Kretschmann wrote lyric poetry under the bardic pseudonym "Barden als Varus geschlagen war." He grafted Norse mythology onto the Ossianic paraphernalia, an approach Klopstock and Gerstenberg also used, but with more success. Most of these poets took great liberties with current literary conventions, something Macpherson had himself done brilliantly.

Rebelliousness found direction and coherence in a fighting spirit that became the hallmark of a group of writers known as the Sturm and Drang school. These men, who had reached artistic maturity around 1770, were inspired by Shakespeare, Ossian, Young's *Night Thoughts* and *Conjectures on Original Composition,* Rousseau, and, to a lesser extent, Diderot. Theirs was an essentially liberal spirit; they resisted tyranny, superstition, and all restrictions on their freedom. Spontaneity was a cardinal principle among them. They exalted nature, made strong emotion a virtue, and distrusted the artificial.

Such attitudes were codified by the movement's founder and pioneer, Johann Gottfried Herder. Herder's work, especially *Fragments on the New German Literature* (1767), *Voices of the Nations in Song* (1778–79), and *Ideas toward the Philosophy of the History of Humanity* (1784–91), served as a guide for this generation of German writers. Herder believed that ancient folk poetry, Macpherson's discovery of Ossian, and Percy's *Reliques,* should be taken as models in a new German aesthetic, and that the "natural" genius of Shakespeare demonstrated the heights that a people might attain through natural free expression. Herder exhorted writers to search for poetic inspiration from within their own national consciousness.[16]

The Ossian influence on Herder remains significant, yet the most important work of the new movement came from Herder's pupil, the young Goethe. Goethe began by writing a tragedy, *Gotz von Berlichingen* (1773), that broke with neoclassical tenets for drama. Reveling in his intellectual independence, he embodied the concept of revolt as fully as a knight who opposes treachery while asserting his independence. Sentimentality and melancholy seem at war with the passionate arrogance of Goethe's hero, who declares himself as vigorously as Prometheus or *Fingal*'s Oscar. In the following year Goethe published a second significant work, a more intimate portrayal of a young man's self-conflict. *The Sorrows of the Young Werther* became at once a prototype of the modern psychological novel, though it documents the deepest sentimentality. *Young Werther* furthered the Storm and Stress movement, much as if Ossian's "joy in grief" were now the perfect model of natural feeling. Goethe's translation of the "Songs of Selma" in part 2 of the novel, as discussed earlier, swelled the adulation already offered at the shrine of Ossian.[17]

Goethe's early work initiated the movement, and Friedrich Schiller's *Die Rauber* (*The Robbers,* 1781) brought it to its close. The basic motif of the play reflects this literary revolt: the value placed on spiritual rightness in an individual who struggles against "a cold-blooded and artificial society." Schiller, though he resembled Ossian in his idealism and in his yearning for freedom, never was more than passingly inspired by the poems. Nonetheless, he admitted readily to a fascination for Rousseau, Klopstock, Goethe, Shakespeare, and, indeed, Macpherson himself. Invigorated by their revolutionary spirit, Schiller would join Goethe in opposing rationalism and conventionalism.

The flame of Ossianic influence flickered for a time among a number of great German writers whose achievements late in the century soon outshone it. The apparent simplicity of the poems proved compelling, especially to those minor figures who became caught up in it. Chief among them were the idealistic Göttingen sons of Klopstock: Gottfried Bürger, Johann Miller, Johann Voss, and Ludwig Hölty. Bürger, a balladeer of the first rank, evoked a primitivism of obscure charm in his *Wilder Jager* ("The Wild Hunter"). His *Lenore* (1774), later translated by Sir Walter Scott as *William and Helen,* reminds one immediately of Ossian—its howling ghosts, mourning lovers, and pervasive terror. The leading critics of the romantic school, Wilhelm Schlegel and

and Friedrich Schlegel, entered the debate over the authenticity of Ossian. The older of the brothers Grimm, Jacob, best known for his revival of old German folk songs, championed the poems' authenticity, arguing for their importance as national treasures. The literary, however, was but one dimension of the Ossian influence in Germany.

Musical adaptations of Ossianic material remain fascinating. Five major German composers—Beethoven, Brahms, Haydn, Mendelssohn, and Schubert—and several minor ones wrote music scored to the tales of Ossian.[18] The music, usually short pieces or songs, gave life to a particular scene or setting in Ossian. Mendelssohn created longer, more complex works. His 1830 *Overture Hebrides* (*Fingal's Cave*) and the *Symphony No. 3* (Scotch) in A minor (1842) best reflect Macpherson's influence. Intrigued by Macpherson's settings, the young composer toured the Highlands and Hebrides in 1829 searching for romantic scenery, finding it "all stern, dark, very lonely."

The wild romance of the poems appealed, also, to German painters. Because of Ossian's connection to Norse mythology, as Klopstock and Herder would have it, the movement in art had deep roots. "It was felt by using this national mythology, as well as local history, a more national art independent of the classical past, could be created."[19] Such painters include Philipp Otto Runge, Johan Christian Ruhl, and Fredrich Georg Weitsch, artists of considerable talent who projected grandiose plans for illustrating the Ossianic cycle, either as a series of drawings to accompany a new edition of the poems or as separate paintings. Generally, they completed far fewer sketches, drawings, and paintings than anticipated; but each produced at least one significant painting or series of drawings that transcended the poetry. Together they reinterpreted Macpherson's limited nationalistic purpose.

On France

Late in the eighteenth century a new period opened in French literature. Reaction against the neoclassical tyranny of form and rules marked the transition; nature was, in a sense, rediscovered. A Rousseauistic romanticism—sentiments, feelings, and passions—together with a heightened sense of the individual, typified this shift of attitude. The inner self rather than objectivity became the prime focus.

German writers (as we have seen) took the lead on the Continent in this movement against classicism. The *Weltschmerz* of Herder and Goethe encouraged the reading public's enjoyment of philosophical in-

trospection, mournful sensibility, and the melancholy heart. In France
Rousseau's autobiographical productions—a novel, *Julie, ou La Nouvelle
Heloise* (1761) and the *Confessions,* written between 1765 and 1770
(1781–88)—evoked from his countrymen a respect for the intuitive
operations of the psyche. Rousseau hailed the natural man, whom he
took to be heroic, an innocent in the state of nature. Having cast aside
much of Voltaire and the Encyclopedists as unfeeling, Rousseau as-
serted that emotion was a better guide to truth than reason. The ques-
tion now arose as to whether Rousseau's noble savage, natural man,
would appeal to the modern reader. The doctrine of natural goodness,
the assumption that primitive man was innately benevolent, demanded
a primitive singer. Macpherson's Ossianic poems provided the best
available example of a cultured primitive—a singer whose epic poetry
rivaled that of Homer. Ossian vindicated the notion of a Golden Age,
a time when the individual existed free from the crippling effects of
institutions. The British poets—James Thomson, Thomas Warton,
William Collins, and Thomas Gray—had spread the cult of primitiv-
ism; Rousseau had taken primitivism to be but the first stage of a larger
emotional advance; Ossian came precisely at the critical moment to
justify his views.

Macpherson's Ossianic poems first appeared in French in the *Journal
Etranger* for August 1760, when two fragments (nos. 4 and 12) were
translated by A. R. Jacques Turgot for its Parisian readers. Their en-
thusiastic reception prompted the philosopher and editor of the *Ency-
clopédie,* Denis Diderot, to translate *Fingal* soon after its publication in
London. Two nationally respected journals, the *Correspondence littéraire*
and the *Journal Etranger,* published his translation, to which the latter
added three other Ossian poems. Diderot's admiration for Ossian was
of a piece with his concept of poetic energy. True poetry, he felt, is the
spirit of life; because civilization not only stifles poetic genius, but also
produces a total dissipation of energy, humanity's return to a precivil-
ized state should be encouraged.[20]

Ossian's influence in French cultural life, it is fair to say, began in
the last decade of Louis XV (1715–74) and declined into relative un-
importance during the monarchy of the "Citizen King," Louis Philippe
(1830–48). Between 1776 and 1848 fourteen separate editions of the
poems appeared in France, of which the most significant was the first.[21]
The translator Pierre LeTourneur had superb credentials for the task:
he had published translations, in 1758, of Richardson's novels and, in
1769, of Young's *Night Thoughts,* and he had begun his prose transla-

tion of Shakespeare (1776–82). In his preface LeTourneur bestows on Macpherson the honorable title of bard, assuring readers that the Scot had discovered Homer's equal, a singer whose poetic richness rivaled that of the Bible. Macpherson seeks a reader, LeTourneur argued, who will ignore the contrasts between Homer and Ossian and, instead, emphasize their similarity in adhering to the dictates of nature.

Strangely, the only other of these fourteen editions to capture the French (specifically Corsican) imagination was not in French, but Italian. The poet and translator Abbé Melchiorre Cesarotti was a teacher of rhetoric in Padua when he wrote to Macpherson in April 1763 praising the Ossian poems (the *Fingal* volume) and promising to translate them into Italian. Macpherson, flattered, sent him a second volume of Ossian (*Temora*) containing notes and an essay "to throw light on its [Ossian's] antiquity." Cesarotti completed the translation in January 1773 (dated 1772), assisted by an English friend, Charles Sackville, who translated the English Ossian into Italian prose from which Cesarotti then worked, and who later paid for the publication of the Cesarotti edition. Cesarotti's critics have felt that he took too many liberties with the originals, that his translation was too much influenced by the romantic poets.[22]

His greatest admirer, however, shared none of these reservations. Napoleon, whose favorite poet was Ossian, had first read the Cesarotti translation in his late teens. Enamored of Corsican honor and French chivalry, as he was of classical heroism, Napoleon immersed himself in the poems. At the close of his Italian campaign in 1797 he awarded Cesarotti a lifetime pension for his translation. Before sailing for Egypt, he argued with the playwright Antoine Arnault about the relative merits of the *Odyssey* and of Ossian—Napoleon preferred Ossian. Throughout his campaign he carried with him only two books: Goethe's *Werther* and Ossian. "I like Ossian," he said, "but for the same reason that I like to hear the whisper of the wind and the waves of the sea."[23]

Napoleon believed that poetry had the power to inspire men to great deeds and to awaken the warlike spirit of a nation. At the same time, Ossian appealed to his fatalism and superstition. He understood the Celtic heroes of the poems, men driven to valorous deeds, kept alive forever by the songs of the bard. Certain scholars have judged his passion for Ossian a mere affectation by a man whose public persona was as the impartial defender of France and a restorer of her lost glories. Nevertheless, aside from his love of war and confidence in force, Napoleon signaled the new romanticism, at least in one respect, in his love of Ossian. Reportedly, his favorite poem, "Darthula," caused him such sentimental anguish that he could read it only when surrounded by his officers, who might by their presence lessen the pain.

As well as respecting the propaganda power of poetry, he recognized that artists and their paintings can serve as potent political weapons. Napoleon influenced an entire group of painters, not only by his military victories fondly depicted in numerous works, but also by his proclamation of revolution and romantic idealism. His patronage encouraged artists to devote themselves to him and his passions: Napoleon's admiration for Macpherson was a spur to their own, particularly if they sought court recognition or advancement. French painters thus turned to Ossian later than their German counterparts and for quite different reasons. The picturing of Ossianic scenes reached its height between the time Napoleon was elected First Consul (1798) and his consolidation of the empire (1810).

Three French painters have been associated frequently with Ossian: Franco Gerard, Anne-Louis Girodet, and Jean-Dominique Ingres. Gerard and Girodet had been chosen in 1800 to decorate the great reception hall of Napleon's summer residence, Malmaison, with paintings based explicitly upon themes in Ossian. Gerard's *Ossian evoking ghosts on the edge of the Lora* (1801) "is not a scene from the poems but a synthesis of the whole poetry: the old bard . . . is invoking the phantoms who inhabit this land and his songs."[24] Critics agree that this was Gerard's finest work; in no other did he so effectively assimilate the atmosphere and sensibility of the poems. After the fall of the empire, the painting was lost at sea while en route to its new owner, the King of Sweden, but fortunately Gerard had managed to paint three copies.

Girodet's *Ossian and His Warriors Receiving the Dead Heroes of the French Army* (1802) is one of the most complicated allegorical paintings of the century. One critic has called it "an incredible tangle of human and animal forms, of light and shade, of the real and fantastic, all confounded in a weird, decorative arabesque."[25] The tension, at times fusion, between classic and romantic, which was characteristic for the period, is nowhere more apparent than in Girodet's painting. Later, he would paint *The Funeral of Atala* (1808), inspired by Chateaubriand, who was himself under the influence of Macpherson.

Ingres' neoclassical *The Dream of Ossian* (1813) was painted as an oval ceiling decoration for Napoleon's bedroom in the Quirinale Palace in Rome, but the emperor never occupied the palace, and the painting was sold in 1815. Later Ingres, as director of the French Academy in Rome, bought it back in the hope of restoring it; it was badly deteriorated, but the restoration was never completed. The serenity of the work stands in marked contrast to Girodet's frenzy; its grandeur and formal strength are in keeping with the style of the classical epic, and with Macpherson's own intentions.

Generally, the French depicted Ossian according to classical dictates, though occasionally an artist's conception broke out in romantic fantasy. For the most part, these artificial compositions remain curious concoctions within an established neoclassical school: art done in response to a patron who was at once irresistible, charming, proud, and capricious.

Napoleon's love of Ossian may serve as a bridge between the early response of Diderot and Rousseau and the reactions of Mme de Staël, Chateaubriand, and Lamartine in the nineteenth century. Joining Herder in viewing literature as "the expression of the deeper emotional and spiritual nature of a people,"[26] and rejecting neoclassical standards, Madame de Staël drew a distinction in her best critical work, *De la Littérature considerée dans ses rapports avec les institutions sociales* (1800), between the classic literature of the South and the romantic literature of the North: the achievement of the Mediterranean countries as opposed to that of the English and Germans. To illustrate this distinction, she compares Ossian and Homer. Northern literature displayed courage, romantic sentimentality, and mystic vision—all characteristic of the primitive Ossian. Homer, a more sophisticated ancestor of the pre-epic northerner, revealed the true impulses of his people, as in folk literature. Macpherson's poems, in their concern with nature and imagination, enjoyed a closer affinity with the new political ideals of the French. Thus Mme de Staël attempted to correlate the political revolution with literary progress, and, in so doing, she found the Ossian poems exhilarating and pertinent. She was, with Chateaubriand, an enthusiastic and energetic precursor of romanticism, and not the first in a long series of talented writers and critics who felt strongly the influence of Ossian.

Her contemporary and uneasy rival, Vicomte François-Auguste-René de Chateaubriand, achieved far greater eminence. An unmistakable romantic, Chateaubriand held a passion for the medieval, the exotic, the natural world, and for melancholy self-examination. In temperament somewhat Byronic, he set the pattern for the doomed hero of the nineteenth century who pessimistically views the world as a source of continual frustration. Imbued with this spirit of imaginative melancholy, he produced a remarkable collection of romantic tales, a prose epic, historical studies, a work of Christian apologetics, and his memoirs.

Because of the disturbances of the French Revolution, Chateaubriand set out in 1791 for America, where he remained for five months gathering impressions of the people and land. Soon after his return, he was forced into exile in England (1793) and not allowed to reenter France until 1800. His experiences in America had enlarged his perspective and given him material for subsequent reflection. In England he discovered Ossian in John Smith's *Galic Antiquities* (1780). A pale attempt to capture Macpherson's success with further translations from the Gaelic, this work became popular outside of England. Its ostentatious sentimentalism proved irresistible; Chateaubriand soon read Macpherson's Ossian in the LeTourneur translation, thereafter proclaiming himself his "most impassioned disciple."

Reminiscences of Ossian occur throughout Chateaubriand's writing, though with greatest frequency and expressiveness in the early work. *Atala* (1801), a romance, was intended to illustrate a section of his prose epic, *Les Natchez* (1826), but he included it with *René* (1802) in his major work, *The Genius of Christianity* (1802). Through *Atala* Chateaubriand gained early recognition; he attempted to demonstrate "the harmony of the Christian religion with scenes of nature and the passions of the human heart." The strength of this tale, set in Louisiana along the banks of the Mississippi River, derives from the psychological exoticism of the characters, the picturesque descriptions of nature, and the melancholy grandeur of its story. The work offers the reader a sophisticated eloquence, giving new expression to the sublimity of Macpherson's themes. Chateaubriand's reliance on the primitive Indian narrator Chactas to tell his tale of "old unhappy far-off things" to René, a young French exile, evokes an immediate comparison with Ossian. Atala's suicide and burial recall similar events in Ossian, particularly the burial of Malvina.

In *René,* originally published as an episode in the *Genius* but issued by itself in 1805, Chateaubriand cites Ossian in order to illustrate his theme, the poetic and moral beauties of Christianity:

On the mountain peaks of Caledonia, the last bard ever heard in those wildernesses sang me poems which had once consoled a hero in his old age. . . . The Christian faith, itself a daughter of the lofty mountains, has now placed crosses over the monuments of Morven heroes and plucked the harp of David on the banks of the very stream where once the harp of Ossian sighed. Loving peace even as the divinities of Selma loved war, it now shepherds flocks where Fingal once joined battle and has strewn angels of peace amongst clouds once occupied by murderous phantoms.[27]

Chateaubriand elevates Ossian to the same pantheon of singers as David, the pastoralism of the Psalms and of Macpherson being made to seem morally equivalent—high praise, indeed, for the Scot.

No French writer of this period appreciated Ossian more or exercised a greater influence on the romantic movement than Chateaubriand. In his *Memoirs* he writes in melancholy Ossianic voice of the execution by order of Napoleon of the Duc d'Enghien, great-grandson of the famous Prince de Conde and a cousin of the Bourbons.

On various occasions the whole forest has fallen under the axe. People of bygone ages have hunted in these preserves, once so noisy, now so silent. What was their age and what were their passions when they halted at the foot of these oaks? What dreams occupied their minds? Obscure men that we are, what are we beside those famous men?[28]

Chateaubriand's melancholic rhythms brought the Ossian influence to bear on the greatest achievement of French romanticism: lyric poetry. Casting aside the old rules, reviving meters and verse forms condemned by early seventeenth-century purists, and experimenting with new ones, the romantic poets wrote lyrics filled with idealism, passion, and a love of nature. The major figures—Lamartine, Vigny, Hugo, Musset—wrote memorably at the height of a movement that lasted from Lamartine's publication of *Meditations* in 1820 to Hugo's *The Burgraves* (1843). But among these four, Alphonse de Lamartine was most deeply indebted to Ossian: "we don't find again in any of his contemporaries a similar faith in the Bard [Ossian] and a similar influence from his poems."[29]

Lamartine discovered Ossian early, probably at the Jesuit college at Belley in 1813; once he remarked that "the harp of Morven is the emblem of my soul." In *To Lucy*, an Ossianic idyll, he painted dreamscapes and wrote longingly for a lost ideal. As he grew older, he linked Ossian with Dante, observing in his lectures that both poets wrote with plaintive sincerity of love and ideal beauty; purity was a theme important to both. After reading Goethe's *Werther*, Lamartine imagined a depressing landscape where his voice would alone prove capable of reviving memories and feelings long considered dead. His early poems, "Le Désespoir," "La Prière," and "La Foi," achieved immediate fame for their word painting and use of sensuous reaction—both learned from earlier French poets, but also evident in Macpherson. In *Jocelyn* Lamartine ensnared the tenderhearted by sublime passages that seemed to arise unmediated from the poet's soul. If divine inspiration had moved Ossian to recount the wars of Fingal, giving him strength and courage, then Lamartine, who was convinced that he carried the divine spark of genius, might express the agonies of Jocelyn and Laurence.

Not unlike Wordsworth, Lamartine loved solitude; he embraced the harmony within nature and produced poems of silent desperation, grief, and lost love. "L'Isolement," L'Automne," and "Le Lac" recall Macpherson's natural and melodious declamations on the passing of time. The sources of Lamartine's art are diverse: the Old Testament, Petrarch, Young's *Night Thoughts,* Byron; but Ossian was as important for him as they.

Lamartine's devotion to Ossian lasted all his life; Ossian's "melancholy of glory," the shadows, and the tomb of these poems inspired him to write new poetry and join in the grand movement of enthusiasm. In embracing the cult of Ossian, Lamartine associated himself with "serious men of action"—Cesarotti, Goethe, Byron, Bonaparte, and Chateaubriand—all of whom shared a similar passion for the Bard and were members in this fraternity.

In that generation of early nineteenth-century romantic poets most influenced by Lamartine we find several of the more important lyricists contributing at least one thoroughly Ossianic poem. Alfred de Vigny's "Héléna et Oïthona" and "La Veillée de Vincennes," Victor Hugo's "Les Derniers Bardes" and "L'Aigle du Casque," and Alfred de Musset's "La Coupe et les Lèvres" come first to mind. In the 1830s and 1840s Ossian appealed especially to minor poets and amateurs; their fascination with Macpherson's work coincided with its general decline and the rise of realism.

For the decline of Ossian we may consult Chateaubriand's description of Napoleon's death on St. Helena in 1821; for both Macpherson and the emperor, the days of glory are now forever past. "Poisoned by sorrow," exiled from friends and family, remaining indoors nearly all the time, the beaten and dying Bonaparte—slowly and with great care—rereads Ossian: Chateaubriand's poignancy recalls Macpherson's own. Chateaubriand, in fact, becomes the paradigmatic Ossian of his generation when he says of Napoleon, "Who shall tell the thoughts of that Prometheus torn alive by death, when, his hand pressed to his aching breast, he looked out over the waves?"[30]

On America

The Ossianic reception in America has been traced through three phases.[31] The earliest, 1766–75, involved Thomas Jefferson and John Trumbull. Following the American Revolution, a second phase, 1786–1800, produced public discussion as well as debate in both the press and in a number of influential periodicals. Controversy over the poems' authenticity was fully aired; there was lively discourse on the nature of the sublime, the primitive, and the epic. In addition, a host of Macpherson imitators flourished whose interest only served to heighten Ossian's popularity. Finally, in the first half of the nineteenth century the great writers of the American romantic movement—Cooper, Emerson, Thoreau, Melville, and Whitman—all responded vigorously and with conviction to the poems as literature, not just exhibits in a forgery case.

The Ossian poems were first advertised for sale in the *Pennsylvania Gazette* by a Philadelphia bookseller, David Hall, in January 1766. Not until 1790, however, did booksellers cease importing English and Irish versions and offer the first American edition, complete with Blair's *Dissertation*. Familiarity with the poems was extensive, nonetheless; about the time Jefferson moved to Monticello, he wrote of his "daily pleasure" in the poems. In a letter to an Edinburgh friend, Charles Macpherson, Jefferson asked if Macpherson could procure a manuscript copy of the Gaelic original from the author, to "include a grammar and dictionary." Jefferson's hopes were disappointed, of course, since he had asked for exactly what Macpherson could never supply either his enemies or his friends.[32] In the same period John Trumbull, one of the Hartford Wits, read *Ossian* and, in a rush of revolutionary zeal, conceived of writing a mock epic satirizing the stupidity and cowardice of the British. His *M'Fingal* consists of four cantos of Hudibrastic couplets, the first two cantos being published in 1775–76 and the complete work in 1782. Though he never became an American Swift, Trumbull's good-tempered ridicule and the public's general knowledge of the original contributed to *M'Fingal's* enormous popularity.

By the 1790s this American vogue had broadened into general popular interest. A drama entitled *Oscar and Malvina; or, the Hall of Fingal* (1796) was performed in Charleston and Boston, and various journals like the *Monthly Magazine,* the *American Museum, Massachusetts Magazine,* the *Columbian Magazine,* and the *New-York Magazine* carried articles arguing for the authenticity and merit of the poems. Imitations grew in extravagance; one even memorialized George Washington: "The Death of Washington: A Poem in Imitation of the manner of Ossian."

Nowhere was the influence of idealism more important than in nineteenth-century America. The confidence, exuberance, and sense of wonder about the promise of growth for the mind and society identified America to the rest of the world. Ossian was taken as an instance of the hidden wonder, an example of the unusual within the usual. For Cooper, Thoreau, and Whitman the poems suggested an organic unity between man and nature; *Ossian* urged the individual to cherish the belief that human beings are by nature prone to do good, that restrictions of their freedom cause evil.

James Fenimore Cooper, the first successful American novelist, was also the earliest—at least of any importance—to be influenced by Ossian. His indebtedness to European romanticism is well known; his admiration for Sir Walter Scott's glorification of the past and Byron's poetry has received substantial attention by scholars. But no scholar had taken notice of the connection between Macpherson and the Leather-Stocking Tales until Georg Fridén published his seminal "James Fenimore Cooper and Ossian."[33] Fridén believes that Cooper came to admire Ossian out of a devotion to Byron's early poetry in imitation of the Bard and through his approval of Scott, whose poems and novels have numerous Ossianic characteristics.

As noted earlier, the *Poems of Ossian* were readily available from booksellers and circulating libraries. Cooper undoubtedly had read part or all of *Ossian,* not out of any sense of literary duty but simply because of the poems' popularity. *Ossian* must have appealed to Cooper; it had exploited heroic action in a hundred battles, described kidnappings and violent escapes, mystified readers with disguises and supernatural action, and reveled in the tortures of disappointed love. Cooper made particular use of such stratagems in the frontier setting of the Leather-Stocking Tales.

Beginning with *The Pioneers* (1823) Cooper explored the life of the forest and its inhabitants. The scenery of the Otsego settlement has a dreamlike quality similar in atmosphere to a hundred vistas in Ossian: clouds obscuring dark, forbidding mountains, bursting streams crashing against great rocks, the wind echoing through the forests of the night. The characters—Leather-Stocking, the uncorrupted man of nature who battles heroically against the vices of civilization, and Indian John Mohegan, the broken chief who lives only to remember the days of his youth—suggest obvious parallels to Ossian. Fridén believed that Cooper saw Indians as "representatives of a dying race whose days of glory and grandeur were gone forever . . . remnants of a proud and free people now doomed . . . and therefore fit to take their place in the world of romance."[34] Macpherson's central theme, the transience of human existence, finds its expression in Cooper's Indians, red men who speak metaphorically of "exquisite feelings of heart" and lament the passing of friends and relatives with soulful grandeur. By adopting the creed of the sentimentalists, especially in *The Pioneers,* and by idealizing the Indians and frontiersmen as more nearly perfect than the people found in the settlements, Cooper produced an American version of Rousseau's (and Macpherson's) doctrine of natural nobility. Indian John achieves glory, not unlike the long-dead Fingal and his warriors apotheosized in Ossian's narrative. Leather-Stocking remains an indomitable spirit, never succumbing to the advances of civilization. Fiedler calls the two of them the pagan Noble Savage and the Christian Noble Savage, "confronting each other across the 'ideal boundary,' the fleeting historical moment at which . . . they meet."[35] The sense of exile that pervades *The Pioneers* has its inception in the condition of the Highlanders, a people made outcasts in their own mountains by the English. Cooper felt the mythic desperation of Macpherson and Scott as they recounted the persecution and, in the case of Ossian, the eradication of a race.

The Last of the Mohicans (1826), the second of the tales and the best of the Natty Bumppo series, is strongly reminiscent of Ossian. Cooper's hero, now called Hawkeye, is possessed of both manly courage and modern sentimentality; confronting him are two Indians, Uncas and Magua, who embody the tensions in nature between good and evil. By exploring the soul of the Indian, Cooper would emphasize the intentions, instincts, and passions of the noble primitive, who stood as a symbol of innocence in the as yet unspoiled wilderness.

Cooper's exploration, however, often is impeded by more than a little melancholy. Uncas as the last man of his race emits a pathetic gloom. Yet humanity's sufferings are more poignant for the Indian's courage in the face of implacable doom. When Uncas dies, the moment is imbued with pathos; the event has the significance of the death of Oscar, Ossian's son, in *Temora*; it is not simply the loss of a great warrior or even a son, but the confirmation of a historical ending.

Cooper's idealized Indians, melancholy atmosphere, and metaphorical language owe much to the primitive culture that in 1771 Herder had discovered in Ossian. Cooper hoped to reawaken the myth of the ideal American by relying on "the wild, more lively, and more freely active" Ossianic poem. He felt strongly that America had gone wrong in the first decades of the nineteenth century because its primitive innocence had been lost.

Emerson saw the universe as an organic whole; poetry, he believed should be an idealized representation of human life, of character and emotion. For Emerson, Ossian marked a breaking away from what he considered eighteenth-century formalism and from the shallowness of poets who "have lost the perception of the instant dependence of form upon soul." References to Ossian in his *Journals* and *Essays* make clear his recognition of Macpherson's development as a poet, and his admiration. But he was not blind to Ossian's elusive quality. In comparing him to Dryden and Pope, Emerson found Ossian superior in "the poetry of storms . . . and sentiment . . . yet he wants their knowledge of the world, their understanding, their wit."[36] Emerson admired the controlling power of the authorial voice and found in Ossian a source of inspiration. But the message from the poems remained a sensual (aural) stimulus, not intellectual. Like Coleridge, he sensed in the works an embarkation toward new horizons.

For Thoreau, the poems were even more compelling. He was fully aware of the questions raised about the authenticity of the Ossian poems as Emerson had been earlier. Yet, where Emerson had paid little attention to the issue, Thoreau accepted the poems as originals translated from the Gaelic. Though he was wrong, of course, his appreciation underscored an important point: insofar as the poems revealed a people who remain true to themselves, they corroborated an essential aspect of Thoreau's own philosophy. Fingal's insistence on the unity of man and nature, never articulated but made clear in his every act, found a receptive soul in Thoreau. Emerson, speaking of Thoreau, said, "his eye was open to beauty and his ear to music," and clearly Thoreau found both beauty and music in these poems. In a memorable passage in *A Week on the Concord and Merrimack Rivers* (1849) he observes that in Ossian "the phenomena of life acquire almost an unreal and gigantic size seen through his mists . . .; they lead such a simple, dry and everlasting life, as hardly needs depart with the flesh, but is transmitted entire from age to age."[37] Thoreau argued that the poet's words should not only have an intellectual effect on the listener but also reach out to his entire being. Ossian, Thoreau implies, has met this requirement primarily through his sensuous and evocative language—in Thoreau's words, "a gigantic and universal language." Since Thoreau believed that words originated in nature, their very existence evidence of a guiding spirit, he found Ossian particularly congenial. He discovered numerous instances in the poems where man and nature are at one. "Their joy and their sorrow are made of one stuff, like rain and snow, the rainbow and the mist." They "vibrate and pulsate with life forever."[38]

Longfellow and Lowell had little regard for Ossian, and even less for Thoreau, who they sensed had been duped into believing the poems authentic—a mistake they would not have made. But Melville reflects the Ossianic influence in the chapter called "Dreams" in his Polynesian romance *Mardi: and a Voyage Thither* (1849), in which he alludes to the "many souls" he had from time to time become or had subsumed as a result of his experiences and his reading. The "chapter on 'Dreams,' " says F. O. Matthiessen, "is a parable, not merely of the birth of his inner life, but of the way in which this fresh consciousness demanded new ranges of language for its expression."[39] Ossian served him, in many respects, as an admirable sourcebook—of adventure, romance, and airy philosophizing. One reviewer for the *New York Daily Tribune* noted acidly that *Mardi* was "a monstrous compound of Carlyle, Jean Paul [Richter] and Sterne, with now and then a touch of Ossian thrown in." A London reviewer called "the book . . . a wonderful and unreadable compound of Ossian and Rabelais.[40] With an enthusiasm comparable to that of the German romanticists Melville, admiring their "nature" and "pathos" and believing them "the soul of melancholy," had taken the poems to heart.

Walt Whitman, in his preface to the 1855 edition of *Leaves of Grass*, displays a profound grasp of the *Poems of Ossian*:

Past and present and future are not disjoined but joined. The greatest poet forms the consistence of what is to be from what has been and is. He drags the dead out of their coffins and stands them again on their feet. . . . He says to the past, Rise and walk before me that I may realize you. He learns the lesson . . . he places himself where the future becomes present.[41]

In his notebooks he frequently records his enthusiasm for Ossian. As a young man, he would carry with him on his solitary boat trips the Bible, Shakespeare, Ossian, Homer, Dante, Aeschylus, and Sophocles.

Though Ossian could lay no claim to being a classic, Whitman saw no inconsistency, apparently, in placing it alongside volumes that could. Later he would say of the poems: "I have had more or less good from what they give out."[42] If Ossian has an effect on the sensitive reader, it is as a force altering the traditional expectations of the poet's role, particularly if the force is embodied as a character in the poems. Macpherson found, as would Whitman, that the poet's genuine material lay in his own place and time; he recognized that highest responsibility of the poet—to move through to the timeless and eternal. In his own misty, often monotonous way Macpherson sought truth as an open-ended process. He had Whitman's daring in the quest, if not his democratic vistas, and both men wrote out of a sense of destiny. Whitman's debt to Ossian deserves to be remembered as more complex than his often-quoted resolve, after a lengthy reading of the poems, not to adopt a windy style. Instead, it suggests a shared intimacy, one the poet affirmed in a generous comment: the *Poems of Ossian*, Whitman wrote, are "the stanchest friends of my other soul, my poems."[43]

Chapter Seven
The Histories and Other Work

By the end of 1763 Macpherson had given four years of his professional life to Ossian. Never again would he single-mindedly devote himself to the bard, though the public was destined to regard the two as inextricably linked. The success of the poems had brought him literary and financial rewards, but with his achievements came as many enemies as friends. Troubled by the attacks of disbelievers and of those with anti-Scottish bias, Macpherson happily accepted Bute's appointment to a small government post in the colonies with a modest pension. This posting to the New World, however, quickly became tiresome, and Macpherson may have felt, as Leslie Fiedler has noted (in another connection), that "in the Ossianic poet only the fictive singer is real; it is Macpherson who does not exist."[1] In 1765, at the age of twenty-nine, he determined that the moment had arrived when he would exorcise the spirit that had possessed him: he would return to London and take his proper place in the world.

Macpherson took up work as political correspondent for the Tory government and was appointed supervisor of the government's newspapers. As the leading government writer for the Pitt, Grafton, and North administrations, he was on occasion provided with documents that were unavailable to the public. However, he was refused access to both the royal archives and the State Paper Office; yet this obstacle, far from dissuading him, only provoked him into using his superb skills as a researcher and collector of historical fragments. Undaunted, Macpherson embarked upon the most significant scholarly activity of his post-Ossianic period: the writing of histories.

The Histories

The fact that Macpherson took up the writing of history at this point in his life is best understood by recalling his conception of his place in the world. First, as David Hume wrote to Hugh Blair, "people now heed the theatre as little as the Pulpit; History, I think, is the Favorite

Reading."[2] Hume and William Robertson, two of the great figures of British historiography, capitalized upon the public notion that an appreciation of the lessons of history promoted the advancement of society. Macpherson, who had no aversion either to making money or being known, entered the ranks of those engaged in historical composition. He also believed, apparently, that the writing of history would enable him to reclaim a reputation for accuracy and veracity. His favorite phrase of this period was "no object but truth." Others writing history thought of themselves as men of letters, a title Macpherson coveted; they set high standards of accuracy and had humanistic goals. To Macpherson the thought of associating with such men seemed the height of respectability. Never wholly confident of his genius, never secure even as a man of distinction, Macpherson was moved to seek the prestige worn so easily by Hume, Kames, Ferguson, Andrew Brown, John Dalrymple, and Robertson. Finally, Macpherson had a genuine intellectual curiosity about the past. He believed that "a historian worthy of the name, not a mere antiquarian, must combine the new with the old and present a synthesis for the edification of the reading public."[3] If his histories served no present usefulness, Macpherson found no cause to defend them on other grounds. Let the reader but see the progress of the human mind.

His earliest historical work, the *Introduction to the History of Great Britain and Ireland* (1771), was an inquiry into the religious, moral, intellectual, and political life of the English, Scots, and Irish. Although he proved unequal to the role of cultural anthropologist, his enthusiasm for Celtic antiquity—not to say, bias—marks him among the first to appreciate the importance of the Celtic race and language in European history.[4]

As had happened before, Macpherson's critics were severely divided on the merits of the work. John Pinkerton, a Scottish historian, antiquarian, and friend of Horace Walpole, viciously attacked the work as "empty vanity, shallow reading, vague assertion, and etymological nonsense." Hume, renowned for his reason and objectivity, complimented Macpherson's "genius and good writing," but rejected as antihistorical his findings regarding the origins of Celtic culture. Nonetheless, with Macpherson famous as the translator of Ossian, the history went through four editions in ten years. Macpherson had found success once again, ultimately receiving the high honor of having Edward Gibbon, in the *History of the Decline and Fall of the Roman Empire* (1776–88), acknowledge the work as his source on Caledonian antiquity.

In the early summer of 1769 Hume had informed his London publisher William Strahan of his decision not to write a continuation of his *History of England, from the Invasion of Julius Caesar to the Revolution in 1688* (1754–62). In view of the work's popularity, he had hoped to bring his account up to the accession of the House of Hanover. Strahan and his associate, Thomas Cadell, encouraged him to change his mind, but without success. By 1773 Strahan had informed him that he had decided on either Macpherson or John Dalrymple as the author of a "continuation of your History." Frustrated and resigned, Hume offered a qualified recommendation of Macpherson, who has "Style and Spirit; but is hot-headed, and consequently without Judgement," and he wished his "Continuators good success."[5]

In 1775 Macpherson published two volumes of *Original Papers, Containing the Secret History of Great Britain, from the Restoration to the Accession of the House of Hanover.* In the same year he also produced a *History of Great Britain,* based on *Original Papers* and covering the same period. His research for these two works recalls, in its complexity, his search for the Ossianic poems.

Macpherson was refused access to the British government repositories for documents on the period, but he was able to examine the materials collected by the Jacobite historian Thomas Carte (1686–1754), who had taken full notes from the state papers of the exiled Stuart king, James II. These were made available to Macpherson by Cadell, who had purchased the papers for £300 from the husband of Carte's widow. Macpherson acquired further material from the memoirs of James II during a visit to the Scottish Jesuit College in Paris, where he also gained access to the archives of the French Foreign Office. Most useful to him were a series of letters and diaries belonging to David Nairne, under secretary to Melfort, the secretary of state to James II in exile, describing the events immediately following the accession of William and Mary. After making translations from the French, Italian, and High Dutch, and securing copies of the papers in English, Macpherson published the most sensational extracts of the entire collection in the first part of the *Original Papers.*

The second section of the *Papers* contained extracts from the family papers of the house of Brunswick-Luneburg or, as they are better known by historians, "the Hanover papers." Consisting mainly of the correspondence between 1695 and 1719 compiled by George I's confidential secretary John de Robethon, the papers were among the effects of Colonel Robethon, the secretary's son, and were sold to Matthew Duane in 1752. Duane gave Macpherson complete freedom to extract and translate from them. Included in the collection were holograph letters to Robethon from William III, Louis XIV, Marlborough, the Elector (George I), and others at Anne's court.

Macpherson, quick to grasp the value of such materials, transcribed or translated their most telling instances of Whig intrigue during the last years of Queen Anne's reign. This happened at a time when most Englishmen in public life recognized that the Hanoverian succession might be supplanted by the Catholic Pretender with the assistance of France, and had made their piece with both Hanover and the Jacobite court at St. Germain. Macpherson made use of Robert Harley's correspondence with the Electress Sophia, to whom Harley vowed his devotion, though at the same time he was entertaining the idea of bringing back the Stuarts. Bolingbroke too sent his assurances, but, as the Hanover papers show, the elector felt that the Tories could not be trusted. These apprehensions, though generally unfounded, caused the Tories great harm when George I came to power. In an attempt to put to rest persistent anti-Tory bias Macpherson chose the most damaging papers in preparing his case against the high-handed Whigs. Even if some readers rejected this partisan analysis, he concluded that the papers would at least appeal to their interest in observing "the secret springs of action, the private negotiations of parties, the intrigues of ministers, and the motives of sovereigns."[6]

Macpherson had utilized a relatively new technique in the development of modern historical methods. His direct use of sources revealing the attitudes and thoughts of the chief participants in a particular event gave his narrative immediacy and credibility. In publishing long extracts from the original documents he followed Robertson and Hume in what has become the accepted practice of allowing the reader his own conclusions and offering him an opportunity to test the narrative.

Critical reaction to the *Papers* and the *History* was immediate, the Whigs accusing Macpherson of rendering the history of England in terms sympathetic to Jacobites and Royalists. The Tories, however, delighted in his reliance on materials showing Bolingbroke and his friends acting honorably toward the Hanoverian junto and in his revelation of "treasonable" letters between the Duke of Marlborough and James II. Horace Walpole, son of the great Whig statesman Sir Robert Walpole, vented his anger in a letter to the poet William Mason: "I stopped dead short in the first volume; never was such a heap of insignificant trash and lies."[7] Soon after, Hume wrote with uncharacteristic petulance to Strahan that "Macpherson's History (was) one of the most wretched Productions that ever came from your Press."[8] Hume's bitterness was prompted in part by the easy popularity of a work he himself had chosen not to write and that soon made its author an exceedingly wealthy man. As a historian, however, Hume would probably have conceded that Macpherson had presented more new information on the subject than the rest of their colleagues. Indeed, nineteenth- and twentieth-century historians have relied on the *Papers* and the *History* for their accuracy and because portions of the original material no longer exist.

As the best of the government writers, Macpherson produced two of the most widely read pamphlets of Lord North's ministry (1770–82). *The Rights of Great Britain Asserted Against the Claims of America* (1776) was published anonymously, countering the colonists' reasons for taking up arms against England. The thesis of the ninety-two page essay is that the government's policy was to eliminate traitors by "spirited exertion and victory." Warning his readers that "an anxiety for negotion [is] generally a mark of weakness," Macpherson attempted to prepare the public for a long, difficult war. Three years later he published anonymously *A Short History of the Opposition During the Last Session,* in which he reviewed the conduct of the Whigs during the war, criticized their lack of support during a time of national crisis, and called attention to the dissension that ensued.

During 1778 and 1779 France and Spain had succesively entered the war against Britain. A number of disasters both in America and on the high seas caused deep discontent in Britain, which would ultimately result in the fall of North's government. Macpherson expended considerable energy and talent in an effort to forestall just such an event. When charges of incompetence were leveled at the ministry, he took every step short of slander to trace any Tory defeat to earlier Whig bungling. As Lord North wrote to George III on leaving office in 1782, "Mr. James Macpherson has for many years been a most laborious and able writer. . . . *The History of the Opposition,* the best defense of the American war, and almost all the pamphlets on the side of Administration were the production of his pen."[9]

Translation of the *Iliad* (1773)

On 23 February 1773, fourteen days before Macpherson's translation of the *Iliad* was to be published, William Mason wrote to his friend Horace Walpole: "Pray (in the name of critical astonishment) what can

be Macpherson's translation of Homer? Has he Fingalized? Has he Te-
moraized him? I'll lay my life he has. Homer à la Erse must be curiosity
with a vengeance."[10] Mason's sarcasm was on the mark; critics greeted
the Scot's translation with disdainful curiosity, which soon turned into
open contempt. Why they responded in this fashion, and what Mac-
pherson's Homeric intentions may have been, have received scant at-
tention from scholars.

From the first appearance of *Ossian* Macpherson's friends, in partic-
ular Hugh Blair and Adam Ferguson, had considered him ideally
suited for translating the *Iliad*. Such an expectation was not unreason-
able since Macpherson had a respectable grounding in Greek acquired
at Marischal College, Aberdeen, and his experience as a student of
Thomas Blackwell, professor of Greek and author of an *Enquiry into the
Life and Writings of Homer* (1735), had been fortunate. Macpherson
knew of efforts then under way in Britain to determine the historical
accuracy of Homer; he had joined Blair, Ferguson, and Henry Home
(Lord Kames) in making the case for Ossian as a prime instance con-
firming Blackwell's theory of epic origin. The four primitivists be-
lieved that Ossian deserved to be ranked with Homer as another great
poet of a rude age.

As Blair and Ferguson kept after Macpherson to take up Homer,
they came up against the major obstacle in the way of a new transla-
tion—the *Iliad* of Alexander Pope, published between 1715 and 1720.
For the last half of the eighteenth century Pope's *Iliad* was considered
the most sprightly and varied of the poetic translations. Though Mac-
pherson pointed out its faults as evidence of why another translation
was now required, none of the Scots correctly measured the chances for
displacing Pope, in the opinion of either the critics or the general
readership.

Macpherson found it easy to decide on the Greek text for his source:
Samuel Clarke's 1729 edition had won general acceptance as the stan-
dard, in part because it was based on Joshua Barnes's 1711 edition,
which Pope had used. Macpherson, reportedly, completed his transla-
tion in a three-to-twelve-week period—a remarkably swift piece of
work—and in 1773 his edition came out in two quarto volumes with
a preface and no notes. A few months later he offered a second, inter-
lineated edition, with the Greek and English texts on facing pages. He
included, also, a Latin version and Clarke's ample notes—while delet-
ing thirteen books of the *Iliad* to make room for this apparatus.

In his preface Macpherson speaks of Homer's fame, and of the admiration by later writers which has, in some instances, caused them to imitate his technique at the expense of their own imagination and judgment. He praises Homer's originality and his character development, yet catalogues his faults. He also assures his readers of his strict objectivity, and having done so, moves to his principal point: that other translations fail both in conveying Homer's linguistic simplicity and in sustaining his seriousness. He himself, by employing the free-verse method of Ossian, avoids Pope's "quaintness of modern fine writing." By translating verbatim and providing clarifying epithets, Macpherson aims to suggest the fire and spirit of Homer; his *Iliad* becomes a poem of simplicity and "single-minded structure." Never at a loss for boldness, he boasts that he has made Homer "as much as possible . . . speak English." In its distinctive rhythmic prose and diction the translation—as Mason had feared—in fact recalls "Homer à la Erse":

The wrath of the son of Peleus,—O goddess of song, unfold! The deadly wrath of Achilles: To Greece the source of many woes! Which peopled the regions of death,—with shades of heroes untimely slain: While pale they lay along the shore: Torn by beasts and birds of prey: But such was the will of Jove! Begin the verse, from the source of rage,—between Achilles and the sovereign of men.[11]

Macpherson, knowing that his critics awaited publication, tried to blunt their attacks by declaring plainly his admiration for Homer: "He mixes the gravity of the historian with the dignity of the poet . . . and when he ascends to the sublime, he chuses to shine."[12] Encouraged by men he respected, unfulfilled and insecure despite his recent success with Ossian, and unrecognized as an author in his own right, Macpherson accepted the role of translator halfheartedly. If his translation failed, the blame rested on him. He forgot (if ever he understood) that the translator "must respond consciously and creatively to the demands of his own literature and culture as well as those of Homer."[13] By relying on Ossianic language, he violated the spirit of Homer's poetry; and by trusting in current poetic diction, he doomed his experiment to failure. Hume, sensing the pathos of the moment, said coolly, "it is hard to tell whether the attempt or the execution be worse."[14] The experiment was not, however, without value. Macpherson can be seen working in a new tradition; unlike Pope and other of Homer's translators, he was much less concerned with the *Iliad* as a moral treatise, than he was interested in it as a historical document. Furthermore, his

treatment of Homer as a primitive—though Ossianic—bard antici-
pates the romantic movement of the next generation. One cannot ac-
cuse Macpherson of not being true to himself: his *Iliad* displays none
of the learned, conscious artistry of Pope's; instead, Homer is revealed
as an untutored singer who embodies the grandeur of his age. Finally,
though his translation failed to achieve the simplicity that was its an-
nounced aim, it did project the spirit of the epic, in which emotional
conflict predominates. Pope, however, was not to be superseded until,
in Macpherson's own phrase, "less prejudiced times."

Conclusion

The *Poems of Ossian* has been characterized by those who yearned to
find evidence in support of a primitivist doctrine, as "a dream come
true" and "an answer to a romantic prayer." Its characterizations were
those of the romantic movement: the return to nature, melancholy,
primitivism, sentimentalism, individualism, and exoticism; and its
publication in a highly favorable climate in the last half of the eigh-
teenth century produced an uncommon response from both its disciples
and detractors.

The question of the poems' authenticity has for too long obscured
their value and discounted their influence. The twentieth century has
been, for the most part, more judicious by admitting Macpherson's
intelligence, sensitivity, and poetic capacity. As a Scot, Macpherson
was patriotic when it was dangerous to be so, loyal to his clan when it
would have been simpler to put it aside, and generous in spirit and
material wealth to his countrymen when he could as easily have been
otherwise. His poetry reflects these qualities. It reveals, as well, his
intense pride, crippling insecurity, and deep cynicism. His govern-
ment work, including his lobbying for an Indian prince and his mem-
bership in Parliament, provides strong evidence of his capacity for
backstairs politics, his shrewd awareness of realpolitik.

Macpherson's dualistic nature permitted him to write as Ossian,
whose falsetto voice could sing of the vast, innocent heart of nature,
and then at a later moment shift to another persona and write histories
and pamphlets, while guiding the publicity of a modern government
with the sophistication and cunning of a Machiavellian agent. This
may explain in part Napoleon's infatuation with Ossian, as well as
substantiate the sense of real power informing the words of Fingal and
his sons. Macpherson's involvement in forgery seems relatively less im-

portant; instead, what remains crucial is the inner world glimpsed by more than two generations of poets, philosophers, painters, and musicians. This world portrays heroism and adventure on its surface while suggesting at every point the mystic communion of mankind with powerful feelings, thoughts, and dreams. *Ossian* can be regarded as the record of a sickly culture, depressed and melancholic in its youth. But the poems may also be read not just as paeans to dead warriors but as eternal testimonials to the poet himself—and to poetry. It is the singer who, in the final analysis, is the only one left to perform an act of creation. Ossian's dream, though passive and self-absorbed, controls the reemergence of the warrior. To his great credit, Macpherson saw the value of art in ensuring the survival of civilization, and in a curious way made the poet the only true warrior. For this and his other contributions—though a man of little moderation and great passion—he promoted the best and most enduring interest of human society.

Notes and References

Chapter One

1. James Boswell, *Boswell's London Journal: 1762–1763*, ed. Frederick A. Pottle (New York: McGraw-Hill, 1950), 182.

2. James Boswell, *A Tour to the Hebrides*, ed. Frederick A. Pottle and C. H. Bennett (New York: Isham Collection, 1936), 206.

3. Bailey Saunders, *The Life and Letters of James Macpherson* (1894; reprint, New York: Haskell House, 1968), 40. Other biographical facts are found in the *Report of the Committee of the Highland Society of Scotland*, ed. Henry Mackenzie (Edinburgh: Edinburgh University Press, 1805); Bailey Saunders, "Macpherson, James," *DNB* (1893); J. S. Smart, *James Macpherson: An Episode in Literature* (London, 1905; reprint, New York; AMS Press, 1973); Edward D. Snyder, *The Celtic Revival in English Literature: 1760–1800* (Cambridge: Harvard University Press, 1923), 69–92.

4. The six other poems usually ascribed to Macpherson are discussed in the following chapter. Malcolm Laing, a nineteenth-century editor of *Ossian*, assigns, on the barest of evidence, fifteen more poems to the Macpherson canon. See *The Poems of Ossian*, 2 vols. (Edinburgh, 1805; reprint, New York: AMS Press, 1976).

5. Thomas Graham had a distinguished career as a soldier, raising the 99th Regiment in 1793, and as a general of infantry who served most notably with Wellington during the Napoleonic Wars (1792–1815). He was created Baron Lynedoch of Balgowan in 1814. See Antony Brett-James, *General Graham, Lord Lynedoch* (London: Macmillan, 1959).

6. For a brilliant portrait of John Home, see Alexander Carlyle, *Anecdotes and Characters of the Times*, ed. James Kinsley (London: Oxford University Press, 1973), 114.

7. For a full discussion of the founding and influence of this club, see E. C. Mossner, *The Life of David Hume* (1954; reprint, Oxford: Clarendon Press, 1970), 272–85.

8. To Sir David Dalrymple of Newhailes, 16 August 1760, Letter 176, *Letters of David Hume*, ed. J. Y. T. Greig (Oxford: Clarendon Press, 1932), 1:328–31.

9. Mossner, *Hume*, 415. Alexander Carlyle describes his character vividly in *Anecdotes and Characters of the Times*, 203, 260.

10. Junius championed the cause of "Wilkes and Liberty." John Wilkes, having been expelled from his seat in the House of Commons for his reflections on the king, in No. 45 of the *North Briton*, had been living in exile in France. In 1768 he returned to England and was reelected to Parliament and expelled again. This happened three times. Finally, he was declared ineligible

and his seat given to his opponent. See George Nobbe, *The North Briton: A Study in Political Propaganda* (New York: Columbia University Press, 1939), and Ian R. Christie, *Wilkes, Wyvill and Reform: The Parliamentary Reform Movement in British Politics 1760–1785* (London: Macmillan, 1963).

11. To Adam Smith, 10 April 1773, Letter 491, *Letters of David Hume,* 2:280–81.

12. This undated letter is quoted in Saunders, *Life and Letters of James Macpherson,* 230–31.

13. Macpherson sat for his portrait near the end of June 1772. Reynolds, in his public portrait period, had begun six other works that month, and had been working assiduously all year to complete many portraits, including those of Samuel Johnson, David Garrick and his wife, the writer John Hawkesworth, and the architect Robert Adam. The Macpherson painting now is in the private collection of Lord Wyndham at Petworth House in Sussex; however, a copy is in the National Portrait Gallery, London. See Charles R. Leslie's *Life and Times of Sir Joshua Reynolds* (London: Murray, 1865), 465. George Romney, who established himself as a portraitist in competition with Reynolds and Gainsborough, painted two portraits of Macpherson in August 1779 and January 1780. The second was done at Macpherson's request and remains in the possession of the family. For a further description, see Humphry Ward and W. Roberts, *Romney: A Biographical and Critical Essay . . . Catalogue Raisonné of His Works,* 2 vols. (New York: Scribners, 1904), 2:99.

14. John Macpherson's return for the Cricklade borough in the general election of 1780 was challenged but not declared void until May 1782. James Macpherson's election to the House was arranged by the government, the cost of the seat presumably defrayed by the Nawab.

15. Robert Adam, a Scotsman who had made a distinguished career in England designing public and private buildings, had maintained a separate Scottish office, making annual trips north, of a month or so, each summer. On one of these he designed in Edinburgh the General Register House (1774–92) and the University building (1789–93), which demonstrate his considerable gifts. He also completed during this last decade of his life a number of country homes, as well as several more of his castle houses in Scotland. Adam certainly knew John Home, who may have introduced him to Macpherson. He is known today as the leader of the classical revival in Britain and as the originator of a revolution in interior decoration. For further information see D. Yarwood's *Robert Adam* (New York: Scribners, 1970) and Arthur T. Bolton, *The Architecture of Robert and James Adam,* 2 vols. (London: Country Life, 1922).

Chapter Two

1. Samuel Johnson, *A Journey to the Western Islands of Scotland,* ed. Mary Lascelles (New Haven: Yale University Press, 1971), 117.

2. Saunders's comment reveals his dissatisfaction with Laing's decision to publish these poems, as well as the other fifteen, based on the evidence adduced (*Life and Letters of James Macpherson,* 50).

3. "Death," in *The Poems of Ossian,* 2:259–61. All subsequent citations from Macpherson's poetry are to this edition and are given parenthetically in the text as volume and page.

4. John Macqueen, introduction, *Poems of Ossian* by James Macpherson (Edinburgh: Mercat Press, 1971), 5.

5. Saunders mentions the influence of James Thomson's *Seasons* (1730) here (*Life and Letters of James Macpherson,* 14). But Thomson's feelings for nature remain, for all their other qualities, purposely pictorial. D. Nichol Smith reminds us of Hazlitt's comment on Thomson: "He puts his heart into his subject, writes as he feels, and humanises whatever he touches." Macpherson may have found *The Seasons* compelling though he repressed any tendency to displace the epic action of his work with Thomson-like description. See "Thomson and Burns," in *Eighteenth-Century English Literature: Modern Essays in Criticism,* ed. James Clifford (New York: Oxford University Press, 1963), 186.

6. Thomas Carlyle, *On Heroes, Hero-Worship, and the Heroic in History,* in *The Works of Thomas Carlyle,* ed. Henry D. Traill (New York: Charles Scribner, 1896–1901), 5:2.

7. Smart, *James Macpherson,* 76.

8. Hugh Blair, *A Critical Dissertation on the Poems of Ossian, the Son of Fingal,* 2d ed. (London: T. Becket, 1765), 53.

9. John J. Dunn, "James Macpherson's First Epic," *Studies in Scottish Literature* 9 (1971):54.

10. Ibid., 50.

11. C. S. Lewis, "Addison," in *Eighteenth Century English Literature,* ed. James Clifford, 155.

12. Boswell, *London Journal,* 41–42.

13. Macpherson had believed, as did other loyal Scots, that Keith intended to return to Scotland in 1760. Keith, however, did not arrive at his Aberdeen estate until the autumn of 1763, and "finding the Scottish weather as insufferable as the Scottish temper, the aged Marischal sold his estates and returned to warmer climate." Keith, as governor of Neuchatel, Switzerland, had befriended Rousseau, introduced Hume to him, and served as a guide for Boswell during the latter's 1764 tour of Germany. See Mossner, *Hume,* 429–30, and Frederick Pottle's *James Boswell: The Earlier Years 1740–1769* (New York: McGraw-Hill, 1966), 140–41.

14. The final fifteen poems in the Laing edition are either translations or imitations of classical poets, in addition to three occasional pieces. The editor's inclusion of these miscellaneous poems depends on the barest evidence from the 1760 *Collection of Original Poems,* edited by the blind Scottish poet-prodigy Thomas Blacklock, who had gathered poems printed in various Edin-

burgh journals. Laing is building his case against Macpherson as translator, believing he wrote heroic poetry from the first. Since the authorship of these poems is unresolved, I do not discuss them.

15. *Report of the Highland Society,* Appendix 4, 69.

16. Magnus Maclean, *The Literature of the Celts* (1902; reprint, Port Washington, N. Y.: Kennikat Press, 1970), 121.

17. Smart, *James Macpherson,* 169. Derick Thomson cautions readers about a "misdirection" on the part of Smart and his concern for only Ossianic epics, not ballads; Thomson also points to the lack of proof that the *Red Book* was a source for Macpherson. See *The Gaelic Sources of Macpherson's 'Ossian'* (Edinburgh: Oliver & Boyd, 1952), 3, 75–77.

18. MacLean, *Literature of the Celts,* 172.

19. Thomson, *Gaelic Sources,* 11.

20. Samuel Johnson states an opinion shared by many of his contemporaries: "There are . . . no Erse manuscripts." James Boswell, *Life of Johnson,* ed. R. W. Chapman (London: Oxford University Press, 1976), 578, 588.

21. Macpherson included this piece as "Fragment 7" in the first collection, and the tale reappeared in his last epic, *Temora,* Book 1. See Thomson, *Gaelic Sources,* 59–67.

22. *Report of the Highland Society,* Appendix 4, 57 contains the primary reference; however, Robert H. Carnie, "Macpherson's *Fragments of Ancient Poetry* and Lord Hailes," *English Studies* 41 (1960):18, and Robert M. Schmitz, *Hugh Blair* (New York: King's Crown Press, 1948), 42ff., provide a fuller picture of this issue.

23. To Dalrymple, 4 April 1760, *Horace Walpole's Correspondence,* ed. W. S. Lewis, C. H. Bennett, A. G. Hoover (New Haven: Yale University Press, 1951), 15:65. William Mason was Gray's poetic protégé, close friend, and literary executor. George Lord Lyttelton was an old school friend of Gray who had a considerable reputation as a historian, but as a poet, Johnson remarked, his work leaves "nothing to be despised, and little to be admired" (*Lives of the English Poets,* 2:382). Other references to Gray's interest in Macpherson occur in the *Correspondence of Thomas Gray,* ed. P. Toynbee and L. Whibley (Oxford: Clarendon Press, 1935), vol. 2, and in Appendix L, vol. 3, 1223–29.

24. Gray to Warton, June 1760, Letter 313, *Correspondence of Thomas Gray,* 2:680.

25. The second edition published in August 1760 contained an additional fragment, inserted as 13, with the earlier remaining fragments renumbered.

26. Hugh Blair, preface, *Fragments of Ancient Poetry* in *The Poems of Ossian,* 2:381.

27. John J. Dunn, introduction, *Fragments of Ancient Poetry* by James Macpherson, Augustan Reprint Series, no. 122 (Los Angeles: University of California Press, 1966), iv. J. S. Smart suggests that an even greater deception

was perpetrated because Macpherson had provided the unsuspecting Blair with the outline of the *Fingal* plot for this preface and had written to William Shenstone, in June 1760, of his certainty about the existence of a nine-thousand-line epic. Hume would later corroborate this remarkable story (Smart, *James Macpherson*, 97).

28. "Account of Books," *Annual Register*:3 (1760):254.

29. To Sir David Dalrymple of Newhailes, 16 August 1760, Letter 176, *Letters of David Hume*, 1:328–32.

30. Mrs. Montagu believed from the beginning in Macpherson and in his claims for Ossian; this fascination eventually brought her to Scotland in hopes of meeting others of like mind. See Ian Ross, "A Bluestocking over the Border: Mrs. Elizabeth Robinson Montagu (1720–1800), August 2–27, 1766," *Huntington Library Quarterly* 28 (1965):213–33.

31. *Report of the Highland Society*, Appendix 4, 57. Saunders, Schmitz, and Smart provide information about this scheme; the most provocative facts are in Carnie, "Macpherson's *Fragments*," *English Studies*, 17–26.

Chapter Three

1. *Report of the Highland Society*, Appendix 4, 59.

2. The letters of Home to Bute show that Macpherson was in the Highlands in the summer of 1761, immediately before the publication of *Fingal*. See R. George Thomas, "Lord Bute, John Home and Ossian: Two Letters," *Modern Language Review* 51 (1956):73–75.

3. To Dalrymple, 14 April 1761, *Horace Walpole's Correspondence*, 15:71–72.

4. Gerald P. Tyson, "'Feast of Shells': The Context of James Macpherson's Ossianic Poetry," Ph.D. diss., Brandeis University, 1969, 78. Also see John Wain's illuminating essay, "Alternative Poetry: An Oxford Inaugural Lecture," *Encounter* 42 (1974):26–38.

5. "A Dissertation concerning the Era of Ossian" in *The Poems of Ossian* (New York: Edward Kearny, 1846), 48–49. This essay appeared originally in the 1762 edition; I am using the standard 1773 version, which usually accompanies later editions. Macpherson was relying on such sources as Paul H. Mallet's *L'Introduction a l'histoire de Dannemarc* (Copenhagen, 1755–56) and *Monuments de la mythologie et de la poésie des Celtes* (Copenhagen, 1756), as well as Roderic O'Flaherty's *Ogygia* (London, 1685).

6. "A Dissertation concerning the Era of Ossian," 55.

7. Francis R. Hart, *The Scottish Novel: From Smollett to Spark* (Cambridge: Harvard University Press, 1978), 342.

8. *Critical Review* 12 (December 1761):410. This discussion of the critical reception of *Fingal* is indebted to Larry L. Stewart's unpublished dissertation, "Ossian in the Polished Age: The Critical Reception of James Macpherson's Ossian," Case Western Reserve University, 1971, 37–92.

9. Stewart, "Ossian in the Polished Age," 71.

10. Blair, *Critical Dissertation,* 41, 42.

11. Ibid., 44, 45.

12. Donald Foerster, *Homer in English Criticism: The Historical Approach in the Eighteenth Century* (New Haven: Yale University Press, 1947), 42.

13. For further insights, see Jacques Chouillet, "Diderot: Poet and Theorist of the Homer and Ossianist Revival," *British Journal for Eighteenth-Century Studies* 5 (1982):229.

14. Blair, *Critical Dissertation,* 44.

15. Samuel H. Monk, *The Sublime: A Study of Critical Theories in Eighteenth-Century England* (Ann Arbor: University of Michigan Press, 1960), 112. Monk refers also to Alexander Gerard, *An Essay on Taste* (1759), the most elaborate investigation of taste during the century. See also Walter J. Hipple, *The Beautiful, the Sublime, and the Picturesque in Eighteenth-Century British Aesthetic Theory* (Carbondale: Southern Illinois University Press, 1957).

16. Josef Bysveen, *Epic Tradition and Innovation in James Macpherson's Fingal* (Atlantic Highlands, N.J.: Humanities Press, 1982), 122–23.

17. Blair, *Critical Dissertation,* 121.

18. Ibid., 41, 129–30. Monk, *The Sublime,* 120–29, develops this point.

19. Howard M. Jones, *Revolution and Romanticism* (Cambridge: Harvard University Press, 1974), 251.

20. Blair, *Critical Dissertation,* 97.

21. Edmund Burke, *A Philosophical Enquiry into the Origin of Our Ideas of the Sublime and Beautiful,* ed. J. T. Boulton (New York: Columbia University Press, 1958), 57, 65.

22. Tyson, "'Feast of Shells,'" 123.

23. Bysveen, *Epic Tradition and Innovation,* 92.

24. Jones, *Revolution and Romanticism,* 245.

25. W. Jackson Bate, *From Classic to Romantic: Premises of Taste in Eighteenth-Century England* (New York: Harper & Row, 1961).

26. Sir Walter Scott, review of *Report of the Highland Society of Scotland . . . and The Poems of Ossian . . . Works of James Macpherson,* ed. Malcolm Laing, *Edinburgh Review* 6 (1805):446.

27. See Larry L. Stewart, "Ossian, Burke, and the 'Joy of Grief,'" *English Language Notes* 15 (1977):29–32.

28. William Wordsworth, *Poetical Works,* ed. E. deSelincourt (Oxford: Clarendon Press, 1952), 2:439.

29. Bertram Davis has pointed out Thomas Percy's attraction to *Solomon's Song* "as a beautiful pastoral" worthy of a fresh interpretation; such thoughts grew out of his study of ancient poetry, particularly Macpherson's Erse poetry, which he saw as an attempt to rescue the secrets of the past. See *Thomas Percy* (Boston: Twayne Publishers, 1981).

30. Kenneth H. Jackson, *A Celtic Miscellany: Translations from the Celtic*

Literatures (1951; reprint, New York: Penguin Books, 1982), 186–87; Thomson, *Gaelic Sources,* 42–47.

31. Scott, review in *Report of the Highland Society,* 441.

32. Peter H. Waddell, *Ossian and the Clyde* (Glasgow: James Maclehose, 1875), 290.

33. Thomson, *Gaelic Sources,* 48; Scott, review in *Report of the Highland Society,* 441; and Blair, *Critical Dissertation,* 77.

34. Thomson, *Gaelic Sources,* 49.

35. Jan deVries discusses the father-son motif in *Heroic Song and Heroic Legend* (London: Oxford University Press, 1963), 50–51.

36. Wain, "Alternative Poetry," 34.

37. Raymond D. Havens mentions only thirteen borrowings from Milton in all of Ossian that should be taken seriously. See *The Influence of Milton on English Poetry* (New York: Russell & Russell, 1961).

38. *The Poems of Ossian,* 1:352; Scott, review in *Report of the Highland Society,* 442. Variant spellings of the hero's name include the Modern English "Cuchulain," or "Cuchulinn," and the Irish Gaelic "CúChulainn"; Macpherson used a contemporary spelling, "Cuthullin." I have modernized the spelling in all cases, except in the title "The Death of Cuthullin."

39. Blair, *Critical Dissertation,* 52.

40. Ibid., 78.

41. Thomson, *Gaelic Sources,* 55.

42. Hart, *The Scottish Novel,* 340–47.

43. Both Monk's *The Sublime* and Stewart's "Ossian, Burke, and the 'Joy of Grief'" discuss the connection usefully.

44. Johannes Brondsted, *The Vikings* (1960; reprint, Baltimore: Penguin Books, 1971), 274.

45. Johann W. von Goethe, *The Sufferings of Young Werther,* trans. Harry Steinhauer (New York: Norton, 1970), ix.

46. Harry Steinhauer, afterword to *The Sufferings of Young Werther* by Johann W. von Goethe, 118.

47. Blair, *Critical Dissertation,* 80.

48. For another interpretation of the phrase—"joy in grief"—see Eleanor M. Sickels, *The Gloomy Egoist: Moods and Themes of Melancholy from Gray to Keats* (1932; reprint, New York: Octagon, 1969).

49. William K. Wimsatt and Cleanth Brooks, *Literary Criticism: A Short History* (New York: Vintage Books, 1957), 295–97.

50. Samuel Johnson, *Lives of the English Poets,* ed. G. B. Hill, 3 vols. (1905; reprint, New York: Octagon Books, 1967), 3:299.

51. See Monk, *The Sublime,* chapter 3.

Chapter Four

1. Preface, *Temora, An Ancient Epic Poem* (London: T. Becket & De-Hondt, 1763), xv.

2. Thomson, *Gaelic Sources,* 59; Smart, *James Macpherson,* 41.

3. Review of *Temora, an Ancient Epic Poem,* trans. James Macpherson, *Monthly Review* 28 (April 1763):276.

4. Review of *Temora, an Ancient Epic Poem,* trans. James Macpherson, *Critical Review* 15 (April 1763):201.

5. Blair, *Critical Dissertation,* 68,

6. Ibid.

7. "Castor," "Essay on Ossian," *European Magazine, and London Review* 29 (1796):304.

8. Thomson, *Gaelic Sources,* 59.

9. Myra Reynolds, *The Treatment of Nature in English Poetry: Between Pope and Wordsworth* (1909; reprint, New York: Gordian Press, 1966), 156–59.

10. These impulses within romantic poetry are discussed in Carl Woodring's *Politics in English Romantic Poetry* (Cambridge: Harvard University Press, 1970).

11. Nora Chadwick, *The Celts* (1970; reprint, New York: Penguin Books, 1982), 121. For comments on Macpherson's style, see Howard Gaskill, "'Ossian' Macpherson: Towards a rehabilitation," *Comparative Criticism* 8 (1986):113–46.

12. Ernest Renan, "The Poetry of the Celtic Races" in *Literary and Philosophical Essays* (New York: Collier, 1910), 153. Matthew Arnold, *On the Study of Celtic Literature* in *The Complete Prose Works,* ed. R. H. Super (Ann Arbor: University of Michigan Press, 1962), 3:370–71. William B. Yeats, "The Celtic Element in Literature" (1897), in *Essays and Introductions* (New York: Collier Books, 1972), 173–88.

13. James Beattie, *Essays: On the Nature and Immutability of Truth. . . . On Poetry and Music. . . .* 2 vols. (Dublin: C. Jenkin, 1778), 2:48. First written in 1762 and published in 1770, these essays were highly suggestive to British romanticists; however, Beattie's description of the Ossian poems shifted from "irresistibly striking" to "defective."

14. Blair, *Critical Dissertation,* 82–83.

15. A full discussion of this development is found in M. H. Abrams, "English Romanticism: The Spirit of the Age," in *Romanticism and Consciousness: Essays in Criticism,* ed. Harold Bloom (New York: Norton, 1970), 90–119.

16. Frederick A. Pottle, "The Eye and the Object in the Poetry of Wordsworth," *Yale Review* 40 (1950):32.

Chapter Five

1. A group of scholars have argued that the controversy lasted until the end of the nineteenth century. See Snyder, *Celtic Revival in English Literature,* 82–84, and Henry Okun, "Ossian in Painting," *Journal of the Warburg and Courtauld Institutes* 30 (1968):327–56.

2. To Dalrymple, 28 June 1760, *Horace Walpole's Correspondence*, 2:69.
3. *Private Papers of James Boswell from Malahide Castle*, ed. Geoffrey Scott and F. A. Pottle, 18 vols. (Privately printed, 1928–1934), 1:127–28.
4. Schmitz, *Hugh Blair*, 55.
5. Boswell, *Life of Johnson*, 280.
6. To Rev. Hugh Blair, 19 September 1763, Letter 215, *Letters of David Hume*, 1:398–401.
7. From Hugh Blair, 29 September 1763, in John Hill Burton, *Life and Correspondence of David Hume*, 2 vols. (Edinburgh, 1846), 1:468–70.
8. To Rev. Hugh Blair, 6 October 1763, Letter 217, *Letters of David Hume*, 403.
9. From Hugh Blair, 1 July 1765, ibid., 516.
10. Frank Brady, *James Boswell: The Later Years 1769–1795* (New York: McGraw-Hill, 1984), 56.
11. Johnson, *A Journey to the Western Islands of Scotland*, 114,117.
12. Ibid., 117.
13. Ibid., 118
14. Ibid.
15. Ibid., 119.
16. Boswell, *A Tour to the Hebrides*, 67.
17. To James Macpherson, 20 January 1775, Letter 373, *Letters of Samuel Johnson*, ed. R. W. Chapman, 3 vols. (Oxford: Clarendon Press, 1952), 2:3. Johnson's remarks on Homer refer to Macpherson's 1773 translation of the *Iliad*.
18. Johnson continued his attack by sharpening up William Shaw's polemic against Macpherson in *An Enquiry into the Authenticity of the Poems Ascribed to Ossian* (1781). See Thomas M. Curley, "Johnson's Last Word on Ossian: Ghost-writing for William Shaw" in *Aberdeen and the Enlightenment: Proceedings of a Conference Held at the University of Aberdeen*, ed. Jennifer J. Carter and Joan H. Pittock (Aberdeen: Aberdeen University Press, 1987), 375–431.
19. See Mossner, *Hume*, 418–20, and Stewart, "Ossian in the Polished Age," 207–12.
20. *Report of the Highland Society*, 1.
21. Ibid., 2.
22. Scott, review of *Report of the Highland Society*, 462.

Chapter Six

1. John Sitter, *Literary Loneliness in Mid-Eighteenth-Century England* (Ithaca, N.Y.: Cornell University Press, 1982), 188.
2. Smart, *James Macpherson*, 5, 11.
3. Russell Noyes, *English Romantic Poetry and Prose* (New York: Oxford University Press, 1967), 121.
4. John J. Dunn, "The Role of Macpherson's *Ossian* in the Development of British Romanticism," Ph.D. diss. Duke University, 1966, 163.

5. Samuel C. Chew and Richard D. Altick, *The Nineteenth Century and After* in *A Literary History of England,* ed. Albert C. Baugh, 2d ed. (New York: Appleton-Century-Crofts, 1967), 1171.

6. Mona Wilson, *The Life of William Blake* (New York: Cooper Square, 1969), 6. In other general references to *Ossian* Wilson points to its malevolent influence on Blake's genius—a conclusion not corroborated by a majority of scholars.

7. Northrop Frye, *Fearful Symmetry: a Study of William Blake* (Princeton, N.J.: Princeton University Press, 1947), 184; Harold Bloom, *Blake's Apocalypse: a Study in Poetic Argument* (Ithaca, N.Y.: Cornell University Press, 1970), 63–69.

8. Wordsworth, "Essay, Supplementary to the Preface" (1815) in *Poetical Works,* 2:423–25.

9. Ibid., 3:103. See John R. Moore, "Wordsworth's Unacknowledged Debt to Macpherson's Ossian," *PMLA* 40 (1925):362–78.

10. John J. Dunn, "Coleridge's Debt to Macpherson's Ossian," *Studies in Scottish Literature* 7 (1969):78.

11. To the Rev. John Becher, 28 March 1808, *Byron's Letters and Journals,* ed. Leslie A. Marchand (Cambridge: Harvard University Press, 1973), 1:163.

12. Woodring, *Politics in English Romantic Poetry,* 157.

13. Dunn, "The Role of Macpherson's *Ossian,*" 208.

14. Rudolf Tombo, *Ossian in Germany* (1901; reprint, New York: AMS Press, 1966), 123.

15. Tombo finds Ossianic material in the odes written in 1764, 1766, and 1767, and in the first *Bardeit* and the *Hermannsschlact.* Ibid., 94.

16. See Alexander Gillies, *A Hebridean in Goethe's Weimar* (New York: Barnes & Noble, 1969), 58–71. Herder's thirty-year fascination with Ossian culminated in an important 1795 essay entitled "Homer and Ossian" published in Schiller's journal *Die Horen.* As far as he was concerned, whether the poems were the work of Ossian or Macpherson made no real difference since both could have turned fragments into epics.

17. Tombo, *Ossian in Germany,* 73, and John Hennig, "Goethe's Translation of Ossian's *Songs of Selma,*" *Journal of English and Germanic Philology* 45 (1946):77–87.

18. Dorothy J. Smith, "The Scotland of the German Composers, 1770–1870," *RE:Artes Liberales* 3 (1976):29–46.

19. Okun, "Ossian in Painting," 339. A large Ossian exhibition of paintings was held at the Grand Palais in Paris during 1974. The infatuation of painters for Ossian was remarkable; German and French artists were represented as well as Alexander Runciman in Scotland, John Sell Cotman in England, and Nicolai Abildgaard in Denmark. However, Runciman's most important work was missing, a series of 21 Ossian paintings composed as decoration for Sir James Clerk's new house at Penicuik in 1772; these had

been destroyed in a fire that burned down the house in 1899. (Some of these compositions survive in a series of etchings he based on them.) See Duncan Macmillan's chapter, "An Ossian's Fancy and a Fingal's Fire," in his *Painting in Scotland: The Golden Age* (Oxford: Phaidon Press, 1986).

20. Chouillet, "Diderot: Poet and Theorist," 225–32.

21. The 1810 LeTourneur edition with a preface by P. Ginguene also enjoys an excellent reputation for its corrections to the text and expansion of the notes.

22. See Pottle, *Boswell: The Earlier Years,* 229–30, 514–15 and Saunders, *Life and Letters of James Macpherson,* 198–99. Cesarotti's edition does not anticipate, nor should it, the fact that Macpherson extensively revised his Ossianic poetry in 1773, "producing an English version which a fair number of Continentals did not like and refused to translate." See Howard Gaskill, "On the Continuing Sorrows of 'Ossian' Macpherson," *Eighteenth-Century Scotland* 2 (1988):15–17.

23. J. C. Herold, ed., *The Mind of Napoleon* (New York: Columbia University Press, 1955), 155. Napoleon carried the Ossian poems just as Alexander the Great had carried the *Iliad.* Arnault wrote in 1796 a five-act tragedy, *Oscar, son of Ossian.*

24. Okun, "Ossian in Painting," 348. The primary reference remains Paul Van Tieghem's exhaustive study *Ossian en France,* 2 vols. (1917; reprint, Geneva: Slatkine Reprints, 1967).

25. A. G. Palacios, *David and Napoleonic Painting* (New York: McCall Publishers, 1970), 15. Girodet also painted *The Death of Malvina,* an interesting compromise between reason and fancy. See also Fritz Novotny, *Painting and Sculpture in Europe: 1780–1880,* 3d ed. (New York: Penguin Books, 1978).

26. Wain, "Alternative Poetry," 32.

27. François R. de Chateaubriand, *Atala/René,* trans. Irving Putter (Berkeley: University of California Press, 1957), 91.

28. François R. de Chateaubriand, *The Memoirs of Chateaubriand,* trans. R. Baldick (New York: Alfred Knopf, 1961), 219.

29. Van Tieghem, *Ossian en France,* 2:329.

30. Chateaubriand, *Memoirs,* 307.

31. Frederic I. Carpenter, "The Vogue of Ossian in America: A Study in Taste," *American Literature* 2 (1931):405–17.

32. George F. Black, "President Jefferson and Macpherson's Ossian," *Journal of the Gaelic Society of Inverness* 33 (1925–27):355–61. To Charles Macpherson, 25 February 1773, in *The Papers of Thomas Jefferson,* ed. Julian P. Boyd (Princeton, N.J.: Princeton University Press, 1950), 1:96–97.

33. Georg Friden, "James Fenimore Cooper and Ossian," *Essays and Studies on American Language and Literature,* no. 8 (Uppsala, Sweden: American Institute, University of Uppsala, 1949).

34. Ibid., 55.

35. Leslie A. Fiedler, *Love and Death in the American Novel* (New York: Meridian, 1964), 189.

36. Ralph Waldo Emerson, *The Journals and Miscellaneous Notebooks of Ralph Waldo Emerson,* ed. Ralph H. Orth and Alfred Ferguson (Cambridge Harvard University Press, 1977), 13:138.

37. Henry David Thoreau, *A Week on the Concord and Merrimack Rivers* (Boston: Houghton Mifflin, 1961), 367.

38. Ibid., 371, 401.

39. F. O. Matthiessen, *American Renaissance: Art and Expression in the Age of Emerson and Whitman* (1941; reprint, New York: Oxford University Press, 1977), 385. Melville had purchased a copy of the *Poems of Ossian* in early 1848 for his own library. See Herman Melville, *Mardi,* ed. H. Hayford (Evanston: Northwestern University Press, 1970), 661.

40. Jay Leyda, *The Melville Log* (New York: Harcourt Brace, 1951), 303–4.

41. Walt Whitman, "Preface 1855" to *Leaves of Grass* in *The Collected Writings of Walt Whitman,* ed. Harold Blodgett and Sculley Bradley (New York: New York University, 1965), 716. For further comment on Ossian and Whitman, see Floyd Stovall, *The Foreground of Leaves of Grass* (Charlottesville: University of Virginia Press, 1974), 115–20.

42. Walt Whitman, "Ossian—? for Note Preface," in *Notebooks and Unpublished Prose Manuscripts* in *The Collected Writings of Walt Whitman,* ed. Edward F. Grier (New York: New York University Press, 1984), 5:1808–9. Whitman, who had read Thoreau's remarks on Ossian in the copy of *A Week* (1849), which Thoreau had given him in 1856, was pleased to find they shared a similar appreciation of the poems.

43. Walt Whitman, *Specimen Days* in *Prose Works* 1892 in *The Collected Writings of Walt Whitman,* ed. Floyd Stovall (New York: New York University Press, 1963), 1:283.

Chapter Seven

1. Leslie A. Fiedler, "Images of Walt Whitman," in *An End to Innocence: Essays on Culture and Politics* (Boston: Beacon Press, 1955), 154.

2. To Hugh Blair, 28 Marsh 1769, in John Hill Burton, *Life and Correspondence of David Hume,* 2:421.

3. D. B. Horn, "Some Scottish Writers of History in the Eighteenth Century," *Scottish Historical Review* 40 (1961):15.

4. Macpherson had received much encouragement and materials from his uncle, the Reverend John Macpherson, whose *Dissertations on the Caledonians* (1768, for which the poet had written a preface), was full of novelties concerning Highland life and customs.

5. To William Strahan, 30 January 1773, Letter 482, *Letters of David Hume,* 2:268–70.

6. *The History of Great Britain from the Restoration to the Accession of the House of Hanover,* 2 vols. (London: Strahan & Cadell, 1775), 1:iv. For more details, see Percy M. Thornton, "The Hanover Papers," *English Historical Review* 1 (1886):756–77; J. F. Chance, "John de Robethon and the Robethon Papers," *English Historical Review* 13 (1898):55–70, and his "Corrections to James Macpherson's 'Original Papers,'" *English Historical Review* 13 (1898):533–49.

7. To Mason, 14 April 1775, *Horace Walpole's Correspondence,* 28:192.

8. To William Strahan, 13 November 1775, Letter 511, *Letters of David Hume,* 2:304.

9. Sir John W. Fortescue, ed., *The Correspondence of King George III: 1760–83,* 6 vols. (London: Macmillan, 1927–28), 5:414. For more details of Macpherson's attacks on the Opposition, see Solomon Lutnick, *The American Revolution and the British Press 1775–1782* (Columbia: University of Missouri Press, 1967).

10. From Mason, 23 February 1773, *Horace Walpole's Correspondence,* 28:64.

11. James Macpherson, trans., *The Iliad of Homer* (London: Strahan & Cadell, 1773), 1:1.

12. Ibid., 1:x.

13. For a discussion of Macpherson's effort, see Peter J. Connelly, "Three Eighteenth-Century Translations of the *Iliad,*" Ph.D. diss., University of Minnesota 1970, 97–120.

14. To Adam Smith, 10 April 1773, Letter 491, *Letters of David Hume,* 2:280.

Selected Bibliography

PRIMARY SOURCES

The Highlander. Edinburgh: Walter Ruddiman, Jr., 1758.

Fragments of Ancient Poetry. Edinburgh: G. Hamilton & J. Balfour, 1760.

——. 2d ed. Edinburgh: G. Hamilton & J. Balfour, 1760. This revised edition contains an additional fragment, No. 13

——. Edited and with introduction by John J. Dunn. Los Angeles: William Andrews Clark Library, 1966. A photographic facsimile of the second edition.

Fingal, an Ancient Epic Poem. London: T. Becket & P. A. De Hondt, 1761 (dated 1762).

Temora, an Ancient Epic Poem. London: T. Becket & P. A. De Hondt, 1763.

The Works of Ossian, the son of Fingal. 2 vols. London: T. Becket & P. A. De Hondt, 1765. Contains Hugh Blair's *Critical Dissertation* on the poems.

The Poems of Ossian. 2 vols. London: W. Strahan & T. Becket, 1773. The infamous corrected edition of the poems.

The Poems of Ossian. Edited by Malcolm Laing. 2 vols. Edinburgh: J. Ballantyne, 1805. Reprint. New York: AMS Press, 1974. Important modern edition.

The Works of Ossian. Edited by Otto L. Jiriczek. 3 vols. Heidelberg: Carl Winters, 1940. Facsimile edition of Macpherson's first edition.

An Introduction to the History of Great Britain and Ireland. London: T. Becket & P. A. De Hondt, 1771.

The Iliad of Homer, translated into Prose. 2 vols. London: Strahan & Cadell, 1773.

Original Papers, Containing the Secret History of Great Britain, from the Restoration to the Accession of the House of Hanover. 2 vols. London: Strahan & Cadell, 1775.

The History of Great Britain from the Restoration to the Accession of the House of Hanover. 2 vols. London: Strahan & Cadell, 1775.

The Rights of Great Britain Asserted Against the Claims of America. London: T. Cadell, 1776.

The History and Management of the East India Company, from its Origin in 1600 to the Present Times. London: T. Cadell, 1779.

A Short History of the Opposition during the Last Session. London: T. Cadell, 1779.

SECONDARY SOURCES

Bibliographies

Black, George F. "Macpherson's Ossian and the Ossianic Controversy: A Contribution Towards a Bibliography." *Bulletin of the New York Public Library* 30 (1926): 1:424–39; 2:508–24.

Dunn, John J. "Macpherson's Ossian and the Ossianic Controversy: A Supplementary Bibliography." *Bulletin of the New York Public Library* 75 (1971):465–73.

Books

Arnold, Matthew. *On the Study of Celtic Literature and on Translating Homer.* New York: Macmillan & Co., 1883. A brilliant, but unsatisfying analysis of nationality in literature which concludes that *Ossian* is a work of Celtic antiquity.

Bate, Walter J. *From Classic to Romantic.* Cambridge: Harvard University Press, 1946. The intellectual background of the change in aesthetic taste at the end of the eighteenth century.

Blair, Hugh. *A Critical Dissertation on the Poems of Ossian, the Son of Fingal.* 2d ed. London: T. Becket, 1765. The classic defense of the *Poems* and an important example of eighteenth-century literary criticism.

Boswell, James. *Boswell's London Journal: 1762–1763.* Edited by Frederick A. Pottle. New York: McGraw-Hill, 1950. Reveals Boswell's contact with Macpherson while providing insights into the Scottish community in London.

———. *Life of Johnson.* Edited by R. W. Chapman. London: Oxford University Press, 1976, Information about Macpherson and Johnson's thoughts concerning *Ossian.*

———. *A Tour to the Hebrides.* Edited by Frederick A. Pottle and C. H. Bennett. New York: Isham Collection, 1936. Numerous references to Macpherson and Ossian usually through Samuel Johnson's eyes.

Brady, Frank. *James Boswell: The Later Years 1769–1795.* New York: McGraw-Hill, 1984. A highly competent analysis of Ossian's influence upon Johnson's acceptance of Boswell's invitation to visit Scotland.

Burton, John Hill. *Life and Correspondence of David Hume.* 2 vols. Edinburgh, 1846. An important source on the rise of James Macpherson and Hume's eventual distrust of his countryman.

Butt, John. *The Mid-Eighteenth Century.* Oxford: Clarendon Press, 1979. Contains a balanced summary of Macpherson's achievements.

Bysveen, Josef. *Epic Tradition and Innovation in James Macpherson's "Fingal."* Atlantic Highlands, N. J.: Humanities Press, 1982. Skillful investigation of the manner in which epic tradition shaped the poem.

Carlyle, Alexander. *Anecdotes and Characters of the Times.* Edited by James Kin-
    sley. London: Oxford University Press, 1973. An outstanding collection
    of anecdotes of people and events witnessed during the Scottish
    Enlightenment.
Chapman, Malcolm. *The Gaelic Vision in Scottish Culture.* London: Croom
    Helm, 1978. Chapter 2, "Ossian and the Eighteenth Century," provides
    a competent summary of the topic.
Connelly, Peter J. "Three Eighteenth-Century Translations of the *Iliad.*"
    Ph.D. diss., University of Minnesota, 1970. A comparative study of the
    translations by Pope, Macpherson, and Cowper.
Daiches, David. *Robert Burns.* New York: Rinehart, 1950. Excellent intro-
    ductory chapter on the Scots poetic tradition.
Dunn, John J. "The Role of Macpherson's Ossian in the Development of Brit-
    ish Romanticism." Ph.D. diss., Duke University, 1966. A well-re-
    searched and rewarding study of Ossian's influence on the romantic poets.
Elledge, Scott, ed. *Eighteenth-Century Critical Essays.* 2 vols. Ithaca, N.Y.:
    Cornell University Press, 1961. A very good collection of pieces repre-
    sentative of the most interesting critics of the century; prints the first
    quarter of Blair's *Dissertation.*
Fiedler, Leslie A. *An End to Innocence: Essays on Culture and Politics.* Boston:
    Beacon Press, 1955. A lively and provocative interpretation of American
    culture that manages to adduce a Macpherson-Whitman association.
————. *Love and Death in the American Novel.* New York: Meridian, 1964.
    Discusses the connections between European and American primitivism.
Foerster, Donald M. *Homer in English Criticism: The Historical Approach in the
    Eighteenth Century.* New Haven: Yale University Press, 1947. Extensive
    discussion of the so-called Scottish school of primitivists who urged Mac-
    pherson to publish his translations.
Gillies, Alexander. *A Hebridean in Goethe's Weimar.* New York: Barnes & No-
    ble, 1969. A study of the Reverend James Macdonald who furnished
    Herder with important information on the Ossianic question and intro-
    duced Burns's poetry to German readers.
Greig, J. Y. T., ed. *The Letters of David Hume.* 2 vols. Oxford: Clarendon
    Press, 1932. Valuable evidence of Hume's central role in the Ossian
    question.
Haywood, Ian. *The Making of History: A Study of the Literary Forgeries of James
    Macpherson and Thomas Chatterton in Relation to Eighteenth-Century Ideas of
    History and Fiction.* Rutherford, N. J.: Fairleigh Dickinson University
    Press, 1986. Argues that the forgeries of Macpherson and Chatterton
    reveal the inconsistencies that existed in both the practice and theory of
    writing British history during the period.
Johnson, Samuel. *A Journey to the Western Islands of Scotland.* Edited by Mary
    Lascelles. New Haven: Yale University Press, 1971. Johnson's pursuit of

Ossian in the Highlands and his abruptness with those Scots who accepted Macpherson as translator.

Mackenzie, Henry, ed. *Report of the Committee of the Highland Society of Scotland.* Edinburgh: Edinburgh University Press, 1805. A voluminous and instructive report issued with the intention of settling the Ossianic question; it did not.

Maclean, J. M. N. "The Early Political Careers of James 'Fingal' Macpherson and Sir John Macpherson." Ph.D. diss., Edinburgh University, 1967. Most interesting study of a little-known period in Macpherson's life.

Maclean, Magnus. *The Literature of the Celts.* 1902. Reprint. Port Washington, N.Y.: Kennikat Press, 1970. The work of a twentieth-century Celtic specialist who settles the Ossianic question without denigrating Macpherson's achievement.

Monk, Samuel H. *The Sublime: A Study of Critical Theories in Eighteenth-Century England.* Ann Arbor: University of Michigan Press, 1960. Historical study of the idea of the sublime in eighteenth-century aesthetics.

Mossner, E. C. *The Life of David Hume.* 1954: Reprint. Oxford: Clarendon Press, 1970. The definitive biography of Hume offering considerable insight into the Edinburgh literati, the rise of Ossian, and British cultural life.

Nutt, Alfred. *Ossian and Ossianic Literature.* 1899. Reprint. New York: AMS Press, 1972. A slim volume issued as the third in a series on popular studies in mythology, romance, and folklore; discusses the true Ossianic ballad literature but, for the student of Celtic literature, goes too far in discounting Macpherson's work.

Pottle, Frederick A. *James Boswell: The Earlier Years 1740–1769.* New York: McGraw-Hill, 1966. An intriguing view of the young Macpherson enjoying his Ossian success in London.

Saunders, Bailey. *The Life and Letters of James Macpherson.* 1894. Reprint. New York: Haskell House, 1968. A Victorian appreciation, lacking scholarly apparatus, skewed in Macpherson's favor at all points.

Schmitz, Robert M. *Hugh Blair.* New York: King's Crown Press, 1948. Contains an excellent chapter on Blair's relationship with Macpherson and the *Dissertation.*

Sher, Richard B. *Church and University in the Scottish Enlightenment: The Moderate Literati of Edinburgh.* Princeton: Princeton University Press, 1985. An astute appraisal of Macpherson's connection with, and attraction to, the Scottish literati who did so much to advance the Ossianic cause. Bibliographical essay on eighteenth-century Scotland and the Scottish Enlightenment.

Sickels, Eleanor M. *The Gloomy Egoist: Moods and Themes of Melancholy from Gray to Keats.* 1932. Reprint. New York: Octagon Books, 1969. Contains a valuable study of the mutability theme in Macpherson's *Ossian.*

Smart, John S. *James Macpherson: An Episode in Literature.* 1905. Reprint. New York: AMS Press, 1973. An important and readable study of all the relevant issues.

Snyder, Edward D. *The Celtic Revival in English Literature: 1760–1800.* Cambridge: Harvard University Press, 1923. The standard work on this important intellectual and literary phenomenon.

Stewart, Larry L. "Ossian in the Polished Age: The Critical Reception of James Macpherson's *Ossian.*" Ph.D. diss., Case Western Reserve University, 1971. Excellent discussion of the extravagant claims made for the *Poems* and the personal nature of many of the arguments.

Thomson, Derick S., ed. *The Companion to Gaelic Scotland.* Oxford: Basil Blackwell, 1984. An excellent reference on Highland life and Gaelic culture.

————. *The Gaelic Sources of Macpherson's "Ossian."* Edinburgh: Oliver & Boyd, 1952. The definitive study of Macpherson's sources; essential reading.

Tombo, Rudolf. *Ossian in Germany.* 1901. Reprint. New York: AMS Press, 1966. The standard work on the influence of the *Poems* in Germany.

Toynbee, Paget, and Leonard Whibley. *Correspondence of Thomas Gray.* 3 vols. Oxford: Clarendon Press, 1935. The standard text with full notes, including an appendix devoted exclusively to Gray and Macpherson.

Tyson, Gerald P. "'Feast of Shells': The Context of James Macpherson's Ossianic Poetry." Ph.D. diss., Brandeis University, 1969. The cultural and aesthetic background of the Ossian poems.

Van Tieghem, Paul. *Ossian en France.* 2 vols. 1917. Reprint. Geneva: Slatkine Reprints, 1967. The standard work on the influence of the *Poems* in France.

Waddell, Peter H. *Ossian and the Clyde.* Glasgow: James Maclehose, 1875. A geographical and antiquarian study that stands as probably the most curious work in *Ossian* literary studies.

Walpole, Horace. *Correspondence.* Edited by W. S. Lewis et al. New Haven: Yale University Press, 1937–83. Immense edition of all of Walpole's correspondence; many references to Macpherson or the *Poems*.

Wittig, Kurt. *The Scottish Tradition in Literature.* Edinburgh: Oliver & Boyd, 1958. A respected and useful book on the subject.

Articles

Barratt, Glynn R. "The Melancholy and the Wild: A Note on Macpherson's Russian Success." *Studies in Eighteenth-Century Culture* 3 (1973):125–35. Ossian's legacy in Russia.

Black, George F. "President Jefferson and Macpherson's Ossian." *Transactions of the Gaelic Society of Inverness* 33 (1925–27):355–71. Examines Jefferson's interest in Ossian.

Carnie, Robert H. "Macpherson's *Fragments of Ancient Poetry* and Lord Hailes."

English Studies 41 (1960):17–26. Connects David Dalrymple with the appearance of these poems.

Carpenter, Frederic I. "The Vogue of Ossian in America: A Study in Taste." *American Literature* 2 (1931):405–17. An important summary of Ossian's early influence in America.

Chance, J. F. "Corrections to James Macpherson's 'Original Papers.'" *English Historical Review* 13 (1898):533–49. Offers highly specific corrections to the material published.

———. "John de Robethon and the Robethon Papers." *English Historical Review* 13 (1898):55–70. Discusses the great mass of papers from which Macpherson made extracts and translations.

Chouillet, Jacques. "Diderot: Poet and Theorist of the Homer and Ossianist Revival." *British Journal for Eighteenth-Century Studies* 5 (1982):225–32. The role Diderot played in the diffusion and interpretation of Ossian.

Davies, G. "Macpherson and the Nairne Papers." *English Historical Review* 35 (1920):367–76. Dismisses the charge of forgery made by Arthur Parnell concerning Macpherson's use of the Nairne Papers for his *Original Papers*.

deGategno, Paul J. "'The Source of Daily and Exalted Pleasure': Jefferson Reads the *Poems of Ossian*." In *Ossian Revisited,* edited by Howard Gaskill (Edinburgh: Edinburgh University Press, forthcoming). Discusses the role of Ossian in forming Jefferson's character.

Dunn, John J. "Coleridge's Debt to Macpherson's Ossian." *Studies in Scottish Literature* 7 (1969):76–89. Demonstrates Coleridge's knowledge of and respect for Ossian.

———. "James Macpherson's First Epic." *Studies in Scottish Literature* 9 (1971):48–54. Examines the meaning and reception of *The Highlander*.

Fitzgerald, Robert P. "The Style of Ossian." *Studies in Romanticism* 6 (1966):22–23. An intelligent appraisal of Macpherson's sensibility and literary genius.

Folkenflik, Robert. "Macpherson, Chatterton, Blake and the Great Age of Literary Forgery." *Centennial Review* 18 (1974):378–91. The burden of the past syndrome in the eighteenth century.

Fridén, Georg. "James Fenimore Cooper and Ossian." In *Essays and Studies on American Language and Literature,* no. 8, 1–55. Uppsala: American Institute, University of Uppsala, 1949. A perceptive study of Cooper's indebtedness to European romanticism, in particular the atmosphere and language of Ossian.

Frye, Northrop. "Towards Defining an Age of Sensibility." *English Literary History* 23 (1956):144–52. Comments usefully upon Ossian's "diffusion of sense" and places the poem in a genre of associative poetry.

Greenway, John L. "The Gateway to Innocence: Ossian and the Nordic Bard as Myth." *Studies in Eighteenth-Century Culture* 4 (1975):161–69. Finds the poems quite modern in their fusing of a nationalistic construct and classical humanist culture.

Grobman, Neil R. "David Hume and the Earliest Scientific Methodology for Collecting Balladry." *Western Folklore* 34 (1975):16–31. Refers to Hume's "Of the Authenticity of Ossian's Poems."

Haywood, Ian. "The Making of History: Historiography and Literary Forgery in the Eighteenth Century." *Literature and History* 9 (1983):139–51. Analyzes Blair's preface to the *Fragments of Ancient Poetry* as both a historiographical and a literary phenomenon.

Henning, John. "Goethe's Translation of Ossian's *Songs of Selma.*" *Journal of English and Germanic Philology* 45 (1946):77–87. Shows Goethe's awareness of the power of Ossian for his own work.

Horn, D. B. "Some Scottish Writers of History in the Eighteenth Century." *Scottish Historical Review* 40(1961):1–18. Surveys the achievements of Scots historians, including a balanced appraisal of Macpherson's career as a historian.

Hudson, Wilson M. "The Homer of the North Translates Homer." *Library Chronicle of the University of Texas* 4 (1950):25–42. The genesis, publication, and reception of Macpherson's translation.

Macbain, Alexander. "Macpherson's Ossian." *Celtic Magazine* 12 (1887):145–54, 193–201, 240–54. Still considered by scholars to be the best presentation of the controversy.

McGuinness, Arthur E. "Lord Kames on the Ossian Poems: Anthropology and Criticism." *Texas Studies in Literature and Language* 10 (1968):65–75. Considers the Ossian poems as a perfect illustration of Kames's primitivistic theory.

Manning, Susan. "Ossian, Scott, and Nineteenth-Century Scottish Literary Nationalism." *Studies in Scottish Literature* 17 (1982):39–54. Argues that Ossian provided Scott with "a mythologising impetus" that met his nationalistic requirements.

Muller, Wolfgang G. "Das Asyndeton als Archaismus [in James Macpherson's Ossian Poems]." [Asyndeton as Archaism in James Macpherson's Ossian Poems.] *Anglia* 96 (1978):89–107. The stylistic use of asyndeton, the absence of syntactical links that produces an uneven style, in Macpherson's work. In German.

Murphy, Peter T. "Fool's Gold: The Highland Treasures of Macpherson's *Ossian.*" *English Literary History* 53 (1986):567–91. A sophisticated redefinition of fraudulence as it applies to Macpherson's *Ossian.*

Okun, Henry. "Ossian in Painting." *Journal of the Warburg and Courtauld Institutes* 30 (1967):327–56. An excellent review of European painters influenced by Ossian.

Parnell, Arthur. "James Macpherson and the Nairne Papers." *English Historical Review* 12 (1897):254–84. Unsuccessful attempt to impugn the documents Macpherson used in writing the *Original Papers*; an interesting piece of Whig revisionism.

Scott, Sir Walter. Review of *Report of the Highland Society of Scotland . . . and the Poems of Ossian . . . Works of James Macpherson. Edinburgh Review* 6 (1805):429–62. An intelligent and balanced appraisal of the work done by the Highland Society, including an unusually fine explication of the *Poems.*

Sher, Richard B. "'Those Scotch Imposters and their Cabal': Ossian and the Scottish Enlightenment." In *Man and Nature: Proceedings of the Canadian Society for Eighteenth-Century Studies,* edited by R. L. Emerson et al. 1:55–63. London, Ont.: University of Western Ontario Press, 1982. Explains why Ossian was so attractive to the Edinburgh "cabal."

Smith, Dorothy J. "The Scotland of the German Composers, 1770–1870." *RE: Artes Liberales* 3 (1976):29–46. Examines the influence of primitivism and nationalism as revealed in Ossian in the music of Schubert, Brahms, Schumann, and Mendelssohn.

Stewart, Larry L. "Ferdinando Warner and the Ossianic Controversy." *Notes and Queries* 20 (1973):421–23. Corrects our understanding of Warner's *Remarks on the History of Fingal* (1762).

———. "Ossian, Burke, and the 'Joy of Grief.'" *English Language Notes* 15 (1977):29–32. Shows that Macpherson used the phrase "joy of grief" as Burke had defined it in *A Philosophical Enquiry into the Origin of Our Ideas of the Sublime and Beautiful.*

Thomas, R. George. "Lord Bute, John Home and Ossian: Two Letters." *Modern Language Review* 51 (1956):73–75. The letters provide information concerning Macpherson's Highland journeys in search of materials for his epics.

Thomson, Derick. "'Ossian' Macpherson and the Gaelic World of the Eighteenth Century." *Aberdeen University Review* 40 (1963):7–20. A highly informed lecture delivered on the bicentennial of the publication of *Fingal.*

Thornton, Percy M. "The Hanover Papers." *English Historical Review* 1 (1886):756–77. Shows the historic importance of these documents for Macpherson's histories and to the period 1695–1719.

Wain, John. "Alternative Poetry: An Oxford Inaugural Lecture." *Encounter* 42 (1974):26–38. A witty and astute paper arguing that lessons can be drawn from the Macpherson and Ossian story: that the shift of taste in the 1760s has been paralleled by the literary upheaval of the 1960s.

Index